W. H. Lizars. Sc.

ALLINGTON.

C.P. TREVELYAN

1870-1958

Portrait of a Radical

C.P Trevelyan, 'Ancient of Days', c. 1950

C.P. TREVELYAN

1870-1958

Portrait of a Radical

A.J.A. MORRIS

ST. MARTIN'S PRESS
NEW YORK

Published by St. Martin's Press, Inc.   175 Fifth Avenue, New York, N.Y. 10010
Printed in Northern Ireland
First published in the United States of America in 1979
ISBN 0-312-11212-4

Library of Congress Cataloging in Publication Data

Morris, A. J. Anthony.
   C. P. Trevelyan, 1870-1958

   Bibliography: p.
   Includes index.
   1. Trevelyan, Charles Philips, Sir, 1870-1958. 2. Great Britain-Politics and government-20th century. 3. Statesmen-Great Britain-Biography.
DA566.9.T7M67 1978   941.082'092'4 [B]   78-13022
ISBN 0-312-11242-4

Printed in Northern Ireland.

CONTENTS

LIST OF
ILLUSTRATIONS

PREFACE

In this book I have written a simple narrative account of C.P. Trevelyan's parliamentary political life. It has been based primarily on his letters and those of his family and political colleagues. Whenever and wherever possible, I have allowed Trevelyan to speak for himself.

I could not have completed this book without the aid of many people, and in particular; Mrs Pauline Dower who was invariably helpful and encouraging; Alistair Elliot, Keeper of special collections at the University Library of Newcastle upon Tyne; Margaret Young and Linda Robinson, who made sense of my drafts and turned them into the finished typescript; Carl Thornton who solved all the design problems; Jim and Diane Gracey and the staff of Blackstaff Press; and finally, but far from least, Cis, Anthony and Fiona — for putting up with me.

There would have been one other name to add to the above list — Howard Weinroth. I dedicate this book with affection to the memory of a fine scholar, teacher, and the best of friends.

A.J.A.M.
Belfast, 1977

IN MEMORIAM

HOWARD S. WEINROTH

Rest, comrade, rest:
Cull we sad flowers to lay on your sad breast:
There till the world awakes to love, we leave you:
Rest, comrade, rest.

HERITAGE AND EDUCATION
OF A RADICAL:
1870-93

The Trevelyans came originally from the parish of St. Veep, near Fowey in Cornwall. A house there that existed at the time of Domesday Book still bears the family name. Before the nineteenth century, however, there was only one notable ancestor, John Trevelyan, member of Parliament, who, for his enthusiastic support of the Lancastrian cause, was arraigned by the Yorkists for piracy. For the next five hundred years the Trevelyans pursued a quiet, country life until, by the latter half of the eighteenth century, the family enjoyed a degree of importance in local if not national affairs. In 1777, by a judicious marriage, the Wallington estate in Northumberland was added to the family estates in Somerset.

Charles Edward Trevelyan, a minor scion of the family, was born at Nettlecombe in Somerset in 1807. For a lifetime's distinguished public service he was awarded a baronetcy, and because of the (for him) fortunate lack of direct heirs, he inherited the Wallington estate. At eighteen he had sailed to India, and in less than three years secured fame and fortune — by reporting the embezzlement and malpractices of his superior. His honesty, courage, and abilities were rewarded by rapid promotion in the Indian Service, and his career was crowned by appointment as Financial Secretary to the Treasury.

In 1835, Charles had married Hanna, sister of the historian, Thomas Babington Macaulay. They had three children. Their second child and only son, George Otto, was educated at Harrow and Trinity College, Cambridge. After graduation, he in his turn went to India to serve as his father's private secretary. There he first established his name in the world of letters and, returning to England, made his début in Society in 1864, determined to devote the rest of his life to the professions of politics and literature. He entered Parliament in 1865 as member for the borough of Tynemouth, early electoral success purchased by an obliging relative, Sir Walter Trevelyan, who secured the Chirton estate and with it a sufficient number of votes to unseat the Tory member. The constituency was abolished by the 1867 Reform Act, but in 1868 friends secured George's nomination for the Scottish Border Burghs, which constituency continued to return him to Parliament without fail until 1886 when, temporarily, Trevelyan supported the Unionists over the vexed question of Irish Home Rule. Charles Trevelyan's early fond hopes for his brilliant son were not to be disappointed. A promising career in Parliament was complemented by a burgeoning and satisfying reputation as an author.

In 1865, George met, and fell in love with Caroline, the daughter of Robert Needham Philips, a Manchester merchant and the Liberal member for Bury. However, the young couple were forbidden to marry because of the opposition to the match of Caroline's uncle, Mark Philips. His wishes were not easily to be discounted, for Robert Philips' fortune was dependent upon that of his elder brother. The young couple's devotion throughout their enforced separation finally undermined Mark Philips' resolution. The elderly bachelor uncle relented his opposition and in September 1869 George Trevelyan married Caroline Philips. The first of their three children, Charles Philips Trevelyan, was born on 28 October, 1870.

There were two younger sons: Robert Calverly, born in 1872, who became a poet and scholar, and in 1876, George Macaulay, the historian. Each was to enjoy a distinguished career, but Charles as the eldest son carried a particular burden of family pride and expectation. The Trevelyans were members of that small yet politically influential upper middle class with its own special aura of country gentry. Though born to privilege, the young Trevelyans were constantly reminded of their responsibility and duty to serve others less privileged than themselves. This permanent and demanding concomitant intruded upon an otherwise comfortable heritage.

The family in the course of a year would stay in three different houses. In London during the 1870s and 80s, Charles lived for the greater part of the year at Ennismore Gardens in a comfortable town house that had belonged to his paternal grandfather. Here, while his father's days were filled by political duties, he might any evening see coming for dinner — that great conversational and dyspeptic institution of late Victorian and Edwardian times — the present, past and future giants of metropolitan, social, political and literary life. To the child, his father must have seemed a somewhat remote figure, part of that greater world of 'affairs', a secret life as yet still closed to him. His much adored mother was quiet yet determined, seemingly a passive foil to the imposing character of his admired father. However, in the early years, constant adult companionship came for Charles, not from his parents but his nurse, Mrs. Prestwich. She was his teacher, arbiter, comforter, much loved and loving friend.

The Trevelyans always spent Christmas and often Easter in Warwickshire at the country house of Robert Philips. There an 'almost too hospitable grandpapa' would preside over the feasting and holidaymaking, taking a benign interest in the antics of his daughter's trio of sons. Welcombe was a vast mansion of fat red brick, hidden amidst trees upon a gentle hill rising from the green water-meadows of the Avon. The house had been built in mock Elizabethan style by Mark Philips in the 1860s. For the children's amusement there were walks through dingles and country lanes to nearby Stratford, or to the more distant old market town of Warwick with its ancient gates and fine parish church. There were visits to the theatre, and on wet days, the never failing pleasure of playing 'Soldiers'. In his *Autobiography,* the youngest Trevelyan brother described the esoteric delights of this family pursuit.

> My father and elder brothers were always playing with the help of regiments of small lead soldiers made in Germany, a realistic war-game (Napoleonic period) by elaborate rules which the Trevelyan family evolved for itself and perfected over a number of years. 'Soldiers'..., made wet days welcome, and united us three brothers, till well after we were all grown men, in the freemasonry of our own peculiar game, in spite of occasional quarrels over its conduct, which was de-cided, not by mechanically applicable rules, but by our opinion as to what was militarily possible.[1]

The gentle charms of Welcombe pleased Charles but, like his father, it was Wallington Hall and the Northumbrian countryside that captured his love and allegiance.

Wallington Hall was where the family spent their summer holidays. George Trevelyan inherited the estate and the baronetcy on the death of his father in 1886. The house is built upon the site of an ancient border castle, the original stronghold of the Fenwick clan. The last of this family, Sir John Fenwick, in the reign of Charles II, had become bankrupt, and the estate was then purchased by a great Northumberland mine owner, Sir William Blackett. This proved to be a splendid transaction, for the bulk of the purchase price was in the form of an annuity of £2,000 upon Fenwick's life. Unwisely, Fenwick could not resign himself to the Glorious Revolution, and his plotting with other Jacobites against William III led to his arraignment for treason. With good conscience, as a sturdy, loyal Whig, and with commendable business acumen, Blackett voted in every parliamentary division for Fenwick's Bill of Attainder. This in time brought the unrepentant Fenwick to the block and, incidentally, swiftly terminated the annuity. What Blackett earned by loyalty the Trevelyans secured by marriage to a Blackett heiress. However, it was Sir William who began the building of much of the present house and another

Blackett, Sir Walter, who invested the fortune he made from mining and commerce in the lavish internal decoration by Italian artists and the design of the parklands by a talented local man, Capability Brown. The central hall was not completed until 1855. The house stands in wooded country upon the banks of the Wansbeck. Within ten miles are the great mining districts of Northumberland whose riches partly furnished the rural beauties of the estate. Upon the other side at a distance of some six miles begin the long expanses of moorland, stretching away to the Cheviots. The heather and white grass moors provided excellent sport, and for the boy learning to shoot, there was plentiful and easy 'game' in rook and rabbit.

At Northumberland in the summer, Warwickshire at Christmas, and in London while Parliament was in session, Charles passed his early years, happy and untroubled. In the summer of 1880, his parents decided it was time their eldest son should begin his formal education. A small preparatory school, The Grange, was chosen because the headmaster, the Rev. C.G. Chittenden, for the times held liberal views on educating young boys. Chittenden's newest charge was despatched by his anxious parents accompanied by detailed notes concerning his health and academic prowess. The headmaster replied:

> I am much obliged for your notes. Such information is always valuable. I am not at all concerned to learn that you do not think him clever, and that he learns slowly; but I am very glad to hear that he is *reasonable*. A reasonable boy is, in all aspects, a more satisfactory pupil than a merely clever boy. You may depend on our not expecting too much from him.[2]

Mrs. Chittenden and her daughters helped to make a new boy's first days in unfamiliar surroundings as friendly and as welcoming as possible. Charles soon settled to the new routine.

> Three times there is play-time, after breakfast, and after morning lessons, and after dinner. We have French lessons three times a week... there are half-holidays twice a week, Thursday and of course Saturday. Monday is history. But I like tea best of all.[3]

Should he ever feel miserable and lonely, there was the comforting prospect that he would soon be joined by his brother, Robert. When writing to him about life at the The Grange Charles was quite clear about the educational priorities. 'You will not have lumpy puddings, I don't think, if you come here.'[4] But unfortunately, the parents did not consider the prospect of two brothers sharing the same preparatory school a wise one, and the Rev. Chittenden, sentiment no doubt tempered by thoughts of lost fees, reluctantly acquiesced in the decision.[5]

Charles did not shine with any particular distinction in his lessons, but he gained his removes at the end of each quarter and in a year had progressed from the fourth to the first class. Despite his own confident estimate of his abilities as an embryo classical scholar — 'I like doing Xenophon very much, we have done one sentence'[6]— his lack of progress at Latin and Greek was a matter of considerable anxiety to his father. The phlegmatic Chittenden was not unduly concerned.

> I am afraid my boys often *seem* backward, but it is really a gain that a boy should be able to construct a simple Latin sentence before he begins to translate much — as it is in Greek, that he should read the characters fluently before he attempts much else. Charles seems to be a very intelligent boy. Like most intelligent boys he gets weary of the amount of Latin and Greek grammar made necessary by our Public School system: but that is the fault of the system rather than the boy.[7]

All boys were obliged to write home at least once a week, an exercise that more than once stretched Charles' capacities as a correspondent. However, he always had decided opinions to express about his masters. He had his favourites, as he told his maternal grandfather. 'Mr. Pearce is an awfully jolly Liberal tutor who often reads us something out of the *Daily News.*'[8] But there were others upon whom he looked with less favour.

> I don't know why it is Mr. C. gets such masters. Ploughman is an awful brute... He would like an autograph of Gladstone. *I leave it to you whether to send it to a Conservative who is always swearing at him.*[9]

If Ploughman was not favoured because of his politics, his faults were mild compared with those of a Mr. Robinson who 'hates me almost more than anyone else because Papa is in the Government and he is a most furious Jingoe'. But Robinson's reign of terror was short lived, and soon Charles was writing home 'Good news. Mr. Robinson has been expelled for pulling and boxing our ears, and I should think Mr. Chittenden did not care to keep him for other reasons I gave you, but he only spoke of that one.'[10]

For a boy who enjoyed good health, Charles was unusually nervous about himself. His mother was always inordinately concerned with his physical well-being. But Chittenden wisely realised that the boy's symptoms of nervousness were connected with his lack of confidence in his ability to satisfy the expectations of others. Here were the first signs of that debilitating depression that was to dog Trevelyan's fortunes as an undergraduate. However, at The Grange the boy's confidence grew as he progressed through the school. By the Summer quarter of 1883 he was Head-boy, and Chittenden reported:

> There are very few pupils of whom I can write with more pleasure than I can of Charles. He is learning to discharge the small practical duties of his position well, and promises to make a good 'Head-boy', which at one time I thought doubtful.[11]

It had long been decided that Charles would go from The Grange to Harrow. In December 1883 Chittenden suggested the boy might attempt a scholarship. 'He would not be likely to get it, but it would do him good to have such an examination in view.'[12] The parents were uncertain about this proposal. To them it was a novel consideration to enter for any academic prize without expecting success. Nevertheless, Chittenden pursued his plan.

> If he knew that you and Mr. Trevelyan would be greatly disappointed by his failure (the most likely result) he might become more anxious than would be good for him; but if he knows that he is only expected to do his best, it will give him, I think, a wholesome stimulus to exertion. Indeed, I already see the good effects of the prospect of such an examination.[13]

Chittenden was allowed his way. But though Charles toiled at his classical studies there was to be no scholarship. This apart, however, the boy's last year at The Grange was a success. In his final report the headmaster noted:

> There is not one of my pupils with whom all my associations are so pleasant as with Charles... I was gratified to find how warmly he felt towards us all... I shall watch Charles's future with the deepest interest as he seems to have in him something more than mere school and college success.[14]

In September 1894 Trevelyan began his new life at Harrow, that school where, to Macaulay's delight, George Otto Trevelyan had been 'buried under laurels — first in the examination, Gregory Medal, Peel Medal, every prize he had contended for without exception'.[15] The son could never hope to repeat the father's brilliant academic successes. But he was to boast one distinction that did not fall to his father — membership of the School's football team. Harrow was always to retain a cherished place in Trevelyan's affections.

The letters to his parents he wrote regularly from Harrow contained much more news than had his 'duty' epistles from The Grange. Those to his mother almost invariably contained reference to his health, which generally was excellent, and food, of which there was never enough. Those to his father, even from the earliest days, were laced with political gossip. Letters from his parents to Charles, particularly those from his father, usually — though unnecessarily — contained admonitions to work. In the diary he kept for his last two years at Harrow, Charles recorded, after a rather poor examination result: 'I am not disheartened or disgusted. I am only disappointed. I have worked very hard. But my scholarship is too poor... Perseverance must take the place of scholarship.'[16] His father never understood why it was that his eldest son could not cope so readily as he, or his youngest sons, with the classics. Nor did he comprehend how his exaggerated expectations placed an unfair burden upon a son who, as a result, dismissed his talents in other activities as worth little. Yet, in the same manner, Charles could be blind — could rate his brilliant younger brother for a healthy idleness and censure his plausible excuses. Nor was he too kind in his judgment of the young Churchill who at Harrow, though manifestly a prime duffer, was altogether too cocky and insouciant. Charles wrote to his father:

> Had the pleasure..., on Thursday, of shaking hands with Randolph Churchill; an honour I should think the Tories thought I was not exactly entitled to... He was bringing his son down here for what is known among us by the expressive name of the 'skews' exam. I should have thought *his* son ought to have at least aspired to the highest exam if not the schol. They can't take higher than middle shell if they come in for the 'skew'.

> [And later] Lord Randolph's son has taken Third Fourth. He is last but one in the school!! An ex-Chancellor of the Exchequer's son!!![17]

Even a casual reading of Trevelyan's letters to his parents for the years he was at Harrow reveals his pleasure and delight in the place. If he did not shine in the classical sixth, he made up for this on the games field. In the Summer he proved himself an above average miler, and a wicket-keeper batsman of competence if not brilliance. But it was in Harrow football that he shone, though his enthusiasm for the game was not always looked upon with favour by his masters.

> Yesterday evening I got a terrible jaw from Vanity for playing footer in the front of the House. I set a bad example was his chief point. I quite agree with him. I keep to rules pretty well generally except when I have the footer fever on.[18]

Harrow football was violent enough, but Harrow's politicking in the 1880s could be more than a little robust. It took courage to admit support for the Liberal cause. Fifteen year old Trevelyan provided his father with the following graphic, if somewhat breathless account, of Harrow's involvement with the 1885 general election.

> We have had one of the most exciting and interesting weeks that I have known. The Conservatives in the School are absolutely furious. There is a Liberal Committee room nearly opposite Dr. Welldon's, and on the windows are posted various Liberal placards. The Conservative candidate, Ambrose..., an awful ass who can't speak decently from stammering, a regular chaw who has to hold his head up to see out of his eyes because he is too slack to raise his eyelids — has not put up any placards yet. So the Conservatives in our House, with the help of a rich banker, Baring, whose son is in the School, got a placard... [and] ... they had about five hundred printed. While all this was going on, the Conservatives in the School grew more and more enraged with the Liberal Committee

rooms. Till yesterday they contented themselves with hooting and knocking at the door. Then, they began to pelt the Bobbies. One had his hat knocked off, so the Inspector collared one of the rowdiest chaps. Then about six police joined in and they got Robinson and Johnson down to the police office and they are to be tried tomorrow.

In the fight, the head of Haycocks, Tom Fowler, was collared by two policemen. But one of the policemen was caught on the nose which sent him flat on his back, and Tom Fowler managed to escape, though later he was caught. He gave the Bobby one in the belly. It must have been an awful joke. I wish I had seen it. I consider the Conservatives awfully feeble for not rescuing them. There were not more than 10 police at the most, and 200 boys ought to be able to do for them.[19]

But Trevelyan's interest in politics was not limited to the antics of his schoolfellows at the hustings. At fifteen he was already developing the instincts of a seasoned political campaigner.

Reverses must come but let us hope for the best from the counties. They know who has given them the franchise. I don't see how the Tories can get a sufficient majority to beat both the Home Rulers as well as us. I noticed how small a majority James had at Bury, and Dilke at Chelsea. Scotland, however, is loyal to us still. What a majority the G.O.M. [Gladstone] got... I should think if no party got a large majority, there will be another election within two years would there not? Our motto must be till then NIL DESPERANDUM.[20]

In the summer of 1889, Trevelyan left Harrow and, that autumn, entered Trinity College, Cambridge. That he should have gone to Trinity to continue his education was as inevitable as had been the choice of Harrow as his school. The family connections with the College were long standing, bridging three generations. Macaulay had been an undergraduate there. In the late 1850s, George Trevelyan had distinguished himself by being placed second in the University Classical Tripos. Though convinced that he merited the honour, he had not been elected to the expected Trinity Fellowship. However, even this loss and disappointment had been repaired in 1885, when he was elected to an honorary fellowship. Sir George's undergraduate successes had not been limited to the academic field. He had enjoyed the company of a wide and distinguished group of friends, and his contributions to the Union and Cambridge literary circles had afforded him pleasure and the admiration and applause of his contemporaries. During his long life Sir George never ceased to sing the praises of his *alma mater* where he had experienced so much success and so many rewards. He looked upon Trinity as an ancient Athenian might have viewed Athens — 'a self-contained republic of high average intelligence, inclined to look upon the rest of the world as "Boeotian", small enough in size..., but interesting and important enough to escape provincialism..., inspiring.'[21] What could have been more natural than to wish his eldest son should enjoy these same privileges and pleasures that once had been his? But there was a fault in this ideal scheme. Sir George was pre-eminently a reading man, as were his two youngest sons. Charles Trevelyan neither possessed the mind nor the temperament to suit him for academic life. However, as a dutiful eldest son, he would strive to be what his father wanted and supposed him to be.

Trevelyan elected to read history. A genuine interest in the subject and his weakness at classical studies dictated in that particular at least, the eldest son could not follow in his father's path. The historical tripos was then a comparative innovation at Cambridge. The formal provision for teaching history to Trinity students was meagre. Of the college's sixty fellows, not one was an historian. The claims of mathematics and classics to almost all the spoils were, as yet, unchallenged. Those university lectures that were available were not intended to cover all sections of the tripos. So a student was obliged to rely largely upon his own reading. When Master of Trinity, Trevelyan's younger brother was tartly to observe: 'This I expect was bad for the weaker and good for the better man.'[22] The tripos then, was not divided into two parts, so, having passed his 'Little Go' with some distinction, Trevelyan was faced by almost two years of reading, much of it unsupervised, broken only by the occasional and lesser demands of college examinations. There was a final year of revision before a candidate presented himself to the university examiners.

Of the Trinity fellows, many would have been familiar figures, either as friends and visitors to the Trevelyan home, or as the frequent subjects of his father's conversation. The Master of Trinity, Montagu Butler, was a life-long and much admired friend of Sir George. For twenty-five years Butler had been headmaster of Harrow before returning to Trinity. There he genially presided for a further, incredible thirty-two years, fortified by a second marriage in 1888 to a young wife whose attachment to the tenets of Christian Science happily allowed her to ignore all Butler's ailments, and thus, according to Bertrand Russell, 'prolonged his life for some twenty years beyond what otherwise might have been expected'.[23]

Charles Trevelyan had many acquaintances at Trinity, but few friends. This lack of intimates was a constant, self-recriminatory theme in his letters from Trinity to his parents. In 1892, he wrote to his mother:

> I am utterly desolate and alone, with not a single person to talk to, to sympathise with. Many are friendly — many would have been friends if I had kept them. No one ever had such opportunities as I had. But I have let them all slip. I have only one friend in Davies, and now he is far away.[24]

For one who from birth had enjoyed so many social advantages, Trevelyan cut an amazingly gauche figure in society. He supposed himself disadvantaged in any company other than that which chose endlessly to discuss politics. He developed a superficial arrogance to disguise his uncertainty. In *The New Machiavelli*, where the Webbs and their circle are brilliantly, if sometimes cruelly lampooned, Wells wrote of Willie Crampton (Charles Trevelyan) 'lying in wait conversationally', having 'no sense of self exposure, the gallant experiments in statement that are necessary for good conversation'. He would rather 'watch one talking with an expression exactly like peeping through bushes. Then..., as it were, dash out, dissent succinctly, contradict some 'secondary fact, and back to cover. He gave one twilight nerves.'[25] Trevelyan had been brought up in a home where, amongst the male members at least, declamation was the more usual form of communication. He was more used to a company regaled by lengthy discourse on the niceties of parliamentary procedure, the tyrannies of the House of Lords, the fatuity of royalty, or the pleasures of classical literature, than to be entertained and be entertaining with unselfconscious, inconsequential chatter. 'I cannot get on with people,' he once wrote despairingly to his mother. 'I do not care to take part in their drivelling conversations and flabby amusements. And I have not the wit to make them talk and do anything worth the while of a rational being.' If, with the natural impatience of youth, he was sometimes less than charitable in his assessment of others, he was always least sparing of himself.

> The world is composed chiefly of the dull. Only now it comes out that I am dull too. I cannot interest those who are not interested already... It is not I wish people to think me clever. But what is the use of any worthy ambition, what is the use of caring for a cause, if there is no chance of ever being able to express a single thought that comes into the brain or a single spark of the enthusiasm that wants to break out?[26]

When he entered Trinity, the one ambition above others he was determined to satisfy was to cut a successful figure in the Cambridge Union. In the first month of his first term, he was afforded an opportunity to impress that body. The occasion was not a success; inexperience betrayed ambition. 'It was all the more bitter,' he confided to his father, 'as a good many men were expecting something. However, they have been very good to me afterwards... I'm certainly going to stick to it, and shall speak later in the evening next time however much I may bore the company.'[27] While recovering from this initial, unsuccessful foray in the Union, Trevelyan practised the arts of debate as a regular attender at meetings of less formidable bodies, the Decemviri and the Magpie and Stump. Yet, even before these less exacting audiences, he was frequently overcome by 'feelings of inferiority... I do not even reach the mediocrity which I am capable of attaining.'[28] By his second term, however, he could report that at last he had succeeded in making a short speech in the Union, and, 'at any rate finishing at the end of a sentence and not in the middle of one. I am sufficiently satisfied at having been audacious enough to make a fool of myself.'[29]

At the end of his first year Trevelyan stood for election to the Union committee and was elected second of the six successful candidates. 'Considering how little I have spoken it is very unusual. I suppose I got all the Trinity and Liberal votes.'[30] News of this unexpected success was not as pleasing to Sir George as his son had hoped. His father advised him that for the sake of his studies he should abandon any ideas of office in the Union. His spare time was already sufficiently filled by his duties as secretary to the University Liberal Club. Trevelyan, after much thought and hesitation, reluctantly acceded. In January 1891, he wrote of how much lighter his spirits were now because he had decided 'to settle back out of the Union course. I felt how thoroughly I was doing the right thing..., though now I can argue with the readiness of conviction for resigning my prospects there.'[31]

Increasingly concerned about Trevelyan's academic fortunes, Sir George considered every possible particular. Nothing that might prejudice the chances of a first class degree should be hostage to chance. His own infrequent attendance at Chapel while an undergraduate had led to a period of suspension. Now, he insisted, his son should be diligent in his attendance at service. Dutifully, Trevelyan replied to his father: 'I will attend to what you say although I am on the whole inclined to disbelieve in it affecting any longer the chances of scholarships or fellowships. I will do as you suggest rather than follow my own inclinations.'[32]

Trevelyan generally enjoyed excellent health yet during his second year at Trinity, he was increasingly plagued by nervous depression. Consequently, he became morbidly concerned about hs health. But it was fruitless to seek a physical reason for what was a spiritual indisposition. In his last year, the prospect of approaching examinations weighed heavily and depression, once spasmodic and brief-lived, became frequent and intense. For this condition, Mackenzie, the family doctor, prescribed a dietary regimen, gentle exercise, a break in his reading, a tonic — but all to no avail.

> I have kept Mackenzie's regulations very fairly, but they do not seem to have the least effect. I have just gone on getting steadily worse as the term advances...[33]

Mackenzie prescribed, his father remonstrated, his mother consoled, but Trevelyan discerned more clearly than them the real cause of his dilemma. 'I think I realise now that it has been the prospect and the feeling that I was not up to the standard in the work that has ruined my time here.'[34] He had long known that he would not get a first. He had to admit to himself the sort of man he was rather than the sort others supposed or wanted him to be.

The conclusion was inevitable, for neither hope nor the best meant advice of anxious parents could help. The only consideration remained he must 'face the ignominy of getting kicked out of the window with a second, with none of the compensating advantages of the recollection of social and intellectual enjoyment which other people profess they have.'[35] In the summer of 1892 Trevelyan heard he had gained second class honours in the historical tripos.

> Things are past the point of redemption. Oh it is so horrible. All my courage is gone, all my strong self confidence, all my hope. The very brightness of my prospects as the world would say, is a curse on me! What can it lead to but the repetition of the same miserable story of inadequacy and inefficiency in the end?[36]

Trevelyan was not yet twenty-two. It was as well he should have ended his tirade with a question, when almost all his long life lay before him.

For a young man, passionately committed to the Liberal cause, who had long decided that his career should be in politics, the summer of 1892 offered the best possible opportunity to forget the tribulations of the past year. The parliamentary session had been cut short, for in mid-summer Salisbury, the Tory Prime Minister, had advised the Queen to dissolve Parliament. At the time, the Tories enjoyed a majority of sixty-six in the Commons. The subsequent general election in July provided the ideal anodyne for Trevelyan's bruised feelings. With work to be done and a cause to promote, there was no time to sit and brood about his personal fortunes. As his father faced a comparatively easy task in defending his majority in Glasgow, Trevelyan eagerly volunteered his services to Charles Fenwick, and canvassed in his interest among the Northumbrian miners in the Wansbeck division. Fenwick was triumphantly returned to the Commons as part of the Home Rule majority in the new House.* In August the Tory Ministry was ousted on a vote of confidence, and Gladstone, now but three months short of his eighty-third birthday, formed his fourth and last Administration. Though even then the effort must have seemed hopeless, Gladstone decided he must settle the running sore of the Irish problem. As in the short-lived third Liberal Cabinet in 1886, John Morley was appointed Chief Secretary for Ireland, and this meant that he was obliged to seek re-election. In July the Liberal cause in Newcastle had suffered a mortifying repulse with the Tory candidate heading the poll and Morley's Liberal colleague coming last. There could be no question of Morley being returned unopposed. If the general election auguries meant anything a defeat for Morley seemed certain. Fresh from the triumph shared with Fenwick, Trevelyan now gave his support to Morley and despite the doleful omens, the Liberals won a famous victory. Thus, in less than two months, Trevelyan had been involved in two campaigns where the

---

*There were 273 Liberals; 81 Irish Home Rule Members; and one Independent Labour Opposed to them were 269 Tories, and 46 Liberal Unionists.

Liberals' Irish policy had been triumphantly affirmed by the electorate. His family's previous involvement in Irish affairs had not always been so happy. *

After the excitement of the hustings a less pleasant prospect appeared. Trevelyans parents decided it would be excellent training for their son to spend some time at Dublin Castle as a private secretary to Lord Houghton recently appointed by the Liberal Government as Lord Lieutenant of Ireland. They thought it time Trevelyan became better acquainted with the pleasures of fashionable Society. Though strikingly handsome, Trevelyan was uncomfortable and withdrawn when in company, intolerant of the platitudes that pass for polite conversation, and particularly ill at ease when obliged to talk with young women. His parents fondly supposed that a period at the vice-regal lodge might soften the hard edges of personality and save their eldest son when in company from being 'invariably reduced to ineffable stupidity.'

It was October before Trevelyan first met his new chief at Crewe House. Lord Houghton appeared much younger than he had expected, and much less talkative. As to Houghton's political intentions in Ireland, Trevelyan, even by this first, brief acquaintance was convinced 'he will not go it very strong... Ld. H's trousers are not of a fast cut.'[37] Going to Ireland 'with a whole crowd of other ADC's' was, Trevelyan admitted, for him 'rather too much like going back to school. There's the same sense of having got among a lot of incompatible companions and the dread feeling that one will never get on with them.'[38]

Within a few days Trevelyan was regretting ever having agreed to go to Ireland. 'God knows whether I shall ever be fairly comfortable in any berth. But, it was the height of folly to allow myself to get into this most uncongenial place that I could have selected in the globe.' As to his mother's hope that he would enjoy the pleasures of Society away from home, he told

*For Sir George Trevelyan's period as Irish Secretary, when he was sent to Ireland to replace Burke who, with Lord Frederick Cavendish had been assassinated by an Irish gang, see, G.M. Trevelyan, *Sir George Otto Trevelyan: A Memoir* (Longmans, 1932), Chap. V, *passim*. The strain of his dangerous office kept for two years, left a permanent mark. Mary, Lady Monkswell, a family friend, recalled: 'As Sir George was not *born brave* he had a most sickening time, it almost drove him mad — the Irishmen were determined to get him — they used to send him word that they were going to mutilate his boys at school. When he came back after two years of the fear of death his hair was white and the eye-lashes of one eye were white.' (E.C.F. Collier (Ed.) *A Victorian Diarist* (John Murray, 1944), ii:204.) Victoria de Bunsen recalled Sir George's attendance at morning service with her family at Waltham Abbey, armed with a pistol in his pocket to guard against possible assassins. (V. de Bunsen, *Charles Roden Buxton: A Memoir* (Allen and Unwin, 1948), 10.) In October 1884, Sir George was rewarded for his courageous services, being given the more congenial post of Chancellor of the Duchy of Lancaster. But his fortunes were still not quit of Ireland. In March 1886, he resigned office unable to agree to the principle of complete Home Rule for Ireland. In the general Election that year, he stood as a Liberal Unionist and was defeated. His infatuation with the Unionists was short-lived and within a year he re-entered Parliament again as a Liberal. He was violently pilloried in the Tory press as a turn-coat and political weathercock. As a child, Charles Trevelyan had played during his school holidays in the grounds of his father's lodge, but seems to have been more discomforted by thoughts of crossing the Irish sea than fears of Irish hoodlums.

her that she could not have been more mistaken. 'The one certain effect of my being here will be that I shall never go anywhere in London in the evening as long as I live.'[39] It was never Trevelyan's habit to promise or undertake anything by halves.

The most obvious cause of his discontent was his under-employment. His secretarial duties for Houghton were minimal. Enforced idleness was made more irksome by attendance as a spectator at much ceremonial for which he felt nothing but contempt. He did not want to fill his time with reading and study; there had been quite enough of that for the moment at Trinity. What Trevelyan wanted, he described as 'one touch of nature — I am sick of intellectual excitement…, of Macaulayism, Trevelyanism; intellectual cleverness in general seems so unsatisfying'. Until now he had allowed himself to be 'cramped by years of duty, of fear of reputation and career'. Now he must seek his true self, though that process would be easier if he was allowed 'to see the machinery of government working', rather than 'prance about in gold lace and white inexpressibles through an Irish season in Dublin Castle'.[40]

With understandable surprise Trevelyan discovered at Dublin Castle there were no more than 'ten Home Rulers in a hundred, and that an outside estimate'. He earlier had calculated that, himself excepted, he was 'now in a society where there is not a single Home Ruler save the Lord Lieutenant, a ludicrous position indeed'. This in part explains why, whenever possible, he took himself off into town or country to talk with Home Rule friends and meet the Irish people. 'I believe it gives a certain confidence in us to them to see at least someone from the Castle going among them and talking to them as a friend.' The bland official lack of concern for the interests and opinions of the Irish people long remained a bitter memory. A decade later, in a letter to Molly Bell, he was to recall how 'over the gates of Dublin Castle stands the figure of Justice, but looking inward with *her back turned to the people*'.[41]

Trevelyan maintained that Houghton's greatest asset was an ability to go through his public duties mechanically, and there was little doubt that he was a better choice for office than had been his Liberal predecessor, Lord Aberdeen. Within a month of his coming to Ireland, Trevelyan admitted that he was totally disenchanted with his master. 'I cannot get on comfortably with him,' he wrote. 'There seems to be a perpetual brick wall between us. I think it is that he is interested in his Vice Regal duties, and that I, though successfully concealing my contempt for them, cannot be easy while sharing them.'[42]

An exaggerated sense of isolation in his opinions made Trevelyan increasingly intolerant and critical of his companions. He informed his mother he feared his heart was hardening into dislike of most of the other ADC's.

Tonight Ld. H. was at play with some of the party. I stayed with others. Afterwards one of the men spoke of politics and Home Rule bitterly, in that high-handed, disdainful, superior way that only Tories can speak, spurning their hearer's opinions, getting the ruder and the more blatant if they see he objects. He spoke of the Irish as ruffians, and used the worst sort of language towards them. He knew no better. There was no retort without the eloquence which I do not possess. Such are the pleasures of belonging to a Home Rule Government.

Later, in the same letter, Trevelyan expressed the main source of his irritation and exasperation, and at the same time begged his parents to excuse his tirade for there was no one else to whom he could complain.

By God, I will have my revenge one day on these supercilious gentry. *This* I shall have learnt to serve me through life, that courtiers are the most narrow, the most ignorant, and of all men the most weak because they do not count the strength of their enemies.[43]

The laboured passage of Gladstone's Second Home Rule Bill through the Commons' in Ireland was marked by increasing Unionist activity. Trevelyan advised his parents to ignore the exaggerated accounts in the press, particularly *The Times*. In January 1893 he wrote to his father of how some wild duck shooting had been magnified into firing upon the bailiffs, and of a barricade raised by tenants 'which might have been of Parisian dimensions from the reports, and yet would not have taken a single carman more than a minute to remove'. Despite all the prejudiced reports to the contrary, 'the people [were] thoroughly determined to be peaceable... [for] they understand the political situation'.[44]

The Unionists are beginning to put on the steam here... The press is full of column after column of resistance. The rich are subscribing, the Ulster working men are shouting, while the Home Rule Bill is dramatically rent and thrown to the winds. The Church too is praying and thundering. But such effervesence is necessary, and there is no violence yet. But against the years and years of petitioning, struggling, obstructing, hating and mourning of the rest of the country, it is very insignificant.[45]

The excitement afforded by the Unionist campaign was a brief interlude to lighten boring routine. The depression that had plagued his last year at Trinity returned with added intensity. He wrote, 'It is very wretched not to have a single person to talk to near me. It is most utterly lonely.' He doubted whether 'even for the sake of learning something more of Ireland..., the odious experience' was worth continuing. If it had not been for the people he knew outside the Castle, then, he vowed, he would not live there another hour. An Easter walking tour accompanied by his brother George afforded a pleasant interlude. Idle hours were sometimes whiled away with conversation lessons to improve his French. But when urged by his father to occupy at least some of his time with studying the Irish problem, he excused himself to his mother as having, by his experience in Ireland, become nothing less than a 'contemptible dilettante'.

By June 1893, it was apparent to Trevelyan's parents that for their eldest son to stay any longer in Ireland served no useful purpose. In May he had urged upon them his utter conviction that the sooner he left Ireland the better. Further gentle parental remonstrance proved unavailing, and eventually Trevelyan was allowed to have his way. Depression was immediately forgotten as he planned how he might spend those first weeks free at last of Ireland. A few days in London, then Wallington for a month where he hoped to invite some friends — 'a fair-sized, lively, Liberal, youthful party. And you,' he informed his mother, 'will make an excellent chaperone, though we are not a troublesome herd as we are all very proper.'[46]

In September 1893, the Home Rule Bill was finally passed by the Commons. Within the week it was rejected by the Lords. Trevelyan began in earnest his preparations to secure and fit himself for a place in Parliament. For the moment he had done with Ireland, but his experiences there long influenced his political attitudes.

MAKING A BEGINNING
IN POLITICS:
1893-99

Though only twenty-three, Trevelyan could confidently expect that his ambition of becoming a member of the Commons would soon be realised. Two generations of Trevelyans already had given eminent service to their country. If he was somewhat inexperienced in matters of administration, time would remedy that. The most important considerations were satisfied: he was a committed Liberal and he was rich. This last was crucial when most members were expected not only to support themselves, but also to give generously to their constituency and party funds.

Sir George's influence within the Liberal party, and particularly in the Scottish constituencies, ensured Trevelyan would not have too long to wait for nomination to a suitable seat. Towards the end of his unhappy stay in Ireland he had written to his father:

> I cannot tell you how much I appreciate the manner in which you have taken the greatest trouble to make the political world realize my existence and have kept on the alert for any favourable chance of getting me a good seat at the next election.[1]

Soon after writing this letter there was a sharp, if temporary, breach between father and son. On a short visit to the Isle of Man Trevelyan fell hopelessly in love for the first time. With an extraordinary naïveté — a close friend had professed astonishment at Trevelyan's admission that at twenty-two his 'heart had not been touched by the tender passions' — he had declared not only his love, but a proposal of marriage, only to be rejected. Trevelyan's father rated him for 'forgetting the responsibilities of his position'. The former good relations between father and son were, however, soon restored. Trevelyan declared he would never again forget his 'duty, which no one can think so highly of as I do myself. I should never mar my prospects of doing good to the people for the sake of any love for woman. This is far the strongest passion of my life.' If he had done wrong by his profession of love, then 'it was not to my own prospects or to Papa's generosity and loving plans for my future, but to her.'[2] The parties agreed the whole incident was best forgotten.

In October 1893 Trevelyan was approached by some Mid-Lanark Liberals, and asked to offer himself as their candidate. This was an excellent prospect as it was a safe Liberal seat. The only apparent disadvantage was that a much more experienced parliamentary campaigner, Edward Caldwell, was a competitor for the Liberal favours. Trevelyan lightly dismissed his rival as 'a second-rate intriguer'. The constituency party thought otherwise and selected the older man. At the conclusion of this brief contest, Trevelyan wrote to his father:

> I hope you are not very disappointed... I cannot say sincerely that I am. I worked as hard as I might... But, I felt in a somewhat false position being pushed not solely owing to my own qualifications... I ought not to have the way made smooth for me too much.[3]

In a letter written that same day to his mother, he confided:

> It is the same with me everywhere and with everything — in college work, love and politics; everything made easy for me up to the crucial point..., false encouragement of kindly but bad judges and inadequacy at the finish. I feel again here that I have been pushed with the best intentions and no doubt full belief in me, without the foundation of work and knowledge which is necessary.[4]

However, this preliminary essay into constituency politics had not been without its more positive lessons. Though he had spoken 'with perhaps greater satisfaction to myself and to the audience than I have ever done before, making points clearly and often forcibly', he recognised his inability to conceal ignorance of local problems. He had given his audiences an impression of political innocence. Nor had he helped his case by his lack of tact when answering questions by refusing to show enthusiasm or interest where he had none. 'I feel..., my failing is a lack of mastery of a subject or situation... I cannot capture understanding. I am an enthusiast with no sound material basis of knowledge to force my theories and build my reforms.' He refused, however, to be plunged into depression by his reverse. On the contrary it was patently his 'duty' never again to seek a safe constituency unless unanimously asked to do so.

> The young must gain experience by hard knocks and must win their spurs tilting on jaded nags before a full-breathed charger is given them to ride in comfort and security. I am ready to fight a seat where there is a reasonable

chance. I should win it through sheer vigour.[5]

This optimistic estimate was to be put to the test sooner than he might have supposed.

Dolly Tennant for years had been a favourite guest of the Trevelyans. She was known to the public as a 'lady artist' whose work had been exhibited at the Royal Academy and the Grosvenor.[6] In May 1890, the press announced her engagement to the famous African explorer, Henry Morton Stanley. A journalist savagely remarked that 'Dorothy Tennant always said that she would marry a lion; and she will certainly be marrying the king of the beasts.'[7] Dolly's engagement was not received happily by Trevelyan, then still at Trinity. He had written to his mother:

> When I brought the news to a select company..., there was a perfect wail of indignation... Stanley is not a favourite — men of importance and be-dinnered heroes of the hour do not come off best with undergraduates — and when it was known that Dolly was engaged to him, the cry was at once 'Then this is the result of lion hunting'. Such intellect to be married to such conceited boorishness![8]

Dolly determined that her husband should become a member of Parliament, if for no better reason than it was the only way she could contrive to keep Stanley in England and protect his uncertain health. Eventually, the explorer was persuaded to stand as Liberal Unionist candidate for North Lambeth in the 1892 election. Narrowly defeated by his Radical opponent, Stanley's rough handling by rowdies at the hustings blighted his meagre enthusiasm for Dorothy's ambitions on his behalf. Only with great reluctance did he agree to remain as a candidate, but on the understanding that while he would make speeches, he would never again degrade himself by asking a man for his vote, or 'do any silly personal canvassing'.[9] In the next election, therefore, the burden of Stanley's campaign fell mainly upon his wife.

Early in December 1893, Coldwells, the Radical-Liberal member for North Lambeth, gave notice of his intention to quit the seat at the next election. In close contact with Coldwells, Sir George Trevelyan actively promoted his son's candidature for nomination to the vacancy. From a short list of four names, Trevelyan was chosen by the local association's executive. Some members were not happy with the way Trevelyan had been selected. They would have preferred Frank Smith as their candidate. Despite entreaties that he should remain silent, Coldwells' former agent, James Woollen, publicised their grievance in the columns of the local daily, but this ploy intended to discomfort Trevelyan misfired. His 'timely piece of indiscretion' made warm adherents of those who formerly had been cool in their support of Trevelyan. Nevertheless, in his letter accepting nomination, Trevelyan particularly stressed that his selection had been 'ratified by large public meetings held in each of the polling districts of the constituency'.[10] Rumblings of discontent continued, and though Coldwells frequently sent comforting letters to his young successor that he should not be concerned, Trevelyan remained unconvinced. The expected threat to Trevelyan's candidature did not materialise. Defeated on a snap vote of censure over cordite supplies in June 1895, Rosebery, despite the opposition of most of his Cabinet colleagues, resigned. Salisbury formed his third Administration bringing five Liberal Unionists within his Cabinet, and then Parliament was dissolved for general election.

In North Lambeth, Trevelyan's preparations for the contest were well in hand. In December he had written to his father: 'We shall have all arrangements ready by Xmas for the literature to be ready within a week of ordering it. We shall know exactly what streets require most canvassing so that they can be tackled first the moment the election comes.'[11] However, insufficient attention had been paid to the register of electors, a mistake that Trevelyan was never again to make.

Trevelyan's manifesto boldly proclaimed his ambition was 'to serve the public' and 'to labour in the cause of progress'. He represented his support for a bewildering array of proposals from Home Rule to local option; the rating of ground values and the municipalisation of gas and water supplies and of the tramway service. He wanted to engage his opponent upon these issues alone, but his agent, a much more experienced and unscrupulous campaigner, did not despise the electoral value of circulating those leaflets that had served the Radical cause so well in 1892. These contained a calculated list of 'atrocities' perpetrated by Stanley in 'Darkest Africa' during the Emin Pasha Relief Expedition. Innuendo was given greater credence by the local Radical press when, on the eve of the poll they affirmed, 'Mr. Stanley's course through Africa has been like that of a red hot poker drawn across a blanket. He nightly sleeps on a pillow of blood.'[12]

On polling day the rival candidates drove round the constituency, Stanley accompanied by his wife in a victoria, and Trevelyan cutting a more dashing figure in a four-in-hand, 'the ribbons expertly handled by his lady companion'[13] That evening, a large, noisy crowd gathered outside the Board School in Hercules Road where the count took place. Impatient of delay, the crowd became threatening, and a detachment of thirty policemen was required to protect the candidates from the attentions of rival supporters. When eventually the poll was declared, it showed a Unionist gain.

H.M. Stanley (Liberal Unionist) 2,878
C.P. Trevelyan (Liberal Radical) 2,473
Liberal Unionist majority 405

Most of the crowd received the news with obvious and noisy disfavour. The

South London Press reported: 'North Lambeth has fallen into the pit that has been so assiduously dug for it by the Primrose League and kindred agencies during the past three years.'[14] Trevelyan was bitterly disappointed. He told a local newspaper reporter:

> I could easily run off a list of superficial reasons why we lost. But, the real cause of the Radical collapse in London lies very much deeper. Coercion, blankets and beer would be useless against genuine conviction. The Londoner is not yet alive to what politics may do for him... The Progressives of London, whether Parliamentary or County Council, will only recover London by patient inculcation of the principles of bold social reform.[15]

Trevelyan retained his candidature of North Lambeth for only another six months. The increasing animosity shown him by members of the local association persuaded Trevelyan his connections with North Lambeth were best soon severed. That decision taken, he made no secret of his relief at 'finally being rid of the business'. The constituency was 'politically in a pitiable state'.[16] Despite this sour ending and the disappointment of defeat, Trevelyan's candidature had provided him with valuable, much needed experience. He listed these gains in a personal survey he wrote later that year.

> I now feel fully prepared for intervention in public affairs... Where once I lectured, now I speak... This training has helped me over the Asses Bridge of rhetoric. [My] rage at what is bad and oppressive is growing while it is tempered by experience.[17]

Trevelyan had described himself as a Radical to his constituents, but it was no accident that he had sounded more the temperate note of Fabianism than that of revolutionary radicalism. Neither inheritance nor intellect disposed Trevelyan to assume a revolutionary stance in politics. He was better read in military history and strategy than political philosophy. Like many another of his contemporaries, the greatest outside influence upon his early political beliefs was the writing of John Ruskin. It was not Ruskin's 'most sincere love of kings' that attracted Trevelyan, but the ideal the writer shared with Carlyle and Froude of the hero who, in true chivalric spirit, strives to serve the poor, the weak and the oppressed. The rhetoric of heroism compensated for a guilty consciousness of the sufferings of England's labouring masses. Ruskin provided the language for an assault upon injustice and inequality while eschewing any firm criteria for detecting social ills or creating legislative remedies. That nothing, or anything, could be said to follow from Ruskin's arguments, was of no significance. Tone, not content, was all important. Hence the appeal to Charles Trevelyan, a young man born to privilege yet made uneasy in its enjoyment by his social conscience.

Ruskin's writings equipped Trevelyan with a broadly based philosophy of purpose in politics. It was his friendship with the Webbs, and consequent involvement with the Fabians, that afforded precision and direction to his aims. His close contact with the Webbs dates from the time he returned from Ireland to live with his parents in London. From the spring of 1894 he became a frequent visitor at 41 Grosvenor Road. Of the famous partnership, the formidable Beatrice would always remain the more impressive character in Trevelyan's eyes. H.G. Wells in *The New Machiavelli*, caught exactly the Webbs' appeal to a young, impressionable, prospective politician like Trevelyan.

> It was natural I should gravitate to them for they seemed to stand for the maturer, more disciplined, better informed expression of all I was then urgent to attempt to do.[18]

Wells also captured the vision of that new generation of young Liberal politicians that the Webbs so carefully cultivated; a group 'all tremendously keen upon social and political service, and all greatly under the sway of the ideal of a simple, strenuous life, a life finding its satisfaction in political achievements and distinctions'.[19] What the novelist failed to reveal was the sense of gaiety and fellowship that lightened even the Fabians' most serious enterprise in those early years. In a letter to his parents, Trevelyan described a 'typical Fabian gathering'.

> We* most of us travelled down together yesterday. At Victoria, a quarter of an hour before the train started, there was a line of cabs reaching for a quarter of a mile from the station, packed with luggage and eager, fussy, indignant hands and faces bobbing in and out of the windows... At Eastbourne, a bus came to meet us with red wheels and a coachman in livery. This is how the Fabian Society go on, when not posing democratically. It was as if the Duke himself had given us the run of his stables to get us up Beachy Head.
> Here we have monopolized the Hotel, except the bar, which is filled with tourists and fly men during the middle of the day. Till eleven and after five we have the whole place and the whole Head to ourselves. It is glorious weather..., and Mrs. Webb has had to borrow glycerine for her sunburns. I am teaching the whole party to bicycle... Mrs. Webb will soon be proficient. Mr. Webb is hopeless, and with an impatience unreasonable in a man who has devoted years to converting London to Collectivism, abuses the bicycle for not 'balancing' during his first lesson. Bernard Shaw is at this moment industriously tumbling about outside... We have an enormous library contributed by different members of the party which nobody reads because we are either out all day or talking.[20]

Contact with the Fabians brought an entirely new dimension to Trevelyan's

---

*The party was: Mr. and Mrs. Webb, Bernard Shaw, Trevelyan, Herbert Samuel, Graham Wallas, Miss Newcombe who was an artist, and a Mr. Ball, 'an Irish Italian in the Local Government Board'.

political experience. 'I see a good many people,' he told his father, 'from the other side of the picture to which I have been admitted before. The conventionality and narrowness of people are exposed often by contact with Shaw and his friends.'[21] Trevelyan was enchanted by Shaw's humour and roguish intellect. 'He is very much what I hoped and expected, excessively talkative, genial and amusing, and not unduly aggressive or cynical. He is not full of praise for anything or anybody — but is the perfection of real good nature.'[22] Soon, the staple of Trevelyan's letters to his parents was Shaw's latest inspired diagnosis of what exactly ailed politics.

> Shaw gives the best exposition of the state of things one could hope to hear... His great point is that the ordinary man *cannot*, and that the leaders at present *do not* do any elaborate thinking either about the theory or detail of politics. This indictment is generally absolutely true... The dilettante character of our leadership at present is an evil which we younger men feel more and more everyday.[23]

Of the friendships Trevelyan made among the Fabians, the longest lasting was with his contemporary, Herbert Samuel. Both sought a place in Parliament and a life of public service; both were Liberals, yet together they explored the possibilities of Socialism, to create a new Radical impetus among Liberals — Samuel with an inveterate caution that belied his youth; Trevelyan with impatient gusto.

For a number of years there had been trade union MPs, but they had always been supported by local Liberal organisations, and had taken their seats in the Commons as members of the parliamentary Liberal party. Keir Hardie's success in winning West Ham for Labour in 1892, and the foundation of the Independent Labour Party in 1893, were sufficient for younger, thinking Liberals to recognise that growing Labour independence might prejudice the Liberal cause in the constituencies. Consequently, 'progressive' Liberals, as they called themselves, were anxious to forestall any further division within radical ranks.

Socialism had been a much discussed subject when Trevelyan had been at Cambridge. In November 1889 he had met and talked with Tom Mann who earlier that year had played a commanding part in organising the successful strike by the dockers. Trevelyan wrote to his father:

> ... You need not be too much afraid of my falling into this bad Socialistic company. A Socialist he is certainly. But at any rate on such questions as he really professes to understand, a very mild one. I have always thought that Socialism was essentially destructive. But all the ends and proposals of Mann are the very reverse and essentially constructive. I should like to talk to you more about what he said.[24]

As long as the Liberal party was 'imbued with a deep and democratic conviction..., supported by the largest mass vote of the working class given to any party, and closely responsive to articulate demands for economic change',[25] then Trevelyan believed it would remain the best *immediate* instrument for securing progress. He long remained sceptical that there was any need for a separate Labour Party in Parliament. He was prepared to repudiate 'the hard unsympathetic view of the individualist', but he was not convinced by 'the Socialist doctrine of a regenerated economic society. The fatal objection to a socialist state,' declared Trevelyan to a meeting of the Newcastle Liberal Club, 'is that there is no security that industry will be more honestly, humanely and intelligently administered that it is by private individuals now.' It was a mistake, however, for Liberals to treat Socialists as enemies.

> The problem for a great many generations to come is..., social reform, and if the Liberal party wishes to hold its own as a great organ of modern pro-gress, it is to this that it must devote itself... The Liberal party must be a national and not a sectional party... The progress of the future must be the progress of all.[26]

The *Manchester Guardian* commented on young Trevelyan's public pleas to his Liberal elders: 'He urges Liberals to activity to redress evils, telling them that "equality of opportunity" is the motto of social progress in these things. Fabianism all over, and nothing very shocking either... If Liberals are wise, they will profit by this.'[27] Meanwhile, Trevelyan grew bolder.

> I have the greatest sympathy with the growth of the socialist party. I think they understand the evils that surround us and hammer them into people's minds better than we Liberals... I want to see the Liberal party throw its heart and soul fearlessly into reform so as to prevent a reaction from the present state of things and the violent revolution that would inevitably follow it.[28]

However, Trevelyan's views on Liberalism and Socialism during this period are most clearly expressed, not in his public speeches, but in the private musings he recorded in his journal.

> How to rebuild and purify is the real problem. And one of the reasons why Socialism is not so happily calculated to deal with this problem is that like all rigid doctrines it is *enragé* with one half of the world and benign to only the other half. It is true that its ultimate goal is an ordered society for all. But it boasts that it will reach it over the wreck of the modern system. It attracts quite as much because of its uncompromising penalties for landlordism and capital as for the new world it offers. This in the long run only angers the average Englishman. To what end this everlasting craving for undoing? ...Socialism is feared because it is thought that it cramps the aspirations and energy of the best men. Very likely it would not, but it is

mainly put before the world as a gospel of the weak or unfortunate. The English see themselves as a strong and fortunate race, and take their pride in it.[29]

In September 1895 Trevelyan was introduced to the Rainbow Circle by Herbert Samuel. This rather self-conscious discussion society of some twenty or so 'Liberals of the Left and Socialists of the Right' — young politicians, journalists and economists — had been formed the previous autumn. The group met once a month, initially at the Rainbow Tavern in Fleet Street, and later at the house of one of the members in Bloomsbury Square. Among the more prominent members were Graham Wallas, J.A. Hobson, Herbert Burrows, William Clarke; and the Secretary was James Ramsay MacDonald. At the first meeting that Trevelyan attended, Samuel read a paper on 'The New Liberalism: its origin and place in politics'. Of the occasion, Trevelyan wrote to his mother:

> Samuel and I have been trying to thrash out difficulties at the Rainbow Circle with the thinking Socialists. I think we make them come down a little from their ideal eminence — certainly we get our own minds clearer as to what we want.[30]

Trevelyan contributed the occasional paper to these meetings. He also wrote articles for the *Progressive Review* and purchased £100 of *Review* stock. This last caused him temporary financial embarrassment, relieved by a cheque from Sir George who willingly made up his son's allowance because, though he counted the purchase 'a little rash', it would 'not be a recurring charge'. The *Review*, a shilling monthly edited by Clarke and Hobson, was intended to 'afford the progressive movement in all its aspects..., a medium of expression'. Unfortunately, the venture was short-lived, foundering upon an insufficient circulation and an acrimonious relationship between Clarke and MacDonald. The *Review's* swift demise was not the end of the Rainbow Circle, but other interests and engagements led Trevelyan to take little part in their discussions despite gentle chiding from Samuel. 'Alas the Rainbow Circle wants to know whether you wish to continue your membership. You didn't attend once last session. Shame!'[31]

Samuel was now Trevelyan's closest confidant in political affairs. Samuel readily cast himself in the role of elder statesman, a cautious curb to Trevelyan's extravagant enthusiasm for any idea that might breathe new life into Liberalism. In May 1895, a little before his unsuccessful campaign in North Lambeth, Trevelyan had written to Samuel:

> I have been talking to one or two of our progressive Liberal candidates about the want of some nucleus of advanced opinion in the party. There is no organisation representing the Radical Labour view. There has never been any discussion to form a definite programme of what should be the mini-

mum creed for a candidate... We thought to start some activity to repair these wants... Our immediate object would be to have the great questions of social importance thoroughly thrashed out first by some half dozen or dozen of us who are mainly interested in them — ...We want you· very much to come — it is essential of course that you should join with us if the matter develops.

Samuel's response was circumspect. Surely it was not for young men such as themselves to promulgate programmes on their own authority for the public's diversion? In the circumstances, it would be wiser to concentrate upon 'the permeation of existing institutions'. Quite unabashed by his friend's response, Trevelyan replied that if they were to follow Samuel's counsel then straightway they must

> consider by what means it would be possible to utilize the Liberal Federation for the expression of the views of the active and progressive elements of the party instead of as now merely reiterating its approval of the Newcastle Programme...

Nor did Trevelyan's schemes end with using the Liberal Federation. There was the Eighty Club which R.B. Haldane was attempting to revivify.

> He [Haldane] thinks it might be possible to use it as an organisation for the expression of advanced Liberalism if carefully handled. His idea is that if you and I and some others could undertake to organize it afresh, we might make it a valuable nucleus of progressive effort.

'Pussy' Haldane would never have a more eager aide for his designs than Trevelyan. 'Haldane wants you and me to go round and have a smoke with him after dinner on Tuesday. I will certainly go,' wrote Trevelyan. But Samuel would not have any part in their 'conspiracy'.[32]

Another friend, Graham Wallas, suggested a course of action to Trevelyan that would more profitably engage his energies than plotting with Haldane to save Liberalism from itself. 'Wallas is very anxious that I should take a vacant seat on the London School Board,' wrote Trevelyan to his father. 'Everyone approves the idea,' he told his mother. But the caucus, by a majority of one, chose another candidate. 'It would have been very interesting work,' but 'I do not care very much,' Trevelyan wrote, while patently caring a great deal.[33] However, his disappointment was short-lived for within a year he was co-opted as a member of the London School Board.

Trevelyan's time now became much occupied with his School Board duties, and particularly in preparing for the forthcoming elections a long polemical pamphlet, *The Cause of the Children*. His researches gave Trevelyan the opportunity to clarify two particular issues to his own satisfaction. Though designed to publicise the Progressives' educational policies, much of the best writing concerned the inter-relationship between Progressivism and a 'true' Imperialism.

> ...True Imperialism does not concern itself alone with the extremities of
> Empire. The heart of the Empire deserves even more attention... To pro-
> vide a stronger and more intelligent generation to take the place — when
> the time comes — of the London of today, is the aim of the Pro-
> gressives... We can be justly proud of our orderliness and external well-
> being. But there is a sterner side to Empire than rejoicing in it. It is
> keeping ourselves fit for it — 'Lest we forget — lest we forget!'[34]

There was romance in plenty, and not a little bombast in Trevelyan's view
of Imperialism in this period. Only a stern sense of an obligation owed 'to
those less favoured by circumstance' than himself, saved the expression of
some of his ideas from bumptiousness. Without a hint of self-consciousness,
he wrote to Samuel, 'The justification of Empire must be based upon the
highest grounds.'[35]

Though not himself a candidate for election, Trevelyan campaigned for the
Progressives with his customary energy and enthusiasm. In three weeks he
made eighteen speeches in London, Leeds, Otley and Cambridge University.
He had good reason to be pleased with his efforts. 'I have not done badly,' he
admitted to his mother. 'I spoke nine times really well, twice badly, and the
rest decently.'[36] The election was a triumph for the Progressives. Trevelyan
wrote, 'There never was such a perfect election...'[37]

The rigours of electioneering had been pleasantly interrupted when
Trevelyan had acted as best man at Herbert Samuel's wedding. 'As the only
gentile present', he wrote that he had 'got Samuel married without a hitch.'[38]
Before he met his wife, Samuel had intended to accompany Trevelyan upon a
world tour. Trevelyan told Samuel that he had refused Wallas's suggestion
that he should stand for election to the School Board because he had decided
'the next step [was] to get into the House... I want to give all my energies to
that..., and to direct political writing or speaking to the end of making
Liberalism rather more of a reality'.[39]

Twice in 1897, Trevelyan unsuccessfully sought a Liberal candidature. In
February he had lost nomination for the Bridgeton division of Glasgow to Sir
Charles Cameron. 'Sir Charles,' wrote Trevelyan to Samuel, 'is chiefly, I
believe, a disestablishment man. The future religion of Bridgeton is humanity
not free Presbyterianism — but let us not scorn any form of good.'[40] In
September he had attempted to be nominated for Barnsley. The immediate
prospects had seemed promising, but for all the optimistic calculations,
another candidate was chosen.

After the School Board elections, Trevelyan had hurried north to Newcastle
and given three lectures on labour disputes and arbitration. The choice of
subject was bold and timely, for the city was involved in a bitter dispute
between the electrical engineers who had been locked out and their

employers. Among local Liberals, Trevleyan's forceful championship of the men created a most favourable impression. They offered him a nomination which he rejected. 'They cannot get me. It is not good enough as they would probably insist on running some half-Tory business man as the second candidate,' he wrote. However, the real reason for his refusal was that an altogether better prospect had materialised.

> The Elland people seem to want me. I am going down there sometime this month to speak two or three times. If I am favourably impressed with the place, and they with me, I shall probably close with them. By all reports it is a safe seat. If I got in, it would probably be for me a permanent seat if any could be.

This time there was to be no disappointment. Trevelyan accepted the offer of the Liberal candidacy when the sitting member would retire. 'Oh. How I like my constituency,' he wrote. 'I am going a good walk this afternoon to get a larger view from the top of the hills.' [42]

The Elland constituency had been created by the Redistribution of Seats Act, 1885. Previously, it had been part of the north division of the West Riding. In four elections Thomas Wayman, the Liberal candidate, had been returned, though each time with a diminished majority. Though there were some patches of agriculture, the major interests of constituents were either industrial or commercial. The *Bradford Observer* claimed:

> He who would fitly represent the people in the House of Commons, must have sympathy with the aspirations of a hard-working, clear thinking, thrifty, independent and ambitious race of men and women who have long since cast aside all subservience to parson and squire and require from Parliament nothing less than a steady improvement at a reasonable pace of their own workaday and holiday conditions of life. [43]

That a Liberal majority of more than three thousand had been whittled away in ten years to little more than three hundred, was not, according to the public pronouncements of the Liberal Association, a matter for concern. In 1895, the deplorable result had been due entirely 'to the Unionist candidate seizing the advantage of a passing wave of reaction'. [44] Trevelyan thought otherwise. 'The lowering of the majority is probably more due to Wayman's want of liveliness than a reaction. They say he has one speech and one only, and even at election times he has been known to refuse to deliver the oration more than four times.' [45] The local Liberal association was in disarray. There was no adequate organisation. The immediate and imperative requirement was to appoint a new and competent agent. Trevelyan wrote to his father:

> Today I have been seeing the recommended agent, W.N. Marshall, who is now at Stockton. He has the very strongest record and seems to be a quite first-rate man..., of real capability, experience and tact, and I do not wish

for a better man. I want to know if I may engage him. The situation is this. He wants £175 a year. The first year I should have to find the money... I have given the [local association] to understand that as I am going to pay election expenses, 2/3 of which they had to find at the last election. I shall expect them to pay all the registration expenses and eventually part of the salary of the agent. Otherwise I cannot get a first-rate man. I quite understand that this is a large sum to ask you to give. But I should not feel easy in leaving the constituency in second-rate hands with the possibility of an election next year... The other day at Headquarters they said positively that no good man could be got under £180, and I certainly should not like to leave for so long if there was only an inferior man in charge.[46]

The particular cause of Trevelyan's anxiety and haste was that, in little more than a month, he was due to begin a world tour with the Webbs. The arrangements at Elland, however, moved forward swiftly and smoothly. Sir George contributed the necessary money for the agent's salary — 'Please thank Papa for his liberality; I am sure it is a good investment in the long run to have a really good man'[47] — and a series of somewhat breathless meetings throughout the constituency were successfully concluded.

I had a rattling meeting in the Tory centre yesterday, and the hedging local paper has almost as friendly an account of me as the Liberal organ. Altogether things are going swimmingly...[48]

Trevelyan's fortunes with the Elland electorate now could be safely left in Marshall's capable hands. Within the week, Trevelyan was on his way to America in the R.M.S. 'Teutonic', 'comfortably berthed', though not quite as well catered for as the Webbs. They, so he informed his mother, 'with true Fabian simplicity have engineered themselves a state cabin!'[49]

Trevelyan chronicled in a detailed diary,* his nine month journey around the world, sent home to his family in the form of letters. His writing was always vivid, and his observations highlighted by a gentle humour. His travelling companions, having completed their monumental work on trade unions, were now planning their study of local government. The Webbs' comparative researches were to be conducted in the major urban areas and invariably they acquired the best available hotel accommodation. This was too comfortable, too restricted, and too slow a mode of progress for their restless fellow 'investigator'. Trevelyan wanted to see *everything*, and an incredible toughness of spirit and boundless physical energy allowed him almost to achieve his impossible aim. He liked much of what he saw, and most of those he met in North America; he disapproved of a few things and persons. But he was constitutionally incapable of being indifferent to anything or anyone.

While Trevelyan was in America, war was declared with Spain. His mother

*The diary has been published, edited by Trevelyan's daughter, Pauline Dower, *Letters from North America and the Pacific* (Chatto and Windus, 1969).

was greatly alarmed that he might be taken prisoner by the Spaniards, as he was expected to cross the Pacific by an American boat. The Webbs also were not a little anxious upon this score. But Trevelyan thought the whole thing was rather a joke.

> You will have received a letter from Webb by this time to say that we may have to risk capture by the Dons between Honolulu and New Zealand. It seems unavoidable, but the risk is so trifling that I do not mind it. It will be a spice of excitement and will warrant packing my revolver on the top instead of the bottom of my trunk... I expect Webb and I together would impress a privateer captain with the importance of the British flag. I do not fear a Spanish prison. I only fear a Spanish hotel, and the long voyage to it.[50]

There was never any real cause for anxiety for they were able to book passages to New Zealand upon a British steamship. The long journey was pleasantly broken by a short stay at Honolulu where the Webbs asked serious questions of local officials and concluded that they were both more honest and efficient than the majority of local administrators in America, while Trevelyan, for once, relaxed in the sun or went surfing with the Princess Kaiulani, whose acquaintance he had made several years earlier in London.

Less than a month was spent in New Zealand, yet Trevelyan visited both North and South Island, packing in enough excitement, adventure and interest to have occupied most men for a lifetime. An incident within a few days of their arrival illustrates his spirit and determination never to be thwarted. The Webbs and Trevelyan were to visit Napier, but the bridge over the Mohaka was down and recent storms had turned the river into a raging torrent. After 'due dissuasion from Mrs. Webb, anxious for justification in case I was drowned', Trevelyan decided to cross the torrent by means of a single rope stretched between the two banks. After 'an affectionate farewell' to the Webbs, who stood as helpless observers of his escapade — 'the crossing was of course impossible for the unathletic Webb or even the masculine vigour of Mrs. Webb' — hand over hand he traversed the river successfully, at the cost of a soaking from the spray, blistered and cramped hands, and the loss of a valise that was borne away to the Pacific upon the flood. The watchers upon the far bank cheered their intrepid companion and then returned to their inn, virtual prisoners.

> They will have to wait however long it takes. It is a pity they are not on their honeymoon. But, they are still sufficiently devoted to enjoy some hours *tête à tête* a day. But I am afraid the meagre literature of the inn and my bag which Webb will ransack will hardly fill in the interstices of more than 24 hours.

Meanwhile, Trevelyan walked the six miles to the nearest point where he

C.P. Trevelyan, the new Liberal MP for Elland, c. 1900

could get a coach to Napier, meeting a tramp on the way whom he persuaded to join him as a travelling companion. The next day, despite the rigours of his adventure, Trevelyan explored Napier as planned and took a guided tour of the meat freezing factories![51]

The reason why Trevelyan enjoyed his stay in New Zealand better than any other part of his world tour was quite simple.

> Here is a land which is home. I can hardly believe that I cannot step into a train to take me in a few hours to Wallington. All the people are English in gait and dress. In this rainy winter season they carry macintoshes, and the main street of Auckland looks as if it were full of rather townified border shepherds... The first two days in Auckland were about the most simply happy I have ever spent, the sheer delight of being again among the home people.[52]

The sea voyage from Wellington to Sydney was recorded with an unusual economy.

Sunday, September 4.	Discomfort.
Monday, September 5.	Respite.
Tuesday, September 6.	Misery.
Wednesday, September 7.	Recovery.[53]

To be in Australia after New Zealand was to be back in the great world again, of 'large business houses, fine public buildings and government offices', and the streets 'alive with rush and bustle'. But the charms of metropolitan life soon faded in comparison with the siren call of the great out-doors, unexplored and untamed. Trevelyan's diary records his continuing fascination with much of what he saw and learned. He still maintained an exhaustingly full programme of engagements; of tours and interviews, speeches and parliaments, factories and farms, schools and colleges. There was, however, a new note in his letters to the family. The tour had been of immeasurable worth, but how he longed to be once more immersed in English politics, to play a part himself rather than stand observer of the deeds of others. From Sydney, he wrote to Samuel:

> I think the chief effect of my tour politically speaking, is to make me more of a land reformer than before. The availability of land is the supreme difference between old and new Britain.
>   But these generalizations are not much use. I look forward to long talks with you, soon after I get back, which will be by the new year. You will have to tell me about home politics which seem mournful rather. I guess the Liberal party wants a little new blood don't you?[54]

The passage from Australia to England was uneventful. Trevelyan admitted that, like a returning schoolboy he numbered the days until he should once more be among his family. But if the delights of Wallington meant much, the fortunes of English politics intrigued and beckoned the more for his having been away from them so long. The day after his return, Trevelyan was writing to Samuel, 'What a disgusting position of things in the party. I have still to hear the inwardness of it.'[55]

But now was not the ideal time to concern himself over-much with the idiosyncracies and foibles of the Liberal leaders when there were immediate, personal issues at hand. Trevelyan's attention was better engaged in securing the Elland constituency which he had so long deserted. His world tour, however, afforded a convenient peg upon which he might hang his pre-by election strategy. So in bitter January, armed with a magic lantern, he went to Elland with tales of America and the warm Pacific. The local Tories were not blind to this tactic, and had a trick or two themselves to play. They made as much capital as they could out of his lectures, as 'an imitative ode in the manner of Kipling' indicates.

> 'As got a lantern too,
> Clever Chawles;
> With a magic slide,
> Limelight Chawles.
> An' 'e'll lecture, an' 'e'll spout
> Till the bally gas goes out
> An' the people rise and shout,
> 'No more Chawles.'
>
> As a bloke 'e's right enuff,
> Dear ole Chawles,
> But 'is politics is stuff
> Rubbish Chawles.
> You 'ave lost your bloomin' way
> As you'll see one Wednesday
> When to Foster* you will pay
> 'Omage Chawles.[56]

Everyone knew that Trevelyan was preparing to inherit the constituency from Wayman, but when would Wayman retire? Alderman Sugden, a local Liberal worthy, and Marshall, Trevelyan's agent, were sure that the sooner the by election was fought the better it would be for the Liberals. Trevelyan reported to his parents anxiously waiting at their London home for news of developments.

Everything, is in train now. Marshall, Sugden and myself discussed the situation thoroughly yesterday. Sugden has no doubt about Wayman's intention of retiring and is quite clear that he ought not to be asked to carry

*Philip Staveley Foster, the Tory candidate.

on any longer. He goes up to see Wayman next week when he will tell him what we want and clinch the matter.

Trevelyan busily rallied his friends for the coming battle. To Samuel he outlined his probable campaign tactics.

We are extremely well organized and I am now very well known. I shall of course fight the election on new Liberal lines and not on criticism of the Tories in the main. I expect I shall certainly be able to set the note as I please.

Trevelyan was determined to show that he was 'ready to risk something to make our people feel that we mean real business if we get the chance'. Nor would he hide the fact that he was a committed Imperialist, no matter what John Morley might have to say on that subject. * Trevelyan's constituents were

all perfectly mad with John Morley. Not all the good people who philanthropise are Little Englanders, and anyway, the 'Manchester Guardian' is read and disregarded on that side of things.

Wayman retired, and at a rousing public meeting in mid February, Trevelyan was formally adopted as the Liberal candidate. He told his supporters that they need have no fears about his essential Liberalism, whether he was an Imperialist or no.

I do not need tutoring by any highly Liberal or progressive or political constituency, for my predecessors have lived and worked in the service of the people. And the ghosts of them would rise against me — or in bodily shape they would come to rebuke me — if I were to fail in my Liberalism, or fail in public spirited performance of my duty at any time.

The Echo evidently approved of the young Liberal candidate.

Some may consider his ideals dreams — some, no doubt, socialistic — but the forcible way in which the arguments in favour of his principles are advanced, seldom fail to impress his audiences. He is a land reformer; a temperance man, will vote for local veto and will ardently support reform of the licensing laws. He is too, a pronounced Home Ruler. How could the son of such a father be otherwise?

Due to Marshall's efforts, the local Association was in excellent order, and in the pre-election period, hordes of willing workers canvassed every quarter of the constituency. Polling day dawned wild, with grey, lowering skies, and the narrow streets of the constituency were swept by frequent rain storms. The candidates braved the elements to encourage their party faithful and were rewarded with a high turn-out of electors. But, while the Tory vote stagnated

*There had been a continuing and acrimonious debate within the Liberal party over the merits of Imperialism. On 17 January, 1899, Morley, speaking to his constituents at Brechin, declared he would no longer play a part in Liberal fortunes as Imperialists acquiesced in militarism.

at its 1895 figure, the Liberals increased their vote by more than five hundred.

C.P. Trevelyan 6,041
P.S. Foster . . . . , ... 5,057
Liberal majority 984

The result could not have been more pleasing.

By the earliest post came a letter for Trevelyan from his father.

My Dear Boy, It is a very great success, and of a sort which proves how very important it was that the fight should come when it did. The seat has not only been won but saved... Congratulate Mr. Marshall for me. It is what he promised us... I am struck by the solid body of Toryism. It was indeed high time that it should be seriously and aggressively attached. It is a great relief — and triumph.

And Trevleyan's mother added in a post-script, 'This is a *real* victory... We are very proud of you and very happy.'   Of the many letters that poured in to congratulate the victor was one from his old, devoted nurse, Mrs. Prestwich.

Dear Mr. Charles, A line to congratulate you on your election and give myself the pleasure of addressing you as MP. I need not say how we all rejoice at your *well earned* success.
Affectly, and respectfully,
   Booa*

The preliminaries were over and done: he was at last a member of the Commons.

Dear Charley I send you my warmest congrats
While all of us merrily throw up our hats.
You have won for the Liberals a rattling success
And may your majority never grow less!!

There was till time to savour Sir Wilfred Lawson's rhyming felicitation. Trevelyan had won the opening skirmish; the greater tests still lay ahead.

---

*The pet name Charles gave his nurse, which everyone then adopted.

OF LIBERALISM, LEADERS AND WAR: 1899-1902

Trevelyan took his place in the Commons on March 14, 1899. 'New blood is welcome in the House,' commented the *British Weekly*, then added tartly, 'but much more on the Opposition side than in the crowded ranks of the Ministerialists.' If the enthusiastic welcome given Trevelyan by the Liberals was to be expected, the Tories also gave him a friendly reception. This was one of the advantages of being 'the son of a man with the largest House of Commons acquaintance of his generation',[1] wrote Trevelyan in his weekly letter to his constituents. A week after his introduction to the House, Trevelyan made his maiden speech in a debate on the London Government Bill. He 'plunged into the discussion with an energy and command of language not unbefitting his father's son and the grand nephew of Macaulay'.[2] What *The Times* tactfully had not mentioned was Trevelyan's very nervous start. Only after frequent efforts addressing the House was Trevelyan able to claim he had at last conquered his nervousness when beginning a speech. 'It is a great thing when you have got over the numbing inability to dare to get up when you know what wants saying at that moment.'[3]

So, the first hurdle in his parliamentary career was successfully negotiated. The obvious pleasure he took in his new work and his growing confidence was reflected in the letters he wrote to his parents that were full of comment upon the personalities and the doings of Westminster. Political commentators were soon speaking of Trevelyan as 'a young Parliamentary veteran'. But it was his independence of thought, and the vigour with which he expressed his ideas, that particularly drew attention and comment.

It would be a great mistake to regard him as merely a unit in the undistinguished ruck of items in the Whips' list of certain votes... He is neither a political adventurer, a party hack, nor a seeker after any of the desirable pickings which reward diligent drudgery in the Tom Tiddler's Ground of St. Stephen's. Beating the party drum is necessary work, there are times when it must be done, and they also serve who only stand and beat. But, Mr. C.P. Trevelyan is not cut out for tasks of that kind.[4]

When Rosebery resigned in 1896, the Liberal party had been left without a recognised or generally acceptable leader. Sir William Harcourt took over for a short time, but then he too resigned. The party next chose Sir Henry Campbell-Bannerman, though many Liberals thought him unsuited for the post. The personal antipathies, the various 'pretenders' to the Liberal leadership felt towards each other mirrored the deep divisions among their supporters, particularly over the vexed question of Imperialism. Rosebery and his young lieutenants, Henry Asquith, Richard Haldane and Edward Grey, called themselves Liberal Imperialists. Harcourt was determinedly anti-Imperialist. Campbell-Bannerman, though to some extent a compromise candidate as leader whom it was hoped might weld together the Liberal factions, was generally recognised as at heart a Radical and 'Little Englander'. The declaration of war by the Boers in October 1899 exacerbated these differences. In December 1898, in a letter to Samuel, Trevelyan referring to the vexed question of party leadership had written:

These petty leaders and their hangers on, what do they matter? What will they matter? Poor old anti-Papal Harcourt. Poor young, much injured, would-be dictator, Rosebery. Perhaps it is the best solution to have both of them temporarily shelved, and some placid Bannerman or busy lawyer Asquith as nominal head, while the body of the party gives birth to its new cause for which none of them are fit to be midwives.[5]

Trevelyan's declared sympathy for Imperialism was bound to attract the suspicion and criticisms of 'pro-Boers' like Francis Hirst. Despite frequently asserting dissatisfaction with Rosebery and the other Liberal Imperialist leaders, and his determination not to intrigue on their behalf, Trevelyan's public actions seemed to belie his intent. In the autumn of 1899, he was the moving spirit in the formation of the Ninety-nine Club, intended to bring active workers in the north of England together in 'the cause of progressive Liberalism'. But the anti-Imperialists in the Liberal party looked no further than the appointment of Sir Edward Grey as the President. To Hirst, Morley and other like-minded Liberals, the Club was just another imperialist clique. For Trevelyan to protest the Club was not intended to promote any sectional interest was, at the least, disingenuous.

I am doing all I can, directing all my efforts in my constituency, in Yorkshire, and generally, to preventing all unnecessary quarrels among Liberals... I do not, of course, conceal my opinion that I think Morley wrong in his attitude. But I am not therefore contemptuous or indignant at his position or that of those who follow him. I recognise that it is based on one great Liberal motive, the cause of peace. But that is not the only thing in Liberalism... It is of course only in private that I express my opinion as to the unwisdom of the violent talk of some of the extreme party. In public I merely try to make them a little more appreciative of the possibility of the existence of another conscientious Liberal opinion.[6]

Trevelyan's views on the Boer War were very simple. He was convinced that the British Government's intervention had been necessary to 'remedy a condition in the Transvaal intolerable to self-respecting Britons'. The war should be vigorously prosecuted. 'We cannot forget the blunders which have marred our good cause before the world,' he told his constituents in February 1900, 'but it is no time to waste breath upon them now when foreign peoples are muttering against us.' He was concerned, however, by the violence done to those who objected to the war. 'It is of no importance whether we approve or not of these ideas,' he told his contituents, 'they have the right to express them and the police and the law must defend them... It is at such times as these that the real extent of our national liberty is tested, and I hope it will stand the test.'[7] In a speech to the National Liberal Federation meeting at Nottingham in March 1901 Trevelyan made a strong appeal for party unity. Liberals should try to be practical rather than exaggerate the difficulties that existed among them. Their time would be better employed in discussing those questions upon which they were all able to agree. He urged the anti-Imperialists to 'accept the greater and larger duty which has been imposed upon us and be the reformers and good rulers of the Empire'.[8] This was the essence of Trevelyan's particular concept of Imperialism. In the end it rested upon the need for Liberals to formulate a programme of far-reaching domestic reform which alone would fit England for her role as an imperial power.

Trevelyan decided there was no point in waiting upon the party elders to come to an amicable agreement before formulating a progressive policy. The initiative must come from the younger Liberals. With his friend Walter Runciman recently elected to Parliament, he planned a series of meetings in the north of England where together they would raise the progressive banner and proclaim the vigour of Liberalism to the people. They must 'smash the Tory Government's reputation and then formulate [their] own programme'. Runciman's almost reckless enthusiasm was much more to Trevelyan's taste than the cautious circumspection of Herbert Samuel. However, Runciman was soon betrayed by his own impetuosity. Trevelyan received an almost hysterical note pouring imprecations upon Campbell-Bannerman's head.

C-B is insufferable and my greatest regret this morning is that he seems to have been reinstated by our wonderful front bench. Is Grey responsible for this?... C-B as far as I am concerned is done. Whether it be rash or not I have pretty nearly made up my mind to go down to my constituency and chuck him... Why not let us and [Charles] Douglas simultaneously in our various constituencies fire the same shot? I have no doubt coming from the three youngest members of our party quite boldly, it would be of the greatest interest, and to my thinking would only make public what we feel privately.[9]

Wisely, Trevelyan refused to accede to Runciman's request. 'To act independently, bravely, originally, even recklessly in *policy,* is what young men can and ought to do. To do the same thing about persons may bring ridicule, where the other can at the worst bring abuse.' It was not that Trevelyan disagreed with Runciman's estimate of Campbell-Bannerman, or that he desired any the less that the leadership of the party should pass to the Liberal Imperialists. But there was no virtue in their further dividing Liberal ranks in a way calculated to make them appear to be self-seeking and disloyal.

The rule in politics seems to be to quarrel with your enemies and not with your friends. And I do not think we should do our cause good by having to spend the next three months in fighting and justifying ourselves with the party. Far better recklessly enunciate an unauthorised programme abroad in the country which I *will* do, ignoring C-B and all his pro-Boer angels. The fact is that if we can keep Grey up to the mark, and get Rosebery and Asquith up to it, they *de facto* at once lead the party, whether *de jure* C-B does or not.[10]

Runciman heeded Trevelyan's advice, but the initial impetus to devise a common programme had been halted.

On 1 September 1900, Lord Roberts, in the Queen's name, annexed the Transvaal. Within two weeks, Parliament was dissolved and a general election called. The ostensible reason for the Government's action was the need to secure a popular mandate for the Transvaal settlement. But the 'Khaki' election in fact was an attempt by the Tories, largely at the instigation of Joe Chamberlain, to cash in electorally on a military victory. Their purpose was betrayed by their not waiting for a new register. However, there was little need for the Tories to be concerned about their electoral prospects. Though their Administration had waned in popularity — since the previous election their majority had been eroded by the loss of twenty-four seats in by elections — the Liberals were far too divided and demoralized to entertain any hope of winning. The Liberals contested fewer seats than in the 1895 election.*

Unlike many another constituency, in Elland, due largely to the efforts of his agent, Jack Marshall, Trevelyan knew that he had the support of an efficient and well-tried organisation. At one point, it even seemed that Trevelyan

*No Liberal candidate stood in 143 constituencies.

might be returned unopposed. Philip Foster refused to stand a second time in the Tory interest, and to their embarrassment the Conservatives were obliged to tout for a candidate. The Radical *Brighouse Echo* greatly enjoyed 'the sight of the Tories, ignominiously supplicating rich London carpet baggers to come down and champion a cause which all their local men regard as hopeless'.[11]

Eventually, a retired army Major, Edward Coates, was successfully dragooned to represent them. If the Tories supposed a holder of the Queen's commission would give them the lead in the patriotic stakes, Trevelyan's supporters had a lapel button manufactured for general distribution with their candidate's portrait surmounting the legend 'Progress and Patriotism'. This was, so the *Echo* assured its readers, 'a clear, short statement of Mr. Trevelyan's principles'!

It was the Major's first venture into politics. 'It is simply a gagging candidature,'[12] Trevelyan wrote to his father. The local Liberal press made the most they could of their candidate's advantage, and confidently predicted a successful result. Trevelyan estimated that Elland Liberals were not divided between pro Boer and Imperialists. George Trevelyan, with his brother throughout the campaign, noted in a letter to his father that 'there was great enthusiasm for Charlie, and *all* the Liberals were enthusiastic for him whatever their views on the war.'[13]

At his adoption meeting Trevelyan made it clear that he was not prepared to fight the election on the war issue alone. 'We are told this is a Khaki election. I tell you at once that so far as the Elland Division is concerned it will be nothing of the kind.' The electorate were asked 'to judge the Government upon their whole past'. It was not that Trevelyan wished to avoid the war issue altogether. He repeated his conviction that it had been necessary for the Government to intervene in the Transvaal but added, 'There can only be a sound solution in South Africa if the settlement can be in the hands of such Liberal statesmen as Mr. Asquith, Sir Edward Grey and Lord Rosebery.' The significance of the names he selected would not have escaped his audience. However, not only for the sake of unity but because he believed it was of more importance, Trevelyan concentrated his campaign upon the lamentable Tory record in domestic matters.

It is imperative that the Imperial Parliament should be made more democratic by providing salaries for members and the payment of their election expenses. The taxation of land values should be the basis of rating. More should be spent upon education; efficient county authorities should be created to control all elementary education and the religious tests for teachers should be discontinued.

Though the Tories have made lavish promises concerning social reform, they have frittered away five sessions without dealing with any of the obvious evils that burden the people. They have done nothing to reduce sweating, long hours or pauperism among the aged. Those measures they have passed to deal with overcrowding and industrial war are worthless. They appointed a Commission on the liquor traffic only to ridicule its findings, and have prevented the passage of even those small reforms upon which the commissioners unanimously agreed.[14]

Attempting to respond to Trevelyan's challenge on the subject of social reform, Coates was quickly bested in a fight for which he was ill-equipped and less than enthusiastic. Some of the major's supporters, disgruntled by his obvious lack of dynamism, attempted to reheat the war issue by posting throughout the constituency notices bearing the legend: 'A Vote for Trevelyan is a pat on the back for Kruger.' But Coates would have none of this and ordered the posters pulled down. 'I will win a fair fight, or not at all,' he was reported as saying. As the campaign drew to its close it was obvious to all that whatever tactics the gallant Major chose to employ, his chances of success were minimal. When the poll was declared, Trevelyan was seen to have increased his majority by more than fifty per cent.

> C.P. Trevelyan 6,154
> Major Edward Coates 4,512
> Liberal majority 1,642

There was every reason for satisfaction and Trevelyan wrote to his father,

> The election was genuinely political and we smashed the Government on their own khaki issue as well as driving home social reform. The election was beautifully arranged by Marshall... We now have the satisfaction of knowing that in every single place in the constituency we can rely upon the local men working the electioneering without outside help... Locally the election is an immense boon to the party — whatever it may be to your pocket. I don't think we shall be much, if at all, over £1,000.[15]

Obviously, there was little wrong with Liberalism in Elland, and Trevelyan was, as Runciman observed in a letter of congratulation, 'a very lucky chap to have such a constituency and such a solid party behind you'.[16] Runciman was well qualified to make that judgment. He had just been edged out at Oldham by Churchill, even though his Liberal colleague, Emmott, had topped the poll.

A recurring theme in the many letters of congratulation that Trevelyan received upon his re-election, was the concern the writers showed for the future of Liberalism, and more particularly, their confusion as to what exactly Liberalism now implied. This is probably best illustrated by the letter Trevelyan received from Fred Maddison. Maddison had been defeated at Sheffield where he had stood as an anti-war Liberal. There had been a split between the pro and anti Imperialists in the local Liberal association. Maddison specifically referred to Trevelyan having been posted as an Imperialist Liberal.

In spite of the I.L. after your name, I am glad to see the good beating you gave to the Tory. To be candid, it has been some disappointment to me that you have considered it necessary to encourage the faction which owns Perks* as one of its apostles, by adding to the sufficiently comprehensive name of Liberal, the word 'Imperialist' which is either a superfluity or a serious contradiction in terms of the political faith we hold. However, this difference..., I hope, is not so much in principle as in method.[17]

George Trevelyan believed that, even in Elland, if it had not been for Marshall effectively organising the Liberals within the constituency, and the forceful advocacy of social reform by his brother, then the Tories would have gained the seat. So great was the confusion, dissension and pessimism in Liberal ranks, they could only be saved from themselves by the inefficiencies and injustices of a prolonged period of Tory rule. Trevelyan's estimate of Liberal party fortunes was not so pessimistic. Writing to Lord Crewe, he pointed out that in Yorkshire at least, the Liberal party had done well. If only 'the infernal personal question' did not always have to raise its ugly and divisive head.

People are perfectly wild with C-B. Thus writes a correspondent, 'The general feeling in Yorkshire is one of despairing disgust. C-B would be quite right in discounting the sectionists if he would go for them *all* and so consolidate the centre consisting of 90% of the party.'[18]

Exasperated by Rosebery's actions both during and after the election, Campbell-Bannerman in a speech at Dundee had delivered a provocative attack upon the Liberal Imperial Council and then talked of welcoming Rosebery back into the fold. Even if the invitation had been intended sincerely, it was not calculated to please Rosebery or any of his supporters. Trevelyan had been staying with Rosebery when Sir Henry had extended his disingenuous invitation. Trevelyan asked Crewe to 'press Lord R the hardest now' as he thought that Rosebery was 'very near the point of making up his mind'.

I wish he could be made to understand how easily he could come back by merely taking a strong line... He would necessarily lead opinion. For there is a vacancy *de facto* in people's minds, even in the minds of those who refuse to intrigue to remedy the pitiful situation by engineering a split.[19]

Trevelyan's conviction was that if Rosebery could be persuaded once more to take up the leadership of the party, the future of Liberalism was assured.

*Robert Perks had been a Liberal MP, since 1892. He was a staunch admirer of Rosebery and with William Allard was to be responsible for the organisational work of the Liberal League. For personal reasons, Perks was particularly disliked by many Liberal MP's. Beatrice Webb described Perks as 'a repulsive being... commonplace... a blank materialist who recognises no principle beyong self-interest.' (*Our Partnership* (Longmans, 1948,), 231-32). Even discounting Beatrice Webb's usual exaggeration, it is clear that Perks was neither an attractive nor persuasive representative for Liberal Imperialism.

But Rosebery, despite the entreaties of his lieutenants, refused to take any worthwhile initiative. Immediately upon his return home after a week spent at Dalmeny with Rosebery, Trevelyan addressed a trenchant letter to his reluctant leader, begging that he might be pardoned the freedom he was taking, but the times were not suitable for standing upon ceremony when 'so many good citizens are seriously concerned at the lamentable want in alternatives in men and policy which the present state of the Opposition presents'.

> You encouraged me to speak freely about politics. I know that most of what I said represents the wishes of the greater number of moderate but keen Liberals who are not pessimists but deplore our present impotence. What we are really afraid of is not that the wrong ideas will permanently take hold of the party. But that if no man or men came forward to give a strong lead, all this disunion and pettiness will indefinitely continue until years hence out of the new generation some new man rises. But why the waste of all these years?...
>
> Many of us have seen by our own experience how utterly helpless old Liberalism is before newer thought. And knowing from our experience in our own constituencies that the party can be brought round as a whole with a little persuasion and strong leadership, we cannot take a line which would inevitably but unnecessarily split the party. An Individualist or Little England Liberal could never get accepted again for Elland. Yet I have not lost a Liberal vote in the process that is worth anything. What I can do in my humble sphere, you and your greater colleagues I am sure can do with the party and the nation. It is not worth the petty squabble of a party, not when a few months of free and constant divulgence of your opinions in the country would convince the weary and the worried Liberal that at last he had men and causes to work for.
>
> 'The people who are simple, blind and rough, know their own leaders after looking round.' But, they have got to see them first. At present they only see those who *cannot* be their leaders except in title.[20]

Rosebery ignored Trevelyan's impassioned plea. If Campbell-Bannerman's reputation and authority among Liberals continued to decline, there was no corresponding rise in Rosebery's status. He remained aloof, remote; and those who courted his interest grew increasingly impatient and indignant with him.

Meanwhile, the war in South Africa, which many had supposed would soon be ended, entered a new phase. When the Boers, after failure by the British Government to negotiate with them, had taken to guerrilla warfare, they had achieved great successes, and the British command had retaliated with farm burning and concentration camps. Even if these tactics could be justified upon military grounds, they caused profound misgiving and anger amongst Liberals. In November 1900, Trevelyan had written to Crewe:

I don't know what you feel. But I think we Imperialists ought to be the first to restrain excesses, if such there are, at any rate to insist the country should know what is going on. If not, all that will happen will be hysterical shrieking by Stead and Lloyd George against the 'bloody and brutal' British soldier.[21]

But the Liberal Imperialists held their peace too long. Provided by Emily Hobhouse with evidence of the cruelty and mismanagement of the concentration camps, Campbell-Bannerman, at a banquet of the National Reform Union in June, asked, 'When is a war not a war?' He answered his own question. 'When it is carried on by methods of barbarism in South Africa.' Campbell-Bannerman's charge was no less than the truth, but it was injudiciously expressed. Many interpreted it as a slander against British troops. In the eyes of many Liberals he compounded his sin by supporting Lloyd George in a motion for the adjournment when the Welshman fiercely attacked Lord Milner. Some fifty Liberals abstained from the division including Asquith, Grey, Haldane and Trevelyan. Two days later, Asquith in a speech to the South Essex Liberals, censured Campbell-Bannerman's 'methods of barbarism'.

'War to the knife and fork', as Henry Lucy amusingly called it, was now fairly joined between the Imperialist and pro-Boer factions of the Liberal party. The Liberal Imperialists arranged a dinner in Asquith's honour, and Trevelyan delightedly wrote to Samuel. Samuel's response was less than enthusiastic and Trevelyan was obliged to write again to his friend giving the reasons why he supported the project with enthusiasm.

I am going..., because Asquith..., wishes to speak his whole soul on Liberal policy. When I was asked I did not hesitate nor do I now despite the timidity or fury of many people. For two years I have been waiting and hoping that one or two capable men, of whom Asquith is the most capable, would come and do their duty in speaking plainly and constantly on all and every subject... Look at the thing like a man in its large aspect. Isn't our party suffering from the timidity of its best men who are always considering what interpretation will be put on their actions, instead of acting, acting, acting till there can be no mistake. I would give Asquith ten dinners if it would make him speak his mind and act.[22]

Samuel was not convinced. It was naïve to suppose that most members of the Liberal party would view this dinner as anything other than an attempted 'take-over' by the Liberal Imperialists. It could only serve a disruptive purpose. Trevelyan did not heed Samuel's advice. He compounded his folly by publishing a letter in the *Westminster Gazette*. It was not that his published opinions were unworthy, but it was not a wise act, particularly for a young politician who could reasonably anticipate office in the near future. His letter offended some, alienated others and was calculated to please no one.

...Of all the wretched effects of the wretched personal suspicions, the worst has been the gagging of some of our best men for fear of misrepresentation of their intentions. I care nothing how one of these breaks through these despicable shackles — a man whom no one dares to accuse of personal self-seeking, or of party disloyalty, but whom most men profess to recognise as a strong man at a moment when England has indeed need of them.[23]

Elders, and in their own estimation, betters, did not welcome Trevelyan's preaching at them. So that no one might be mistaken as to the position he had adopted, Trevelyan addressed a letter to his constituents insisting that, though it was impossible to pretend that for the moment Liberals were in entire agreement, the unity of the party had to be maintained because, 'the time will soon come when all men of Liberal opinions ought to be able to work together at effecting a Liberal settlement of South Africa and pursuing a Liberal social reform policy at home'.[24]

Campbell-Bannerman, feeling the need to strengthen his own authority, summoned a special Liberal party meeting at the Reform Club. There, he had secured a unanimous vote of confidence as leader. However, Grey and Asquith made it quite clear they were not prepared to follow Sir Henry's lead over the war — the single most important issue! Campbell-Bannerman then declared he could accept 'honest differences of opinion', but not organisations designed to perpetuate and accentuate those differences. He appealed to Asquith to postpone his dinner,[25] but this was rejected on the pretext that it would cause 'enormous inconvenience..., countless explanations and misunderstandings'.[26]

For Asquith, the dinner was an opportunity for a show of strength by his supporters as against Campbell-Bannerman's. His ploy, however, did not succeed as Rosebery, who first had refused to preside at the dinner, at a luncheon meeting held that same day in the City Liberal Club, delivered a head-line-catching speech that altogether stole Asquith's thunder. Rosebery, while declaring his resolve to 'plough my furrow alone', charged the Liberal party to 'start with a clean sheet as regards those cumbersome programmes with which it has been overloaded in the past'. Rosebery had talked of the 'organised hyprocrisy' of trying to hide the cracks in the Liberal party. Asquith spoke of reconciliation and the underlying unity of the party. He deliberately turned from South Africa to domestic issues, insisting neatly, that Liberal Imperialism should be linked with a policy of radical reform for Little England. No wonder then that Trevelyan should have been attracted more by Asquith's than Rosebery's vision. At leader level, there was a sharp if temporary breach between Rosebery and the other Liberal Imperialists. This, however, did nothing to bring them closer to Campbell-Bannerman. If anything, Liberal disarray was more evident than before. This was a matter of deep regret to Trevelyan, but Asquith had indicated the path which he had long favoured and therefore he saw no reason why the present situation should not be capitalised upon. Now surely was the opportune moment for the more moderate Imperialist elements in the Liberal party to take over the mantle from the Radicals as the prime instigators of social reform?

With Asquith, Trevelyan exchanged ideas for a programme which would deal with the Irish question, South Africa, education, temperance and land taxation. In late August Asquith wrote to Trevelyan:

> How very glad I was to get your letter. I believe that I am in entire agreement with all you say as to the future. And I am anxious that you should know how warmly I appreciate the courageous and constant loyalty and friendship which you have shown in peculiarly trying times. These are the things which make me feel that public life, with all its drawbacks and disappointments, is worth living, and nerve one to perseverance and endeavours.[27]

Before the year was out, Trevelyan was to do Asquith an even more difficult and signal service when acting as a 'second' in the 'war to the knife and fork'. But his immediate concern was to summon his friend Runciman into the lists for the Autumn campaign in the North when together they could — as intended the previous year — publicise a programme of progressive Liberalism.

With Parliament in recess, Trevelyan spent from mid October to early December stumping the northern political circuit. The comparative calm of exhaustion that had settled over the Liberal party was only occasionally disturbed by sniping between the leaders of the two factions. Trevelyan savaged these desultory yet damaging incursions. 'We ordinary Liberals are sick of these internecine quarrels,' he told a Liberal meeting at Halifax. 'A Liberal's business is to interpret the incapacities, the manifold incompetences and the unpatriotic lethargy of the Government under which we are unfortunate enough to live.'[28] He was obliged to spend more time than he wished on discussing the South African situation, and particularly the concentration camps. To the background of the first rumblings of advance publicity for the speech Rosebery was to give in December to the Chesterfield Liberal Association, and the contradictory rumours as to what exactly the reluctant ex-Liberal Prime Minister intended to say, Trevelyan proclaimed that his earnest wish was for Lord Rosebery to express 'some of the profound anxiety of the great middle mass of Englishmen who do not believe the war is a criminal enterprise, but who are not Jingoes and are anxious at the way this war is being conducted'.[29]

Trevelyan had been disappointed with Asquith's performance during the recess. He had been 'tame'. Asquith's tameness and Campbell-Bannerman's 'lameness and general incapacity', were two good reasons for persisting in the publicising of a progressive Liberal programme because there was bound to be a 'favourable response before long'. Perhaps Rosebery might arouse that response with his Chesterfield speech? Harry Paulton, an enthusiastic Liberal Imperialist, had given Trevelyan a 'hopeful account of Rosebery's state of mind'. Trevelyan 'refuse[d] to be hopeful... If only he would be a man!'[30]

Trevelyan's jaundiced response to Paulton's optimism was probably because once again he was personally involved in another squabble over the fortunes and fate of the Liberal leadership. Early in November, Trevelyan received a letter from Alan Lawrie.

> I write to you at Haldane's request to ask if you will propose Asquith for the presidency of the Eighty Club* at the next general meeting. Campbell-Bannerman is now President but there is an understanding that a new President must be elected every year. As Rosebery and Kimberley have both occupied the position Asquith is clearly the man. Now Harcourt or Morley might be put up... If Asquith could be elected without a fight, so much the better: but if the violent men in the pro-Boer camp are going to run one of their men, it would be much better for us to have our man first in the field, thereby putting on the pro-Boers the stigma of forcing on 'an unnecessary war by barbarous methods'. Therefore, Asquith must be put up at once by someone, and Haldane says that you are the proper person to do it.[31]

It was not a commission that Trevelyan welcomed. He wrote to Asquith asking for his views. He could well have anticipated the reply. 'Of course I shall be delighted if you will take the responsibility of nominating me.'[32] In early December, Trevelyan received an urgent request from Lawrie.

> ...Please come up for the Eighty Club meeting on Friday afternoon. A dead set is being made at the nomination of Asquith..., and I hear that Greenwood is going to call on the Committee to recommend Lord Spencer. We shall want all our forces if we are to defeat this move.[33]

On the day the Committee was due to meet Trevelyan had a speaking engagement in Newcastle. He obviously was unhappy at the way matters were developing and excused his absence by claiming that he could not break a prior engagement. However, he was persuaded to send a letter to the Committee setting out his reasons for nominating Asquith. Though strongly worded, Trevelyan's injunction — 'I hope the Committee will not take any

---

*The Eighty Club took its name from the first year, 1880, of Gladstone's Second Ministry. Originally formed by young Liberals of mildly radical and imperialist sympathies under the leadership of Albert Grey, Haldane had been its first honorary Secretary. Grey's political views, to use Haldane's word, had become 'erratic', and the 4th Earl seceded to form another club — an earlier case of Liberal schism!

It was not merely a dining club that invited leading Liberals to address it, but an important party organisation that published its own literature and provided speakers for Liberal meetings throughout the country. See, *inter alios*, Richard Burdon Haldane, *An Autobiography* (Hodder & Stoughton, 2nd Edn 1929), 80-81.

step that would be seriously offensive to one of our recognised leaders'[34] — would not have harmed his reputation with many Liberals had not parts of the letter been leaked to the press by someone suggesting that Trevelyan was the main conspirator in a plot to get Asquith nominated before the Club's Committee could decide for themselves. Lewis Harcourt and George Greenwood mounted a strong attack upon Trevelyan at the meeting even though he was not present. Herbert Samuel advised Trevelyan he would be wise to publish a denial that he was the fount of the conspiracy.

This squabble for office of a dining and debating club serves to show with what good reason Trevelyan desired, more than anything else, a leader whose personality might transcend such petty conspiracies, who could promote a programme of reform and a campaign of criticism against the Tories, and unite and release the power of Liberalism. Trevelyan hoped that Rosebery's speech at Chesterfield, when he had talked of the Liberal party 'cleaning its slate', might have heralded the breakthrough. He wrote to Rosebery, 'whether you persist or not, there are many of us who will be lastingly grateful to you for the larger spirit you have introduced into politics'. Was Trevelyan referring to Rosebery's injunction for Liberals to put away their 'fly-blown phylacteries'? Until this meaningless phrase was translated Trevelyan was convinced that Rosebery was adopting a conciliatory attitude which would allow for a rapprochement between the Earl and Campbell-Bannerman.

Meanwhile, Trevelyan wrote to Haldane praising Rosebery for his attack upon the Tories and asking why had not Asquith, Grey and Haldane taken an equally strong line. It was not really a fair indictment, but Haldane excused and explained the attitude that until then his colleagues had adopted.

> The nation trusts Rosebery. They do not in like manner trust Asquith, Grey or you and me, and they would not take from us in the crisis in which they are crying to us for help, criticism which they are ready to take from Rosebery... Even now that Rosebery has spoken, it is not for us to abate our concentration or attempt to steady or hinder his purpose. 'He who would accomplish anything must limit himself.' It is only a great figure like Rosebery that can — in such emergency — take this liberty that is allowed to Anius.* All this will change and perhaps is already changing, but the time for more than has been done is not yet.[35]

This picture that Haldane promoted of himself and the other, younger Liberal Imperialist leaders, was not true. Campbell-Bannerman in a letter to J.A. Spender complained bitterly of the activities of Rosebery's 'acolytes', in particular Haldane who, he said, was 'tramping in his heavy way along the path..., of irreconcilable variance.'[36] Haldane in fact, was busy trying to stir the forces of rebellion in Asquith's breast, and Grey was writing to

*Anius was the priest of Apollo at Delos.

Campbell-Bannerman threatening to repudiate his leadership.

Amidst these scenes of wayward passion, one man remained unmoved and unruffled. Rosebery was undisturbed that his speech, which some were pleased to suppose had marked the ground for common Liberal action, was the direct cause of the present undignified shambles. He wrote to Trevelyan;

> It seems to me that I for the moment have done my part, it is for others to do theirs. I hear a great deal of eloquence as to the country rallying to my views. But unless that rallying is crystallised it would be evanescent. Yet everyone seems to think that it is enough to say 'I agree with Lord R', turn round and go to sleep. What I want to know is what people like your anonymous correspondent is going to *do*. Tory or pro-Boer are organising; throwing up earthworks while my adherents (if I had any) are saying 'What an excellent speech!' I want a little of the political spade on my side as well as on the other.[37]

Whether expected or not, Trevelyan responded immediately to Rosebery's challenge. 'The onus for action is with you,' he told Rosebery. 'You have but to summon your willing troops and they will flock to your banner. But, that standard can only be raised by you.' If Trevelyan supposed that his letter would win an enthusiastic response, he was to be disappointed. Rosebery's reply was a rebuff.

> I believe that in certain altitudes a sneeze may bring down an avalanche. That is rather my sensation on receiving your letter. Pray send me a copy of mine if you have kept it so that I may once more see the peg upon which hangs your deliverance...[38]

Chesterfield had proved merely the prelude to a period of bitter internecine strife within the Liberal party ending with Rosebery's brutal repudiation of Campbell-Bannerman, and the replacement of the Liberal Imperialist Council* by a Liberal League with Rosebery as its President, and Asquith and Grey among the vice-presidents. For his part, Trevelyan was angry and disillusioned with the struggles for personal power among the party

---

*The Liberal Imperialist Council had been set up in July 1900. Leading Liberal Imperialists, while they had not formally associated themselves with the Council, inevitably were thought of as sympathetic to its ideals. Immediately before the 1900 election, the LIC issued a list of Liberal candidates that they approved; and after the election, a manifesto asking that a clear distinction should be made by 'patriotic' voters between those Liberals who could be 'trusted', and those whose opinions disqualified them as suitable for office in an Imperial Parliament. Very properly, Campbell-Bannerman denounced the Perks manifesto in the press. However, in a speech at Dundee, by an unfortunate slip of the tongue, when criticising the LIC, he referred to them as the Liberal *Unionist* Council. That really set the opposing factions at one another's throats.

The Liberal League was a much more formidable body than the LIC, which it replaced. Though Rosebery maintained that it had been formed merely to 'stop his friends being drummed out of the Liberal party', many suspected that the real intentions of the League were schismatic and aggressive. Asquith responded to a stern warning from Campbell-Bannerman by announcing that it was never his intention that the League should destroy or weaken the Liberal party's general organisation. Most members of the League then adopted Asquith's limited interpretation of its function.

leadership, and he made no secret of this. He told his constituents:

> Among Liberal members, with a few unimportant exceptions, there is a general feeling of regret that after the Chesterfield speech had found the only common line of action on the only vital question of the time, Sir Henry Campbell-Bannerman and Lord Rosebery can do no better than fall foul of each other over the business of a 'clean slate' and the exact relations of the party to the Irish. IT IS NOT BUSINESS. We should all much prefer that these leaders of ours should concentrate their critical ability on the malpractices of ministers. Their quarrels are more ill-timed as the last week has been abundantly demonstrating the essential unity of the party on practical politics and the disunity of the Tories.[39]

Such public pronouncements were not guaranteed to endear Trevelyan to the leaders of any faction. For the next few years he was to cling to the opinion that if 'C-B and his gang' were 'fat-headed and stupid..., Haldane and Rosebery are as bad in another way. Grey and Asquith are alone fit to lead, but won't try.' As he saw it, 'the only chance' was 'a rush of new spirit in the party demanding capable leadership and much new blood'.[40] Any hope of Liberal unity and resurgence, he believed, could only be brought about by a determined campaign in the constituencies to promote a progressive Liberal policy to which the new young candidates would be committed.

But what end was served by further earnest debate among young Liberals, of this programme and that tactic when their party was in disarray? As in the past, so now, pressure for unity came not from within but from external causes. In March, the Tories promoted a highly controversial education bill. The April Budget included a proposal that a duty should be paid on imported corn. In May, the South African war at last was ended by the Peace of Vereeniging. If the breach between the Liberal Imperialists and the rest of the Liberal party was still wide, at least the ending of the Boer War and growing dissension in Tory ranks encouraged Liberals to focus their efforts, not upon damaging internal disputes, but on censuring the Government. It seemed the tactics that Trevelyan had long been demanding would at last be employed. The long, bitter chapter of Liberal schism and impotence was coming to an end. A time of change and of opportunity was at hand.

CONFUSION, RESURGENCE, VICTORY: 1902-06

W.E. Forster's Education Act, passed by Gladstone's Government in 1870, created a comprehensive system of elementary education in Great Britain. The Act set up non-denominational Board Schools which were financed out of the rates. From the same revenue source, existing Anglican National, and Roman Catholic schools were subsidised. The Nonconformists bitterly resented the subsidising of National schools as this allowed the Established Church to perpetuate its monopoly of elementary education in areas where most of the people were Dissenters. The education bill introduced by Balfour in March 1902 was designed to enlarge the scope of state education by providing for secondary instruction. Educational administration was to be rationalised by bringing it under the control of county councils, abolishing the School Boards, and the distinction between Board and Voluntary schools. Educational debates always attract passionate and ready, if frequently ill-informed, opinion. But in 1902 the debate was conditioned and poisoned by religious prejudice. Earlier attempts to reform the educational system had merely illustrated the religious snare in which any would-be reformer inevitably became trapped. The suggestion that a Liberal Government intended to reform education on a secular basis had been enough for the Roman Catholic bishop of Nottingham to rally the forces of the faithful against Liberalism in the 1900 election with the cry: 'Let us stand up and defend ourselves against selfish, cold-blooded, calculating tyranny..., a tyranny such as was exercised by Julian the Apostate against the early Christians.'[1] Nonconformists, already convinced that the Anglican Church with the growing enthusiasm for ritualism among its hierarchy was proceeding with indecent haste along the road to Rome, interpreted the bill as a direct attack upon them by the Tories at the behest of the Established Church in collusion with the Roman Catholics. Outside Parliament the Nonconformists were rallied by the veteran Baptist minister, Dr. John Clifford. He denigrated the bill as perpetuating and securing all the worst vices of the old system, and coined the effective battle slogan 'Rome on the Rates'. Declared David Lloyd George, 'The ship of state is making its way through the midst of rocks, and what is the Government's proposal? To put the chaplain on the bridge.'[2]

Loyalties aroused by the provisions of the bill traversed divisions within the ranks of the two major political parties. The Labour party really was not involved in this particular struggle. It had already indicated that its own educational priorities were practical not religious. As the Swansea Congress of Trade Unions had resolved in 1901: 'Under our present system an attempt is made to feed the brain while the body is starved.' For the Liberal party, the bill provided an opportunity for the Liberal Imperialists for once to prosecute a cause together with their Radical brethren. 'The very existence of our Empire depends on sea power and school power,' declared the 'Limp' member for Oldham, Mr. Emmott. So, with the exception of Haldane, the 'Limps' joined with the Radicals to attack a Tory measure that, in part at least, was inspired by the Fabians! If, at the beginning, the Tory party was not openly divided, then it was uncomfortably uncertain about the measure. Chamberlain was hostile, though he had so far 'crossed the Rubicon' that he did not, like most of the Nonconformist Liberal Unionists, march back into the Liberal fold. Salisbury was timid, and with good reason, of the passions such a measure would inevitably stir. So it fell to Balfour to rouse himself from his customary pose of indolent indifference, and skilfully steer through Parliament a measure that when implemented surprised him both by its effect and costliness. From its introduction in March to its acceptance in December, the education bill was the most important and controversial measure of the 1902 parliamentary session.

From the first, Trevelyan had recognised the bill's value as the means of uniting the dissident Liberal elements against the Tories. Thus, he might be excused his occasional lapses into cant when addressing constituency audiences, as when he suggested that the Cecils were intent upon reviving the policy of Laud, and conjured the passions of his listeners by portraying them as latter day Hampdens about to rise up in the name of democracy against their persecutors.[3] This, and like splenetic nonsense, most of which Trevelyan seems to have borrowed from the *Methodist Weekly*, was not only foreign to his normal style of oratory, but contrary to the spirit of reasoned criticism he adopted in the Commons where he proved himself a knowledgeable and stout critic of the bill.

There was a personal reason why Trevelyan involved himself as a protagonist in the 1902 education debate. During the passage of Forster's Act, his father had been one of that small group of Liberals who criticised the measure because they felt by encouraging denominational schools it did not provide for a truly national system of education. Trevelyan prefaced his speech on the second reading of the bill in May, by admitting his first instinct had been not to oppose because 'the re-organisation of our system of national education is necessary. A Bill is demanded by the people from the sense of shame in our possessing the worst instructed peasantry in the West of Europe..., and a belief that the time has come when equality of opportunity should be really given to all men.' Because of the faults in the 1870 Act, the Government had found 'progress clogged by a denominational difficulty'. Faced with the alternatives of 'subduing or immensely strengthening the denominational system of the country', the Government had taken 'the latter alternative and I think have made the wrong choice'. From the first, Trevelyan concentrated his attack on the issue of religious tests for teachers in National schools. In his parliamentary speeches, in the dozens of harangues he delivered in the northern English counties, he constantly returned to this particular theme.

It is a much more serious thing to require a man to subordinate his conscience in the matter of religion than to subordinate it in the matter of politics. This is the central evil of this Bill.[4]

Tactically, the controversy aroused by the bill presented the Liberal party with an ideal opportunity, if not to tumble the Tories, at least to strengthen their own ranks. The resurgence of political dissent must be harnessed to the sense of injustice felt by Nonconformists. The portents of such a union were obvious. In a by election at Leeds, a safe Tory seat fell to the Liberal candidate who had fought his campaign on the single issue of the education bill. 'Mr. Barran's victory', Trevelyan told his constituents, 'has put real heart into our party. We now know for certain that denominational privilege, which we are contesting, is as obnoxious to the country as to ourselves... The next appeal to the country will reverse the unpopular policy.'[5]

That promise was for the future. Immediately there was the prospect of a Tory Government visibly cracking under the strain of trying to accommodate its High Church supporters. If only the Liberal front bench would play its proper part. In July, Harry Whitley had introduced an amendment to clause 4 of the bill, attacking a declaration of religious belief as a condition of a teacher's employment. Balfour was obliged overtly to beg for the support of sections of his party, and to remind the Roman Catholics of their required loyalty. In the end the amendment was just defeated. Trevelyan wrote to his mother:

We ought to have beaten the Government, and should have done so but for the sublime incapacity of Sir Henry Campbell-Bannerman who kept the debate going for twenty minutes on a twaddling point and then put on party tellers to frighten off the shaky Tories. The whole of the work is done by the back benches. The leaders either sit down or muddle.[6]

Generally, Trevelyan managed to limit to his private correspondence, comments upon the lethargy and the incapacities of the Liberal leaders. But occasionally he allowed his feelings to get the better of his judgment and required loyalty, and several times he told audiences it was fortunate that the future of Liberalism did not rest upon the favours and performance of their leaders.

A party is made up very much more by the rank and file than it is by the leaders. The fighting of the rank and file over the Education Act in Parliament, and the fighting of the ordinary citizens in the by elections shows that our people, leaders or no leaders, have a grip of Liberal principles that is quite strong enough to enable us to direct a Liberal Government when it comes into power... We can be confident of victory with our own Liberal forces.[7]

The Education Act became law, and the fight against its provisions moved from Parliament into the country, with the Dissenters' campaign for non payment of rates. But in Parliament an even greater issue than education now occupied the interests of most politicians. Protection versus Free Trade was the issue; and the man responsible for promoting this cathartic dispute was Joseph Chamberlain.

In September 1902, while the education debate still raged, Chamberlain had written to his friend Alfred, Viscount Milner, then Governor of the Transvaal and Orange River Colony, 'I think the time has come when, if a further marked advance is to be made in the relations between the Mother country and the Colonies, I must take some step of a rather sensational kind.'[8]   In November, before sailing to South Africa for a holiday, Chamberlain insisted that the shilling corn duty, imposed by Sir Michael Hicks-Beach which his successor as Chancellor, C.T. Ritchie wanted to repeal, should be maintained and used to give preference to Canadian corn. Chamberlain carried his view in Cabinet despite Ritchie's opposition. When he returned to England in March 1903, however, Chamberlain was told that Ritchie was now to have his way. Balfour attempted to effect a compromise by supporting Ritchie's proposal while suggesting there should be an enquiry into imperial preference undertaken that summer. Reinforced in the wisdom of his opinions by Milner's reception of his ideas, Chamberlain arrogantly ignored Balfour. In May 1903, from the familiar platform of Birmingham Town Hall, Chamberlain announced a policy of Tariff Reform. Joe maintained that the country must choose between Imperial unity or a wrong interpretation of Free Trade which had been foisted on the country by Little Englander Liberals of the Manchester School. The Empire could only be saved from disintegration by material ties. There should be preferential duties for Empire goods, and retaliatory duties against the goods of foreign countries. Preference for colonial goods would place a small tax upon food, but this would be insignificant when compared with the advantages that would accrue to depressed British industries.

According to Margot Asquith, her husband's reception of the news from Birmingham was ecstatic. 'It is only a question of time,' he told her, 'when we shall sweep this country.'[9] Despite Chamberlain's appeal that the *raison d'être* of his scheme was the strengthening of the Empire, Trevelyan's response was no less enthusiastic than Asquith's, and for the same reason. The issue of protection and free trade was bound to unite the Liberals. Equally, the Tories were bound to be divided beyond hope of mending their fortunes. Though no economist, Trevelyan was not disadvantaged in the free trade tariff fight. His powerful oratory refurbished old, well-worn arguments, and he was in demand as a speaker, not only upon the now familiar northern counties circuit, but in the Midlands and East Anglia.

Trevelyan's free trade campaign concentrated, not on the subtleties of economic argument, but on the political reality that the polarising of support for free trade and protection drove Balfour — whatever he might say about having 'no settled convictions on the subject' — further away from his errant lieutenant, Chamberlain. Trevelyan derided Balfour's attempts to placate the opposing Tory factions. 'You can ignore Mr. Balfour,' he told an audience at Northowram early in October 1903.

> The forces he has to deal with are far too strong for him to control. This controversy is not with Mr. Balfour but with Mr. Chamberlain... He has raised a question on which all men must decide, and no shuffling or shamming by the present Prime Minister will get him out of his difficulty.[10]

A fortnight later, for the first time in a public speech, Trevelyan mentioned a subject that was to figure prominently in his thinking on the free trade controversy: 'When Liberalism is victorious, we do not want Government of passive Free Traders.'[11]

Sooner than many another Liberal, Trevelyan discerned the essentially negative and conservative aspects of the Liberal free trade campaign. For this reason he had written to Campbell-Bannerman demanding reforms: of education, taxation of land values, of Army administration, readjustment of taxation with a graduated income tax, and of the electoral system. Campbell-Bannerman's reply to this 'manifesto' was affable enough.

> I am much delighted for your letter... You speak definitely of 'graduated income tax', and that is the only point on which I would make a reservation. Not that the end to be attained is not right, but that particular access to it has always seemed to me beset with difficulties.

Sir Henry might have said the same about Army reform, a subject upon which he had earlier instructed his party and the Commons that the best and cheapest reform was to leave the Army entirely alone! He concluded his letter:

> There will be no desire to concentrate public attention on the fiscal question, and on the other matters there ought to be clear and strong speaking. It is Chamberlain and his people who want to sink everything into fiscal controversies.[12]

In private, Campbell-Bannerman agreed with Spencer's estimate of Trevelyan. No one could doubt the young man's enthusiasm, but he showed such little sense of proportion.[13] As to Trevelyan's private estimate of Campbell-Bannerman, he still retained grave doubts about his fitness to be leader, but he seems to have been drawn closer to Sir Henry during this period than in any other before 1906. After a sharp speech by Campbell-Bannerman in the House, it was with unaccustomed warmth and courtesy that Trevelyan reported on his leader's performance in a letter to his mother.

> C-B made an excellent, humorous speech yesterday. It was the best sort of thing he can do — spawky chaff — elaborately prepared for a fortnight before and read, almost every word. However, it was not heart-rending as it usually is.[14]

If Free trade was not to be the exclusive consideration of Liberals Trevelyan proposed its natural complement would be a sound labour policy. And the best specific for such a labour policy, so he maintained, was the taxation of land values. He told a Glasgow audience, 'Cobden never intended to stop at free trade, and neither do I.'[15]

Support for the rating of land values owed its initial popularity to a limited understanding of its effects. It was a leaseholders' movement which had originated in London. With already high rates that increased each year, the occupiers in towns felt that they were bearing the burden entirely while the landlords got away with paying little or nothing. Though land value taxation was mentioned in the Report of the Royal Commission on Housing of the Working Classes in 1885, until the beginning of the new century little was either said or done in Parliament on the subject. Members for urban areas of England where freehold and not leasehold tenure was the rule took little interest and were often hostile. A Royal Commission was set up in 1896 to examine the subject, but until its final report in 1910, successive governments used the Commission as an excuse to defer action. A municipal agitation begun in Glasgow in 1895 spread through Northern England until within seven years it embraced more than five hundred local authorities. A reform that for years had been regarded by most people as the proposal of fanatics and faddists was further strengthened in 1902, by the interim minority report of five Commissioners, recommending rating of urban site values. That same year, Trevelyan introduced a Rating of Site Values Bill which was defeated on its Second Reading. Reporting as chairman to the fifteenth annual meeting of the Land Law Reform Association, Trevelyan did not seem unduly perturbed by this set-back. 'When a proposal has reached the stage of being abused, it is beginning to be formidable.'[16]

Another bill was introduced in 1903, to suffer the same fate as Trevelyan's in the previous year. But in 1904, Trevelyan successfully introduced a rating bill which passed its second reading with a majority of sixty-seven; and in 1905, another rating bill successfully secured a second reading, this time with a majority of ninety. Both bills, like the minority recommendation of the Commissioners, were allowed to drift and were never implemented. Supporters argued that existing rating arrangements placed 'a universal burden on enterprise, industry and building'. The reform they advocated, they believed, would bring land onto the market more cheaply and in greater abundance. 'Free land for building and enterprise,' Trevelyan demanded. 'That is the best answer we can give the Birmingham policy.'[17] To him, the virtues of land value taxation were self-evident. If only sufficient of the Liberal leaders would enthusiastically grasp this sovereign specific instead of mindlessly honouring the worthy but ancient shibboleth of free trade.

> How many people who rightly are working now with a political energy un-exampled in our time to defeat a new bread tax, realize fully that the local rates are nothing better than a house tax, as heavy as the bread tax was in the bad old days?'[18]

Within months of Chamberlain's Birmingham speech, for Trevelyan the free trade issue had become inextricably involved with questions of party allegiance. His interest in imperial problems and Army reform in some degree made him the natural ally of contemporaries like Churchill and Seely* even though they were Tory backbenchers. Both men were to move to the Liberal party in 1904; Churchill over Tariffs; Seely over Tariffs and Chinese 'slavery' Trevelyan was particularly drawn towards Churchill because of the attitude Winston had adopted towards Army economies. In 1901 Churchill had been in the van of those who had attacked the Secretary of State for War's proposed reforms as ineffectual and costly. Trevelyan agreed with Churchill's criticisms, but had concentrated his censures upon the dangers of conscription and the need to make entry to the commissioned ranks open to talent rather than restricted to the aristocracy. In the *British Empire Review*, Trevelyan had written.

---

*John Edward Bernard Seely (later first Baron Mottistone) had the unusual experience of being returned unopposed as Conservative MP for the Isle of Wight in the 1900 election. Crossing to the Liberals in 1904 he was again elected unopposed in a by election. Under-Secretary for the Colonies, 1908-10; Under Secretary then Secretary of State for War, 1911-14. Resigned over Curragh incident.

All Army reform is but vain talking unless the ideal of work for the same motive and the same incentives is planted in the mind of the officer as in the mind of the lawyer, doctor and business man. Seek talent, open the door for it, and let the gentlemanly qualities look after themselves. Those who know England know that the control of men by the silken threads of sympathy and character and courtesy is not the monopoly of any Anglo-Saxon aristocracy.[19]

This was a legitimate radical line of attack upon the Army, and Trevelyan pressed it eagerly and frequently, but to no personal advantage in a party that because of anti-militarist prejudice affected no interest. Thus, a common area of interest and sympathy had been established between Trevelyan and several of the younger Tory members even before the free trade controversy. Therefore, Trevelyan was prepared to offer a palm to them provided they accepted the need for a programme of social reform. This issue was crystallized publicly for Trevelyan when he wrote to the editor of the *Daily News* concerning the 'conversion' of the Liberal Unionist MP, John Wilson, into a Liberal free trader.

As the fight develops there will be more and more anxiety for a working alliance between the two parts of the Free Trade army.
...I have very little doubt that many of the Unionist Free Traders would be ready enough to fall into line with Liberals on taxation of land values and licensing reform. It is essential that they should do so, not for the sake of general progress alone, but for the sake of Free Trade itself.[20]

The letter was bold if indiscreet. Though not mentioned, any attempt to embrace the free trade Unionists raised the spectre of Ireland — 'the great sore in the middle of the Empire' — as Trevelyan had recently described it. With the re-unification of the Irish party under Redmond in 1900, no British political party could ignore the eighty Irish MPs in Parliament, or the influence the Irish catholic vote exerted in many English and Scottish industrial constituencies. Most Liberal Imperialists did not want the Irish issue mentioned, because of the determined Home Rule section within their party. For some time Trevelyan had admitted that 'personally..., I think Home Rule, as understood by Mr. Gladstone, has been decisively rejected by the English people. I believe that we can only give Ireland self-government by degrees.'[21]

Fortunately for Trevelyan, his letter did not start the dangerous Irish hare. Instead it involved him in the almost equally difficult problem of Liberal Labour relations. The day after his letter appeared in the *Daily News* Trevelyan received a reply from one of Wilson's constituents. The real sting in the letter came, not in the implied condemnation of Trevelyan's and the Liberal party's tepid radicalism, but in the threat contained in its last sentence. 'There will be no real improvement until we get Labour members into Parliament at whatever risk of dividing constituencies.'[22] In his public statements on relations between Liberal and Labour, Trevelyan had frequently 'demanded a better and more reasonable alliance between the twin forces of progressivism.' In his private correspondence, however, Trevelyan generally was for seizing the main chance by exploiting better Liberal organisation and finance to insure the swift adoption of progressive Liberal candidates before any Labour forces could be mustered.

This confusion of public and private sentiment was mirrored by the Labour Representation Committee. Of the fifteen candidates they had endorsed in the 1900 election, two had been successful, Keir Hardie and Richard Bell. Bell had run a joint campaign with the Liberal candidate for the two member seat at Derby. He was a notorious Lib-Lab and was later to be expelled from the Labour party when he refused to sign its constitution. Because of Bell's overt association with the Liberal party, the LRC at their annual conference in Newcastle in 1903 adopted a resolution demanding Labour candidates should 'abstain strictly from identifying themselves with, or promoting the interests of any section of the Liberal or Conservative parties'.[23] Yet, at the same time, Ramsay MacDonald, the LRC's Secretary, was negotiating a secret agreement with the Liberal Chief whip, Herbert Gladstone, to avoid unnecessary clashes between Liberal and Labour candidates in certain constituencies.

At a by election in August 1902, in a North East Lancashire constituency, Labour won the seat from the Liberals. In March 1903, Will Crooks took Woolwich for Labour from the Conservatives. In June, the Yorkshire constituency of Barnard Castle became vacant. As at Woolwich and Clitheroe, Barnard Castle was a predominantly working-class, industrial area. For many years it had returned a Liberal member and was 'practically an appanage of the Pease family'. Arthur Henderson, Wesleyan lay preacher, member of the Ironfounders Union, and former Liberal agent, was nominated by the LRC as their candidate. Trevelyan knew Henderson well and liked him. The local Liberal Association then entered the electoral lists with their champion, Hubert Beaumont. He immediately appealed to Trevelyan for aid, but was refused. Trevelyan suggested that fighting Henderson could only endanger the fortunes of other Liberal candidates in neighbouring constituencies. This response to Beaumont's appeal was disingenuous on both personal and tactical grounds. Beaumont wrote again to Trevelyan, this time enclosing a letter he had received from Catterall, the Liberal agent at Clitheroe.

> Great pressure is being put upon me to withdraw, but I think most of the Northern Liberal members do not at all understand the position here. I have the united support of all the local Liberals behind me and I cannot possibly withdraw when they are so strongly against it... Even if I were to withdraw, it is extremely possible that Henderson would be beaten as the strong Liberals say that they would rather vote for Vane (the Unionist) than have Henderson foisted upon them in the way in which a small section of

Socialists hailing from London are trying to do. What I am doing now, all you Liberal members with large working class constituencies will have to do within the next ten years, because if you don't smash the Independent Labour party now…, they will smash the Liberal party as they avowedly say they wish to do.[24]

Henderson, when he had joined the Labour party had taken with him a large part of the local Liberal Association membership. For more than a year Trevelyan had been anxiously trying to secure a suitable seat for Henderson, and had actively lobbied on his behalf for several vacancies. However, Catterall's note, enclosed by Beaumont on the fate of the Clitheroe Liberal Association after David Shackleton's unopposed return for Labour, must have given Trevelyan food for uncomfortable thought.

What has been the result during the last twelve months since our constituency was given away? In the first place, our organisation is falling to pieces…, our subscriptions have fallen 25%, we cannot get a meeting together…, most of our active supporters are openly declaring they will vote Tory if there is a Tory candidate in the field… What effect has it had upon the Labour party… they have been more aggressive. It has encouraged them in a position of independence.[25]

Tales of Labour truculence were less likely to raise Trevelyan's sympathy, or more correctly ire, than the idea of helping Liberals whose allegiance to progressive policies was so tentative that at the first challenge they could contemplate deserting to the Tory camp. In the event, Henderson was successful in a three cornered contest winning with a narrow majority. It was an historic victory for Labour and, coming after their triumphs at Clitheroe and Woolwich, there was widespread speculation that Labour might now win all the working class constituencies. In December 1903, there was an opportunity to test this hypothesis when there was a by election at Norwich. By then, however, Chamberlain's programme had completely altered the immediate outlook in British politics. The Liberal candidate on a free trade platform secured the seat. The Labour candidate came bottom of the poll. Not in the least abashed, Richard Bell was among the first to congratulate the Liberal on his victory. In the coming months, Henderson, Crooks and Shackleton were to be prominently involved with the Liberals in their campaign against protection. Ruefully, the 1904 LRC conference was obliged to rescind its statute, passed only the previous year,' that had demanded Labour candidates should observe strict neutrality between the two bourgeois parties or resign.

Chamberlain's initiative had effected changes in tactics, spirit and allegiances within the parties. For Trevelyan, drawing the younger, free trade elements of the Tory party into the Liberal fold was of more immediate interest and importance than a Lib-Lab alliance. Since his dramatic introduction into politics, Churchill had attracted both Trevelyan's interest and qualified admiration. He had written of him in 1901, 'he is undoubtedly a big man... inordinately ambitious. But, whatever line he takes, he will always bring out the best and most reasonable side of it. I like him, personally. He amuses me and is first rate company with all his egotism.'[26] If you could ignore his bumptiousness, Churchill's dynamism and rhetorical gifts would be no small advantage if secured for the Liberal cause. Trevelyan decided to explore the possibility of an alliance. Winston, meanwhile, had already decided that his destiny lay with the Liberal party, although at the time his personal inclination was for some moderate, central position in a group led by Rosebery or the Duke of Devonshire. The particular interest in the exchange of letters between Churchill and Trevelyan in December 1903, five months before Churchill crossed the floor of the Commons, lies in Winston's hard-headed appraisal of the political possibilities, both personal and general, that arose from the Tory free trade split. Even in this period which was prologue to his becoming a Liberal Minister, Churchill's essential conservatism is as apparent as is Trevelyan's romantic attachment to the notion that a programme of economic and social reform for the benefit of the people could be effectively promoted by an unlikely alliance of backbenchers. With an uncharacteristic humility, Churchill might have acknowledged Trevelyan's greater experience in political affairs, but the exchange between them proved that he, rather than Trevelyan, was the political realist. Churchill had learned already that policies are not promoted by wishes, but by the capture, husbanding and exercise of power. Political ends provided interesting material for discussion by philosophers, but means were the province and the prerogative of the politician. Despite every reason to persuade him otherwise, Trevelyan throughout this period retained a romantic notion of the 'progressive' forces drawn in alliance from all parties, promoting the 'cause of the People' in Parliament. One of his last letters to his constituents before Balfour's resignation contained a vignette of himself with John Burns and Winston Churchill, standing together on the terrace of the House of Commons, 'discussing the lines which social reform ought to take in the next Parliament'.[27]

Though the Tories already had sufficient divisive and debilitating problems with which to contend, a new explosive, political issue made certain that their waning power would not immediately be revived — the introduction of Chinese labour into the Transvaal goldfields. Throughout the Boer War, the Government's supporters had promised as soon as they secured control of the country that the goldmines, hitherto hindered in their development by Kruger's hostility and taxation, would enter upon a period of unexampled prosperity. The conclusion of the war, however, brought not prosperity but depression to the goldfields. It was soon obvious that any hope of the

Transvaal repaying the cost of the war to the British taxpayer would have to be abandoned. The mine owners requested that they be allowed to import Chinese labour to supplement European and native labour. These Chinese were to be indentured, so as to ensure that they would work long enough to repay the cost of their recruitment and transport. They were to be segregated from other labour, confined to compounds and denied, even during their leisure hours, the normal liberties of life. Milner accepted the mine owners' case and, after some hesitation, so did the British Government. This was not a wise decision on any grounds and there was an immediate furore.

Liberal Imperialists were offended because Canada, Australia and New Zealand, all contributors to the war effort, were strongly opposed to the importation of Chinese. The Australians in particular were obsessed with their fear of the 'Yellow Peril', and were not inclined to ignore the Mother country's affront to their declared prejudice. Organised labour was angered by this latest manifestation of the Tory belief that labour was nothing more than a commodity. The unemployed saw themselves as deprived of the opportunity to obtain work on the Rand that they could not get at home. The Radicals, who from the beginning had opposed the war because they claimed it had been waged merely to serve the interests of a group of financiers, saw the Government's action as confirmation of their criticisms. With these practical considerations was coupled a genuine humanitarian concern for the fate of the Chinese 'slaves', whose conditions of transportation, work and domicile seemed deliberately designed to create, in R.C.K. Ensor's memorable phrase, 'moral sinks of indescribable beastliness'.[28]

In concert with J.E.B. Seely and Herbert Samuel, Trevelyan was immediately involved in prosecuting a vigorous campaign against the Government's ordinance. Humanitarian considerations may, in part, have accounted for 'the unusual warmth and vehemence' he showed when addressing his constituents on the subject. 'This crusade to me is moral,'[29] he told them. But he was enough the Liberal politician to recognise what a powerful stick this provided with which to beat the Tories. As chance would have it, Sir Thomas Brooke-Hitching, chosen by the Elland Conservative Association to stand against Trevelyan at the next election, made his acquaintance with the constituency at the same time as Herbert Samuel, in an amendment to the Address, had denounced the importation of the Chinese. Sir Thomas unwisely maintained the opponents of the ordinance were 'old women', and that their arguments were 'unbusinesslike'. Trevelyan eagerly seized his opportunity.

> I can understand the Conservatives in this constituency choosing as the man to fight their battle, one who is in favour of upholding great Church privileges and like humbug, and going back to the old and bad tariff laws, but I confess I cannot understand them going in for a slavery candidate... Maybe we are unbusiness-like..., but I fear this policy above all..., because

I consider it is a stain upon the British name — bringing in slavery..., for no other reason than that of increasing the dividends of what will soon become a more and more ignoble plutocracy.[30]

In and out of his constituency, Trevelyan pursued the Chinese slavery issue in speeches notable for their lack of any spirit of charity towards the Government.

The Government have disavowed all the objects of the war which could in any sense be called high-minded. There are higher things than money. There is national honour, there is national credit, there are national ideals. It is on behalf of these last that I protest against the introduction of Chinese labour...[31]

Viscount Samuel has told in his *Memoirs* how, 'When the case was put in Parliament, in the Press and on the platform, the country caught fire... The Liberal Party definitely declared itself opposed to the whole Chinese Labour scheme.'[32] The Government had gone too far to withdraw, and Trevelyan with other like-minded Liberals took advantage of the perfect weapon with which to smite the Tories. His one concern remained that inadequate leadership might yet cause the Liberal party to founder. Samuel agreed, even if allowing himself a caveat. 'I admire the way you pour the vials of your violent vituperation on the vile villains who lead us,' he wrote. 'I agree on the whole, but believe there may be some obscure grains of common sense among them.'[33] Trevelyan was not prepared to allow himself even that scruple of magnanimity towards his leaders.

The rumours of gross cruelty suffered by the Chinese in their compounds caused Trevelyan to write to Seely, suggesting that together with Samuel, and perhaps John Burns, they should demand an immediate inquiry. Meanwhile, they might send a letter to *The Times*. Seely replied:

A joint letter to *The Times* would do great good, for, as you say, if properly worded it would put us right with the moderate people besides heartening up the extremists. We might also send a round-robin, either to Campbell-Bannerman or to Balfour direct... It may be said that if the government agreed to the enquiry they would use it to stifle discussion..., but we must risk that. Let me know what you think about this, and I will gladly co-operate in whatever plan you decide upon.[34]

Whatever humanitarian reasons might have prompted their initial campaign on the Chinese issue, it had now become primarily a matter of tactics to exploit the problem for the maximum party advantage.

The suggested letter was published in *The Times*, and brought a note from Samuel to Trevelyan.

I saw your letter..., and quite agreed with the substance of it... I hardly think that any useful service would be rendered by a letter to Campbell-

Bannerman. It would result in nothing new, and it would emphasize the party character of the movement against Chinese labour.

Samuel suggested the best course would be to send to Balfour, 'an open letter — almost in the nature of a manifesto'.[35] His advice was followed and the 'manifesto' published in November 1905.[36] With its twenty signatories, giving the impression of all and non party support it proved a very useful exercise in keeping 'live' the Chinese 'slavery' issue, appearing as it did little more than a week before Balfour's resignation. H.G. Wells was one of those who signed the letter. The confusion in men's minds concerning the problem, and the value it afforded the Liberal cause in the election, he captured perfectly in *The New Machiavelli*. Richard Remington is addressing an election crowd as their Liberal candidate:

> 'Chinese labour!' cried the voice again.
> 'You've given them notice to quit', I answered.
> The market-place roared delight, but whether that delight expressed hostility to Chinamen, or hostility to their practical enslavement no student of the General Election of 1906 has ever been able to determine. Certainly one of the most effective posters on our side displayed a hideous face, just that and nothing more. There was not even a legend to it. How it impressed the electorate we did not know, but that it impressed the electorate profoundly there can be no disputing.[37]

Trevelyan's days had not been entirely devoted to politics. Lady Caroline Trevelyan was concerned, now that her eldest son had begun so well upon his parliamentary career, that he should be thinking seriously about marriage. She, at least, knew that behind the reserved and serious front Trevelyan affected in company, there was a very different man, of abounding sentiment. Yet, should she too obviously press her concern in these matters, her son was quick to reply:

> I have promised to tell you if I fall in love or make up my mind to marry anyone... You need not be afraid as far as I am concerned that I shall commit myself in a hurry. It is vastly more likely I shall never marry at all.[38]

Mary Katherine Bell was born in 1881, the last of the three children of Hugh Bell the iron master, and his second wife, Florence Olliffe. Molly, for so she was called by her family, enjoyed a particularly happy and comfortable childhood. Her education was that which convention dictated for girls of her social position.

> My mother's idea was that her daughters should be turned out as good wives and mothers... We must be able to play the piano and sing a bit, we must learn to dance well, and know how to make small talk..., the more

serious side of education did not take any part in the plans my mother made for us... No girl that we knew was trained for any career or profession, nor did girls from our class go to school.[39]

Neither of Molly's parents was particularly interested in politics so that their social circle rarely included politicians. Therefore, when for the first time, at the invitation of Molly's half sister, Gertrude, Trevelyan visited the Bells' home, it was not surprising that she should have thought of him as 'a bird of very different plumage' from the usual guests that gathered at 95 Sloane Street. The young politician, for all his predilection for taking himself and his conversation too seriously, made a not altogether unfavourable impression on Molly. She wrote in her diary, 'Charles Trevelyan, Sir George's son was here. He is a dog.' During the 1902 season, Molly was frequently seen, accompanied by Trevelyan, at parties and balls and on cycling expeditions into the country. People began to talk of a match.

Trevelyan was never a dancing man. At balls he much preferred to seek out some quiet corner where he could engage his partner in earnest conversation. Gay talk and badinage he counted nothing more than a waste of time. 'He was,' his wife later recalled, 'of a type utterly unlike any other man I knew, deeply serious, imbued with a high sense of duty, full of ideals to which I had never given a thought.' Their talk was of colonial preference, tariff reform, the taxation of land values, home rule for Ireland and the raising of death duties — and all with a perfect intensity and seriousness of purpose. Nor would Molly dare to interpolate a lighter theme into this stream of polemic. Had she wanted to say anything, she would have found difficulty in getting a word in edgeways. Upon one occasion, bold enough to say that in time he would find out how ignorant she was on political subjects, Molly won the less than gallant rejoinder, 'I've discovered that already.'[40] Not surprisingly, the friendship was sundered.

Trevelyan was thirty-two, discouraged and miserable. He began to dread 'the long loneliness of life'. When, quite late in the 1903 Season, Trevelyan and Molly met once more at a party he was no longer the domineering partner of the year before. Needing companionship he was now prepared to listen to what another might have to say. He accepted readily the offer of 'platonic' friendship made by his younger companion. Time and their separation had changed Molly as much as Trevelyan.

I had grown up since we had last met, and was no longer such a silly, flirtatious creature as I had been the year before... We were both ready to hold out a welcoming hand, and to enjoy talks and companionship together.[41]

The 'platonic' friendship flourished, but Molly still had reservations about her suitor. He was eleven years older than she, grave where she was gay. Their outlook on life could not have been more different. He was, in Molly's words, 'well educated, well read, thoughtful and determined', while she was but 'a bit of thistledown'.[42] For his part, Trevelyan had no such reservations. What Molly might lack in education and seriousness, time and reading would soon repair. It was more than enough that she accepted the basis of his ideals, his views upon religion and unreservedly accepted his commitment to the cause of 'the People'.

> To get near the People you have *got* to give them yourself and your character... Morley would think he had lost all dignity... I, a little man, intend to be known to those whom I am among. They shall know that their 'great' folk are human beings; that all the world is equal. Oh, my darling Molly, how I talk! Forgive me.[43]

In September 1903, Trevelyan asked Molly to marry him. This time there was to be no rebuff.

Although the period of their engagement was short, they were to be separated for part of the time. Trevelyan had long arranged a series of political meetings for that Autumn which he could not cancel. Meanwhile, Molly spent a short holiday with her uncle, Lascelles, British Ambassador in Berlin. From Berlin came letters to Trevelyan telling of longing and loneliness, of shopping expeditions and parties, of balls in the great state rooms of the Embassy. Amidst the tender confidences Trevelyan bestowed in his letters came news of speeches and rowdy political meetings. But more important was the careful detailing, without any reservations, of his personal political philosophy.

> It is the lesser men that aristocracy (that is, the certainty of position and tolerable or excessive wealth with no compulsory sense of its responsibility and evanescence) injures so deeply... These are irretrievably injured by their position. It can never enter into their imaginations that the whole basis of their comfort or position may be wrong and unsocial. Others may be *too* revolutionary. But not to be capable of being revolutionary is the worst curse of man. Such a man cannot see far down and cannot move with great currents. However, this is vague. But be it noted that all great Englishmen, except what you can count upon your thumbs, come from the middle *working* classes not the *enjoying* classes... Wealth and made position are the only quite deadly poisons I know, and the longer I live, the more firmly I believe it hard beyond all other hardness for a rich man to enter into the kingdom of heaven. I cannot dispose of my wealth or fling it away, and I cannot spend all my time fussing over whether I have the right to do this or that. But there is only one rule which I have evolved which I believe to be any guide at all — that all expenditure must be made to make us efficient for our chosen service, and that all above that is a source of subtle degradation, of blunting our realization of the real facts. I can see no sanction for our unearned wealth except shockingly unjust accident which has selec-

ted us against any hundred thousand others to have it. Rights of earned property I understand. Rights of such property as ours I cannot understand at all... I am trying to make you understand and feel some of this, because without it you will never understand me. The whole of my politics and life is based on it, and the strength of it grows with years... It is the only vital question for those who have not made their own place in life and live exclusively on the labour of others... Of all the truths I seem to have got into my blood, the only two I ultimately care about are:
1. that no human being deserves anything or has the slightest right to complain of any mischance, however huge;
2. that no pleasures can ever be bought by money but only by labour... I want you to be myself, and so I struggle to explain through these lame words my almost inexplicable self.[44]

Before her engagement, Molly, encouraged by light-hearted friends, sometimes had been bold enough to laugh at and chaff her suitor for the earnestness of his opinions. Had she any reason to suppose that Trevelyan was not totally dedicated to improving the lot of his less fortunate fellow-men, the confidences he now gave her in his letters permanently disposed of that idea. Nor should she suppose that he would ever temper those opinions for the sake of personal political advancement. He had a hard-headed appreciation both of his capabilities and the task to which he was dedicated.

When I read Gladstone's *Life* I feel my own nothingness, and I am constantly anxious that in your newness to affairs you should not make pretty dreams for yourself of great successes for me... I have not the quickness, variety or imagination of outlook which can possibly enable me ever to deal with the complicated revolutions of our national politics. I can only do my duty. And so little do I think there is any good chance of rising to very high position with my mediocre store of knowledge and ability, that I shall tend less and less to try for position and more and more to take a line I think right — not for the flattering advantage of being a martyr, but because calculation and intriguing are only of use where there is real aptitude for them. My desire is to imitate Gladstone's openness and rectitude.[45]

There could not now be any doubting for Molly that she was marrying a 'damned serious gowk', as Trevelyan had been affectionately characterised by her father. At first hesitatingly, then with growing certainty, Molly appreciated, if she did not altogether understand, that her future husband would, if he could, sever the leading strings of social and economic convention that stifled the lives of many for the benefit of a privileged few. It did not matter that the privileges Trevelyan was intent upon undermining supported that class to which their families and their friends belonged. His watchword was 'the People's interest', and he did not give a fig that Society should disapprove such 'socialistic' intentions.

Trevelyan rejected the notion of formalised and institutionalised religion. He thought that the clergy of all denominations would better be employed in improving the fortunes of their flocks in the world than preparing them for the promised, and to Trevelyan's way of thinking, dubious pleasures of heaven. In later years, he would sometimes recite to one of his children:

> Though burning at first
> Perhaps may be worst,
> Yet time the affliction will soften;
> But those who are bored
> With praising the Lord
> Will be more so by praising Him often.

Trevelyan was not persuaded of sanctity's virtues by its formal trappings. As he observed after attending a Harrow dinner where the chief guest had been Dr. Randall Davidson:

> He is simply a very nice English gentleman. It is a most respectable thing to be head of the English church. But catch *him* fishing in Galilee Lake with anything except the best gut and artificial fly and impermeable waders! And no fear of him going into the highways and hedges to compel them to come in. Oh, it is a *very* respectable thing to be an Archbishop.[46]

Fortunately, Molly shared his views — even if she did not express them in such an intransigent fashion. Though in married life they did not attend Church, in one particular at least, Trevelyan's views were swiftly overborne. Religious scruple was vanquished by the unremitting demands of social etiquette. Protest though he might his wish that he and Molly should be married in a registry office, Lady Bell would have none of it. In the event, they were married at Holy Trinity Church in Sloane Street, on 6 January 1904; a thoroughly conventional society wedding.

In anticipation of her son's marriage, Lady Trevelyan had altered and improved a property in the model village of Cambo on the Wallington estate. At Cambo House, as they renamed it, the Trevelyans were to spend their time when Parliament was not in session. It was to remain their holiday home until Trevelyan inherited Wallington on his father's death in 1928. Their first London home was a house in North Street but, unable to secure a long lease on the property, they joined with Walter Runciman in building twin houses, 14 and 15 Great College Street, where they lived until Trevelyan finally left Parliament in 1931.

The great advantage of their new London house was its proximity to Parliament. A division bell was installed. This permitted Trevelyan to spend much more time at home than otherwise would have been possible, and allowed Parliamentary dinner guests to attend critical votes in the House, if necessary, between courses — a convenience for them if a nuisance for their hostess. The Trevelyans entertained frequently; a small intimate dinner party usually, with a 'tail' to follow. The guests were often Trevelyan's contemporaries in the Commons and came from both sides of the House. In those early years Churchill was a frequent visitor, always good company but invariably monopolising the conversation. Trevelyan was also fond of bringing home a single guest so that they might dine à *deux* and discuss politics. Occasionally there would be large formal parties that were as taxing on space as they were perplexing exercises in etiquette. 'Did a Bishop take precedence over a baronet?' Molly was to recall such intractable problems. 'When I wrote to Lord Carlisle inviting him to dinner he accepted, adding, "Don't ask anybody higher than an Earl, or I shan't be able to take you in." ' [47] Molly enjoyed such gatherings; her husband much preferred their less formal entertaining.

By her own admission, Molly in those early days of marriage was not the most competent of housekeepers. Trevelyan had counselled her that she would do well to learn of these things from Mrs. Webb, advice that Molly did not altogether follow as may be judged from the generous fare her guests were offered. The couple lived comfortably for, apart from the allowance he received from his grandfather, Trevelyan possessed money left him by his grandfather, and Molly also had money of her own. To staff their ten roomed London house they employed a cook, parlourmaid and housemaid. When the children were born, a nurse and nursery maid were added to the domestic staff. Theirs was a modest household by the standards of the day. The total wages for five permanent staff amounted to £101 a year. But that was in 1905.

All Liberals were agreed in one thing at least; that Balfour could not much longer delay the inevitable demise of the Tory Administration. But, should Balfour resign rather than advise a dissolution, what then would be the best tactics for the Liberal leaders? Should they form a Government and then dissolve, or should they refuse to form any administration until after a general election? Earlier in 1905, Trevelyan had eagerly discussed these various possibilities with Samuel. Both men agreed:

> ...it would be a lamentable blunder to form a ministry before the election. It would divert the public attention from the iniquities of the Government to the omissions from and the admissions to the new Government. It would cause schism in our ranks. What of the Dilke problem?* It does not matter which way it is solved. What of the certainty in the non-party mind that

---

*Sir Charles Dilke, 1843-1911, brilliant Radical Liberal, lost the certain offer of a Cabinet place because of his involvement in a divorce scandal in 1886. He remained a prominent and important member of the radical section of the Liberal party. His friends hoped that in the easier moral climate after Queen Victoria's death, he might receive the office that his abilities deserved when the Liberals came once more into power. In the event,

the old foozler, C-B, was going to try to be Premier or leader of the House of Commons? All that trouble ought to come after not before an election when there is a vigorous party to bring the officials about at once and to settle the matter irrespective of Tory jibes... I suppose a Ministry formation is always a hateful business but doubly so when there is no *man* among the leaders. I am trusting, however, more to time and the quality of the new party.[48]

The Tories stumbled through the 1905 parliamentary session. If in their new found unity the Liberals found good reason to feel truculent, the precarious nature of their combination was revealed when Rosebery, speaking at Bodmin, mounted a determined attack upon a speech Campbell-Bannerman had made a few days before on the subject of Irish Home Rule. Rosebery totally misconstrued Campbell-Bannerman's speech which had been a compromise statement based upon an agreement worked out between him, Asquith, Grey and the Irish party. Rosebery's former acolytes turned viciously upon the Earl, and Trevelyan finally abandoned any remaining hopes he might have retained concerning Rosebery's fitness to be the Liberal leader.

Campbell-Bannerman was certainly proving himself to be anything but 'the old foozler' Trevelyan had supposed. When Balfour resigned, hoping to capitalise upon the rift in Liberal ranks loudly advertised by Rosebery's monumental indiscretion, Campbell-Bannerman, over-riding the hesitation of many of his supporters, formed his Ministry — successfully defeating in the process a plot by Asquith, Grey and Haldane to banish him to the House of Lords. Then as Prime Minister, with a speech at the Albert Hall on the 21 December as a curtain raiser for the general election, he unfolded a programme bolder in spirit and more comprehensive than his many critics had anticipated.

Trevelyan could look forward to his electoral campaign at Elland with more than ususal confidence. It was true that in Sir Thomas Brooke-Hitching (former High Sheriff of London, an industrialist who had made his fortune from the manufacture of perambulators), he had a more formidable opponent than in his previous contests. Sir Thomas had sound local connections, and was a determined, courageous and effective speaker. But his unqualified support for Chamberlain, the Education Act and Chinese indentured labour, was a crippling handicap in the attempt to win a seat that even his own supporters admitted was 'the citadel of a particularly backward kind of Radicalism'.

'It is an inspiring thought,' Trevelyan declared at his adoption meeting at

---

C-B did not give Dilke the War Office. probably because he feared Nonconformist reaction. Morley maintained, however, that C-B's decision from the beginning was a *chose jugée*. In the 1906-10 Parliament, Dilke assumed the rôle of elder back-bench Radical statesman giving encouragement also to the new Labour members.

Halifax, 'that the progressive party is going into this fight united, while the Tories are divided, and divided, not upon a trumpery issue, but the vital problem of Free Trade and Protection.'[49]   Though he was not sparing in his advocacy of that ancient shibboleth of Liberalism, in his campaign Trevelyan made much of Chinese 'slavery', the rating of land values as a panacea for almost all ills, the need for economy in administration, and he vigorously attacked the Education Act.

In no previous election had Trevelyan enjoyed such enthusiastic and unanimous approval from the electorate. The whole campaign was a triumph, and there could not have been a more pleasant introduction to the demands of the hustings for Molly, joining her husband for the first time on an election platform. Polling day, 17 January 1906, was to fulfill and even exceed the most sanguine hopes of Trevelyan's supporters. The declaration of the poll revealed a turnover of more than two thousand votes. Trevelyan was re-elected with a more than doubled majority and the biggest Liberal vote in the constituency's history.

> C.P. Trevelyan 7,609
> Sir T. Brooke-Hitching 3,962
> Liberal majority 3,647

From all quarters came the glad news of Liberal victories. Churchill was in at Manchester together with six other Liberal members and two Labour members. Even the Tory leader, Balfour, had been defeated. The following weeks' results confirmed the Liberal land-slide victory.* After his own triumph, Trevelyan had written to his father: 'We could not have done better.'[50]   But a post card sent to his mother bearing a five word message said everything. 'There *WAS* a Tory party!'[51]

---

*Their victory in 1906 gave the Liberals for the first time in twenty years a majority over all other parties combined. The Liberal share of the vote was only 5.4% more than the Tories' but they gained 400 seats to the Tory 157. The Liberals could also count upon the support of the 30 Labour members, and 83 Irish members, giving a grand 'ministerialist' total of 513 members.

OF LAND, LORDS,
LABOUR AND IRELAND:
1906-14

News of Balfour's resignation in December 1905 was greeted by Lady Caroline Trevelyan with considerable personal interest. 'A *bad* Government has ended as badly as it possibly could,' she wrote to her youngest son. 'Of course, Papa and I are deeply interested in it as it affects Charlie. We feel pretty confident that he will have some office offered him.'[1] To Molly, who was already advertising the certainty that her husband would be promoted from the back benches, Trevelyan gently explained that perhaps his claim was not so obvious to others as it was to her. That this was real and not an affected modesty is confirmed by a letter written to Ralph Wedgwood by his elder brother Joshua, soon to enter Parliament as Liberal member for Newcastle-under-Lyme.

> By the way I heard several things about Trevelyan that would please you. They say he is extremely unselfish and willing to help everybody without aiming at anything for himself and that he alone among the young Liberals is not intriguing for office.[2]

Wedgwood's unsolicited testimonial points to estimable qualities in Trevelyan as a man, even as it indicates certain frailties as a politician.

From Walter Runciman in London, busily engaged in promoting his own claims to office, came a letter on 9 December with an accurate list of the major Cabinet appointments. Runciman added, in a postscript that he certainly would not have interpreted as a self-denying ordinance, 'as in the making of all Cabinets there have been some quite absurd expectations'.[3] Trevelyan told his father, 'it certainly is a Cabinet of all the talents... The Cabinet is Radical, which matters most.'[4] Though the junior posts were still undecided, Trevelyan remained in the North. His brother George, calling on John Burns the new President of the Local Government Board, was invited inside. In the subsequent conversation, the subject of land valuation was soon broached. Burns declared he was anxious to promote the cause at the Local Government Board and had decided he must have as his Under Secretary, a man who 'understood all about it'. He had already rejected one candidate, and would accept no others for the post than Trevelyan, Runciman or Whitley in that order of precedence. George advised his eldest brother to come immediately to London and be available for his imminent summons to office. Trevelyan complied, admitting he 'would feel rather out of it if all my particular pals get office and I don't'. But he was not optimistic about his chances and within twenty four hours he was writing to his wife, 'It is pretty clear I shall not get anything... I can only hope that Runciman has got the place.'[5] Trevelyan wrote next to his parents, regretting that he should have disappointed their hopes in him. Nevertheless he rejoiced in his friends' good fortune. Lady Caroline congratulated her son upon his 'generosity and dignity'. For her part, she could accept his lack of office only 'with a very bad grace... It is abominable that pushing people should come off best.'[6]

From Runciman, whose vigorous promotion of his own claims to junior office had perhaps more than any other factor blighted Trevelyan's chances of promotion, came the stoic avowal, 'I shall never be happy in harness while you are out... You have done mighty work re Site Values, and I hope that if John Burns and I are allowed to push that, you will take us in hand.'[7] If this last was too much like rubbing salt in a wound, Trevelyan made no complaint. But Sir George was not so readily pacified as his son. Once more, Trevelyan was obliged to write to his parents disclaiming any personal desire for office and advertising the excellent qualities of his more fortunate political friends. 'Don't worry about me, I have got a very happy life and can do without being a Mandarin.'[8]

Early in February 1906 Trevelyan, attending a private dinner party, was told by the Prime Minister how much he regretted that he had not been able to find a place for him in December. 'He then said, if I cared to have it, he would make me the Third Charity Commissioner who is unpaid and answers for the Commission in the House. The place is vacated by Griffith-Boscawen.'[9] Campbell-Bannerman intimated there was no need for Trevelyan to make a rushed decision. He consulted both his father and Sir George Young as to the exact duties involved and then accepted the offer.

The post of Third Charity Commissioner, unpaid, was not exactly the sort of official recognition that would satisfy for long even the least fevered ambition. If Charles Trevelyan was loath to advertise his claims for office, others were not so reticent in their expectations of his imminent promotion. At every hint and rumour of change in minor government offices, Sir George expected and Molly waited in vain for Trevelyan's advancement. Nor was Trevelyan unconscious of the loyal expectation and disappointments of his family. In December 1906, after another fruitless bout of rumour-mongering, he wrote to his wife:

> You must make up your mind to my remaining a common-place MP, which I expect will distress you more than it will me... The only reason I am irked at not being in office is that I have no scope for all my energies. I really do not feel any disappointment or difficulty in curbing my ambition, and I can say that with much greater certainty than a year ago.[10]

The rumours of promotion continued. In January 1907, it was confidently predicted that Trevelyan would be going to the Local Government Board. Joshua Wedgwood wrote a gruff letter of 'condolence' to Trevelyan.

> As I understand that John Burns objected to having you at the Local Government Board on the express grounds that you were the head and fount of the offending Land taxes, I cannot be expected to condole with you an exclusion which does you honour — even if it was your way to ask for condolences. With earnest radicals your position will be enormously strengthened, and although I believe that you are absolutely devoid of personal ambition, that is at any rate good for the cause.[11]

For Wedgwood, there could never be a better cause for which a man might pocket ambition than that of land taxation. Not so Sir George Trevelyan who was quite convinced the Prime Minister *ought* to have done better by Charles. He wrote to Campbell-Bannerman telling him as much, to receive by return a glowing tribute to his son's political promise. 'Undoubtedly he stands for promotion,' wrote the Prime Minister, 'but sadly, at the moment, there simply is no vacancy for his talents.'

A year later, when Asquith replaced Sir Henry as Prime Minister, it seemed the ideal opportunity for Trevelyan to be promoted. It was not to be. Molly, quite distraught at this latest and most cruel blow, was comforted by her sister in law. 'I might have known how deep it would go... Isn't it strange to think of those people in Downing Street not realising one atom what they have done. I hope you are being buoyed up by a good, furious indignation as I am.'[12] But indignation was little comfort when so many had confidently asserted that Trevelyan would be offered the post of Civil Lord of the Admiralty. Instead of the notes of congratulation, once again the all too familiar letters of condolence arrived. Wedgwood wrote:

> I am not surprised that they have not found room for you. You are much too nice and honest to do the wire-pulling and press advertising that people with careers find necessary... I know you are too unselfish to mind being left out. You can leave the grievances to your friends... We like you all the better the more this sort of thing happens.[13]

Wedgwood was not being disingenuous. Sir George, stung by this latest disappointment, wrote furiously to Asquith:

> Since our party came in, full recognition has been given to past services of those who, in the old days, served the country and the cause, by the employment of their sons and relatives who were worthy of a chance in the career of administration. Now that several younger men have been placed in office, while my son is left out, I must protest, once for all, that I feel the exception made in our case very deeply.[14]

Only the pain of constant, humiliating disappointment at his son's lack of promotion could, in part, explain such an outrageously nepotic letter. Asquith, meanwhile, had written to Trevelyan. He should not consider himself to have been 'passed over... As soon as a fitting place can be found, then I will ask you to become a Cabinet colleague.'[15]

Walter Runciman, in a letter that barely disguised his satisfaction with his own fortune at being promoted President of the Board of Education, grieved that his happiness should be spoiled because Trevelyan had not been given office. 'Asquith assured me definitely that he wanted you... Don't be depressed.'[16] But this time Trevelyan was bitterly disappointed by this latest blow to his parliamentary career. For more than six months Trevelyan had shown increasingly less interest in his parliamentary duties. If he was to be permanently 'condemned' to his backbench status, then he would be better employed outside Parliament. Alternatively, if he was to remain in the House, then he would take a much more independent and critical stance. To his wife he affected a complete indifference to politics and would tell her little of his parliamentary life. Bewildered by this change of mood, Molly wrote to George Trevelyan asking him if he could explain his brother's strange new state of mind. He replied:

> I think I understand..., Charles is unwilling to talk because he has so little to say of a definite nature. He is happy at home, but bored with 'agitation' now that the period of Liberal legislation has set in... His duty as a supporter of an active Government is to vote and do nothing. Four hundred more or less able men are in the same absurd and wasteful situation... A change of thought would send him back once more fresh and interested in English affairs.[17]

Trevelyan refused to recharge his political interests. He claimed that he was not spending enough time on his domestic life. If he decided to change his mind he had only to stretch out his hand and there would be more than enough public work for him to do. Perhaps he ought to take a more strenuous part in politics, 'but sufficient unto the years are the meetings thereof'. He might, in the new year, make a greater effort.[18]

The long and frustrating period without office ended in October 1908 when Trevelyan was offered the post of Under Secretary at the Board of Education. 'It is pleasant once again to have a Trevelyan in a Liberal Ministry,' declared the *Westminster Gazette*, 'though we need hardly say, his qualifications are a good deal more than nominal.'[19] Sir George, at last, was placated: for his own part, Trevelyan was delighted. 'I am in an office most interesting administratively, and in the midst of a political crisis. Above all I am under my political chum, with whom I have been accustomed to confidences and who trusts me.'[20]

Trevelyan was to remain as Under Secretary at the Board of Education until his resignation from the Liberal Government in August 1914. In July 1909 Asquith offered him a move to the Local Government Board, a department that by then had sunk into impotence under its incompetent President, John Burns. Trevelyan refused Asquith's offer because he was 'quite convinced... [he]... would not be able to get on with J.B.'. Burns, so Trevelyan told his mother, was 'very wroth' at the decision. 'Dear, vain, old fellow! He cannot understand how anyone would not jump at the chance of serving under him.'[21] There was one other attempt to move Trevelyan from the Education Board. In October 1911 Trevelyan asked Asquith to give him a job that would provide him with more work. This was probably only part of the reason why he sought a move. In a Cabinet reshuffle that month, Runciman had been moved to the Board of Agriculture, and J.A. Pease, formerly Chancellor of the Duchy of Lancaster, took Runciman's place. Trevelyan did not have a high opinion of Jack Pease's qualities as a Minister, though he admitted to his wife that his new master behaved 'very nicely' towards him. Asquith intimated that Trevelyan might be offered the Civil Lordship of the Admiralty which would provide 'more responsible administrative work', and the opportunity of advancement 'if I do well'. The scheme foundered because George Lambert, Civil Lord since 1905, stubbornly refused to move. Asquith was sympathetic, but he had problems of greater moment to concern him than the placing of a junior minister in a more congenial or demanding post.[22] So Trevelyan served a frustratingly long period in junior office in one department. In the long term it was to provide him with unrivalled background experience for senior ministerial office as President of the Education Board in the first two Labour governments. But for the moment it was a sore disappointment not to be given the opportunity to prove his qualities and capacity for administration and leadership in another department of state.

By nature, Trevelyan was not a compromiser. He believed that love was the basis of the good life. 'It is true because not only our feelings but our reason sanctions it... Love is the instinctive working of the force which teaches us both to rely on others, and spend our energies in helping others.'[23] But to love your neighbour was not to ignore his faults if they caused suffering to others. He despised the middle class morality with its instinct for hoarding property which it equated with 'respectability'. The Puritan in him abominated the ostentatious display of luxury by the wealthy who were pleased to suppose that the misfortunes of the mass of the people were either divinely ordained, or a crime for which those who suffered were themselves responsible. Trevelyan's political philosophy did not readily admit of shades of nuances of right and wrong. What he believed was 'right', he pursued with all energy. In the excitement of that pursuit he often ignored, to his personal cost, those courtesies of deference that senior Ministers required their junior colleagues to observe at all times. Trevelyan seemed insensitive to the pricks he unwittingly administered to others' self esteem. A heated correspondence with Lord Chancellor Loreburn on the appointment of magistrates illustrates the way Trevelyan's forthright style could alienate a Minister.

One of Trevelyan's influential constituents had complained that there was not a single permanent Liberal magistrate in Elland. The political bias in the appointment of magistrates was notorious, and Trevelyan took little thought in composing his letter of complaint to Loreburn. He received for his pains a stinging reply.

> Really it is very good of you to inform me of the duties of a Liberal Minister and of your opinion of the way I discharge them: very little I fear to your satisfaction. I am afraid your patience will be even more tried than you say it is if you wait till you gain much by writing in the style you adopt... Pray do not forbear on my account from making what complaints you please.[24]

Trevelyan managed to repair some of the damage created by his earlier letter, but if he cherished any hope of promotion it was not the wisest tactic to rouse Loreburn's ire. The Lord Chancellor was one of the Prime Minister's oldest and best friends. Nor was it any excuse that Trevelyan's private opinion of Loreburn's personal and political qualities was, to say the least, critical.

> Loreburn has always been a sanctimonious humbug, capable of a certain tearful and emotional humanity, but is utterly without the vigorous dislike of wealth and privilege which alone make a useful Liberal. He is thoroughly conceited besides, and won't listen to advice. It is useless to hope for anything from him, and the magisterial appointments will get worse not better.[25]

This opinion (unfair only in his last conjecture) Trevelyan had confided to his mother. However, his habit of committing his unreserved and unvarnished estimates of people and policies to paper, and then sending these missives to correspondents whose discretion could not always be guaranteed, was bound to make him appear a risk if appointed a Minister. This consideration would have weighed particularly with Asquith, who kept his Government afloat by constant compromise and adaptation. Another consideration which must have weighed against Trevelyan's chances of promotion, was his determined, constant and enthusiastic espousal of the taxation of land values, a political 'hot potato' that Asquith and most of his ministerial colleagues preferred to admire from a distance rather than to seize boldly.

Under the chairmanship of John Whitley, a Land Values Group to 'initiate and promote land value legislation in Parliament', by Easter 1906 had the support of more than three hundred MPs. Trevelyan was a leading member and it was he who presented their draft bill to the Prime Minister. 'I believe we have turned the corner in regard to land values,'[26] Trevelyan wrote to his wife. But, though the Prime Minister's response had seemed favourable, the parliamentary session continued without any sign of the Government fulfilling its promise to introduce a valuation bill. A further memorial was prepared, this time signed by four hundred MPs, insisting that the proposed legislation should be introduced, at the latest, in the next session. Trevelyan was one of the six leaders of the deputation that presented the memorial to Campbell-Bannerman and John Burns.

> [We] made little speeches of three minutes each. C-B gave us an excellent reply promising a valuation bill. But Burns showed that he is against us and made the most miserable speech conceivable. There is a considerable turmoil, and I am afraid there will be great ructions next session. For Burns never could carry a bill if his spirit is as hostile as it at present appears to be. He is simply a Tory on the question.[27]

It was obvious that John Burns'' hostility to the proposals of the Land Values Group would be a fatal incubus to the success of their plans.

On the opening day of the 1907 parliamentary session, Burns gave notice of the introduction of a bill for the valuation of land in England and Wales. In May 1907, a Land Values Taxation (Scotland) Bill, recommended by a select committee in December 1906, was introduced in the Commons. This bill, passed by huge majorities through the Commons was rejected outright by the Lords. Reintroduced in February 1908, it again passed the Commons, this time with even greater majorities, only to be so thoroughly mutilated by the Lords that the Government decided the measure was best abandoned. To add to the frustration of the land taxers, despite the promise made in the King's Speech in February 1907, the session passed without any sign of an English Valuation Bill. The 1908 session brought merely more unfulfilled promises. In October, all hope was abandoned when it was announced there would be no bill that session, and this despite the firm promise by Asquith in May, when speaking in a debate on a Housing and Town Planning Bill, that Burns would introduce 'at an early date' a valuation bill for England and Wales.

The Land Values Group was bemused by the conduct of the Liberal leaders who constantly affirmed their support for legislation, and then did nothing about it. It became obvious that to achieve anything other avenues of action would have to be explored. The Scottish Land Value Bill had not been the only piece of Liberal legislation vetoed or mutilated by the Lords. A truculent Upper House had rejected almost every important bill that the Liberal Commons had sent them. The Lords, with its massive Tory majority, denied the mandate given the Liberals by the electorate, and, adding insult to injury, claimed to be acting in the interests of the people. This excuse was too patent to deceive anyone. In 1907, Campbell-Bannerman told the Commons that the power of the Lords would have to be 'so restricted by law as to secure that within the limits of a single Parliament the views of the Commons should prevail'. A resolution to this effect was accepted by the Commons after three days of debate by a majority of 432 to 147. 'We cannot expect the House of Lords tamely to submit,' wrote Trevelyan to Lady Caroline. 'I suppose this will mean an election next January.'[28] But the Lords, far from showing concern or any sense of submission to the wishes of the Commons, carried on as before. They were obviously quite indifferent about any resolution concerning their powers that a Liberal House of Commons might be pleased to accept.

In this particular, Asquith's inheritance as Prime Minister and leader of the Liberals on the death of Campbell-Bannerman in April 1908, was no easy one. In February 1908, Sir George Trevelyan had predicted that the future of Liberalism depended upon the party fighting the Lords, an opinion his son enthusiastically shared. But was it realistic to expect Asquith to be bolder than his predecessor Campbell-Bannerman? The answer was provided in the last week of the 1908 session.

The Prime Minister was being entertained to a dinner by Liberal MPs at the National Liberal Club. The celebration was to acknowledge the skilful way in which Asquith had piloted the Licensing Bill through the Commons, but the Prime Minister seized the opportunity to declare war upon the House of Lords. Trevelyan wrote in great delight to his father:

> It is like coming out of a fog into sunshine on a mountain. This is the kind of thing we have been waiting to hear for three years... Campbell-Bannerman just failed to do it. It is the step I have been longing for. There is no going back now. I have always hoped that Asquith, with all his caution, would be very formidable, and now he is proving it.[29]

'Bravo Asquith!' echoed Sir George. 'We have been kicked for seventy years, for the kicking began when Melbourne was P.M. It is time to kick back.'[30] Almost as a post-script to his speech, Asquith had added: 'The Budget of next year will stand at the very centre of our work by which we shall stand or fall, by which certainly we shall be judged in the estimation both of the present and posterity.' As his biographers wrote, Asquith's prediction was to prove truer than at the time he could have supposed. The 1909 Budget was to be the anvil upon which the fate of the House of Lords was forged.[31]

The new parliamentary session began quietly enough with no hint of the drama to come. 'I think the party is in pretty good heart,'[32] Trevelyan reported to his wife; though he showed some concern about the increasing number of Labour candidates being adopted to fight traditionally Liberal constituencies. This must bode ill for the future. In March and early April, Parliament was fully occupied with the Naval Estimates and an anti-German naval scare. The need to raise more money for the construction of extra British Dreadnoughts to meet a supposed acceleration in the German naval building programme was a discomforting, hysterical prelude to the budget.

David Lloyd George introduced his budget to the Commons on 29 April 1909 with an inordinately long speech. In Trevelyan's opinion it was 'not at all up to the occasion'.[33] However, after a detailed study of the budget proposals Trevelyan concluded that the Chancellor had dealt very fairly with the land question.

Apparently all land is to be valued under the Act. So, we shall be in a fair way to getting our valuation complete. Otherwise too, it is excellent..., bold and uncompromising. The more I understand the Budget, the more it is the embodiment of all I could hope for. Certainly it will be a severe year. Now, if ever, I will stick to work with no rest till it is all over...

Papa and Mama, of course, accept the Budget, but they don't wholly like it. I let them talk. They never mentioned the land tax. They pitied the heir who has to pay large death duties on land. It is very curious, the combination of public spirit and yet complete failure to appreciate any of the deeper social effects of taxing large fortunes. They would pay half their fortunes without publicly grumbling, without seeing why they *ought* to have to pay it.[34]

Writing to his mother in July, Trevelyan first mooted the idea that perhaps the true political potential of the budget did not lie entirely in its fiscal proposals but in the unreasoned passions it aroused.

The way the landlords and peers are cursing and whining is all to the good. We shall very soon have a clear cut issue between the many and the few. I am half inclined to wish the Lords would throw it out.[35]

Perhaps the 'Welsh Wizard' had conjured better with his budget than they all had supposed — a social and constitutional revolution in one, wrapped in a speech as dry as dust! But would the Liberal leaders seize the opportunity afforded them? 'I am convinced,' wrote Trevelyan, 'the reaction of the last eighteen months has been stopped.' Should the Government have had any doubts that the budget, and in particular the land clauses, afforded their party an enormous electoral advantage, they were very soon to be convinced. Because of his appointment as a junior Treasury minister, Oswald Partington, member for the High Peak constituency in Derbyshire, was obliged to fight a by election. In 1906 he had scraped into Parliament with a very narrow majority. Few Liberals expected Partington would win — but he did. Trevelyan wrote of this unlooked for triumph:

> The effect of the Budget has been even more rapid than I expected... High Peak was unquestionably won on the Budget and especially the Land Taxes. I frankly did not expect the win and it is a great victory. For, if we can keep that sort of seat we can keep anything! [36]

The budget continued to make painfully slow progress through the Commons. In the constituencies, Liberal morale was high. But in Parliament, Trevelyan admitted that members would have 'died of boredom but for speculation about the Lords'.[37] Those who, like Trevelyan, fervently desired that the Lords in their rage would ignore constitutional convention and reject the budget, were comforted when the Upper House began its proceedings in September in an intransigent mood 'mutilating the Housing Bill and cutting out what little remnant of value it had after the whittling down of it by John Burns'.[38] A speech by Balfour further raised Trevelyan's hopes. 'I don't see now how the Lords can fail to throw out the Budget. But there are still many people who thing they won't.'[39] A week later, hope was dampened if not entirely extinguished.

> I am sorry to say that the King is putting on pressure to prevent the Lords rejecting the Budget. Presumably he dealt with Rosebery last week. He has now sent for Lord Cawdor who is supposed to be a 'rejectors' ring leader. But, I have not yet ceased to hope.[40]

As the budget reached its final stages in the Commons, Trevelyan reported that 'the Tory opposition [was] now a weak thing', though, to the end, they stubbornly continued to fight the land clauses. 'Milner has made a speech practically recommending the rejection of the Budget,'[41] Trevelyan wrote, making it obvious that this was the one thing above all else in politics he then most desired. The budget passed its final scrutiny by the Commons on 2 November with a majority of two hundred and thirty votes. Within the month, the House of Lords rejected it by an equally overwhelming majority. Asquith's response was to move a resolution in the Commons, joyfully accepted by the majority: 'That the action of the House of Lords in refusing to pass into law the financial provisions made by this House for the service of the year is a breach of the Constitution and usurpation of the right of the Commons.'

So the battle lines were drawn. A January General Election was now inevitable. The parties prepared for a contest without parallel within living memory. Even the Peers, by constitutional dispensation, for the first time were allowed to enter the fray. The issue at debate would not be the merits of the budget but whether an hereditary, Tory House of Lords should be allowed to exercise an absolute veto on the legislation sent to it by a Liberal Commons that had been elected by the people.

To his great regret, Trevelyan had missed the last act of the parliamentary drama. An old knee injury had been aggravated by a fall while out climbing in the Lake District. In mid-November he entered a London hospital for surgery. He wrote to Runciman of his 'sorrow at not being present at the greatest occasion of modern times when Asquith makes his declaration'. However, he was not too ill to raise a subject that had concerned him increasingly during the past two years.

> I hope all the energy and wisdom of the most important heads of the party will be devoted in the next week or two to trying to find a *modus vivendi* with the Labour party. It is much too big to be left to the Whips who are not sympathetic enough to arrange it. In truth, Asquith and Lloyd George ought to make it their personal affair.[42]

Trevelyan could never understand why the Labour and Liberal parties could not cooperate to their mutual advantage. When Victor Grayson won Colne Valley for Labour in July 1907 — a seat where the Liberal candidate had been returned unopposed in 1906 — Trevelyan was not disturbed by Grayson's reputation as an independent and revolutionary. 'I don't mind much,' he wrote to Molly, 'though this success will make the Labour men perky and they will be hard to deal with. It means that you and I will have to work very hard to keep my seat safe... But, the people are independent and thinking for themselves. Why shouldn't they have their own man? I dare say I should have voted for him myself. What I have to make them feel is that I am as good a man as any Labour man they could get.'[43] Early in the new Parliament, Trevelyan had been disappointed by Liberal party tactics that allowed the Labour party the credit as the initiators of necessary social legislation. But Trevelyan was ignoring the fact that many Liberals were too much 'Individualists' of the old school easily to unbend enough to support Labour measures. It is interesting that men like Trevelyan and Wedgwood who eventually were to leave the Liberals and join with Labour, at this time denied the logic of their sympathies. Wedgwood lightheartedly touched upon this subject in a letter to Trevelyan in August 1907.

> I have been having a series of meeting with F. Neilson. Great fun, but he does manage to put up the backs of the Socialists in a wholly unnecessary way. At least it is unnecessary in my constituency where they are all my best supporters.[44]

In September 1908, the problem of Lib-Lab relations moved closer to Trevelyan's constituency. There was a vacancy at Newcastle. Labour threatened to run a candidate, and the Liberal nominee was, in Trevelyan's opinion, 'no good... There may be a catastrophe and I expect I shall be sucked into the vortex.'[45] The immediate threat did not materialise but Trevelyan's agent sent disquieting reports that the local branch of the Independent Labour Party was becoming very active, gathering funds, talking of putting up their own candidate at the next election, criticising Trevelyan for the time he spent out of the constituency, and finding fault with his actions in Parliament. The decision of the Miners' Federation to join the Labour party immediately put at hazard the seats of two of Trevelyan's particular Lib-Lab friends, Thomas Burt and Charles Fenwick. Both refused to sign the pledge to obey their party. 'Men who have been independent for thirty years cannot surrender their independence at this time of their lives and promise to vote according to orders,'[46] wrote Trevelyan to his wife. But increasing Labour militancy and independence was the sign of the times, and Sir George's assertion that 'the action of the Labour party [was] mid-Summer madness at this moment'[47] revealed more of anger, a sense of impotence and wishful thinking, than of truth.

However promising the general prospects for the Liberal party were, Trevelyan knew that this time he would have a stern personal test to face. The local ILP was still threatening to put up its own candidate. For once, the Tories had a very strong candidate in George Ramsden, a local man who was a member of the Halifax council. He had been adopted in 1908, and for the past twelve months had been carefully nursing the constituency. Ramsden promoted himself as 'the worker's friend'. The budget should be strenuously opposed for it was 'Socialistic'. Why should there be more taxes when they were taxed enough already? They should 'tax the foreigner instead'. Lloyd George, not Trevelyan, was Ramsden's particular target.

Trevelyan had issued his manifesto from London early in December. It was an uncompromising attack upon the House of Lords.

> I wish to make it clear from the outset that at the coming election I want support on no other understanding than that the new Parliament is to destroy once and for ever, the power of the hereditary chamber to reverse the decisions of the representatives of the people. Their power to delay or reject supplies must be abolished, and they must never again enjoy an absolute veto over ordinary legislation. They have rendered fruitless the most serious work of the present House of Commons.[48]

Once in his constituency, Trevelyan concentrated most of his invective upon the Lords' hatred of land taxes. His meetings were well attended; his audiences enthusiastic; but, for the first time in Brighouse he suffered heckling. The Tory press gleefully reported that the minds of the Liberals were much agitated by the question, 'What will the Labour Party do?' Eventually, the local ILP decided that their members should have a free choice as to how they should vote, but only after the narrow defeat of a resolution that they should support Ramsden. The Brighouse section of the ILP joined with the

Spen Valley Socialists in a determined attempt to unseat their Liberal member, Sir Thomas Whittaker. Trevelyan was not unduly concerned by the machinations of the local ILP. He did make a point, however, of constantly affirming that both he and his father were delighted to see Labour increasing its representation in the Commons as evidence of the growing support for 'progressive policies'.

Polling day for the Elland division was 18 January 1910. Trevelyan was resigned to the fact that he could not hope this time to repeat his bumper majority of 1906. In this, his expectation was realised, but he still won with a comfortable margin.

C.P. Trevelyan 7,469
G.T. Ramsden 4,686
Liberal majority 2,783

While the Tory vote had altered little from 1906, Trevelyan had lost almost nine hundred votes. A half of these were probably explained by Labour abstentions; the rest by Tory 'out-voters'. Sir George congratulated his son on his victory.

> Your majority is splendid. It is about what I expected after what you had told me of your own opinion a week ago. I suppose the Socialists voted against you... We knew that your position was secure and satisfactory... The Stock Exchange is in absolute consternation: which shows what the Tories really think of their prospects.[49]

For once, Sir George's electoral forecast proved incorrect. The huge Liberal majority of 1906 was steadily eroded until the two major parties were left with almost the same number of seats with Labour and Irish members holding the balance. The North of England, Scotland and Wales, held firm for Liberalism. But the Tories swept the South. 'Things go badly,' wrote Trevelyan. 'It is war between industrial and feudal Britain — with the Scotch and Welsh counties ranged out of their place on our side, and Birmingham a traitor on the other. It will be a longer fight than we thought, but, we shall win.'[50] A letter from R.L. Outhwaite, a passionate supporter of land taxation who had fought and lost Horsham in the Liberal interest, placed a new complexion on Tory victories in the South. Outhwaite, after congratulating Trevelyan on his 'splendid win', wrote:

> The work you have done to make land taxation a prominent feature of Liberal policy in the North has helped to create a stronghold against reaction. The North can only save the South if members from the great industrial centres insist that the North shall dictate the policy of the party. I believe the clean sweep made of the county members representing agricultural divisions will prove a blessing in disguise. Now at last it will be

seen that the dependent condition of the landless serfs of the villages is
going to give the Protectionists their opportunity and that the danger can
only be averted by making them independent.

In his long, detailed letter, Outhwaite gave Trevelyan an insight into the
haplessness of the country labourer, and his feudal-like dependence upon his
landlord.

> Polling day was a revelation. So enthusiastic had been the labourers at my
> village meetings that I thought I had stirred them to revolt. The last two
> nights, the labourers did not attend, and on polling day I saw them driven
> to the booths by their lords and masters who polled them like Tammany
> bosses... The agricultural labourers are on the balance, their instincts are all
> against the Protectionists but fear makes them a prey... I do hope you men
> of the North will come to the deliverance of the South.[51]

The influence of Outhwaite's letter is clear in the almost violent missive
that Trevelyan fired off to Sir Edward Grey, insisting that the Government
should now go for the Lords 'neck and crop'. Grey, though as always polite,
by the very coolness and brevity of his reply implied that Trevelyan had not
grasped the fact that the Liberal success depended now more than ever upon
support from Irish and Labour members, difficult allies at any time. However,
Grey assured Trevelyan, 'there is not here..., any disposition to underrate
either the urgency or the importance of the issue of the Lords'.[52]   In fact,
Trevelyan's stratagem was based upon a keen appraisal of the nature of the
Liberal victory and its consequences. He had written earlier to Runciman, 'I
do not see how any course is possible except a perfectly direct policy of
attacking the Lords as if we had a majority of 250. It is obviously the only
terms on which we can keep Irish and Labour support for a moment. Nor will
the Northern Liberals tolerate any other course... Defy the reactionaries and
the nation will want to be ruled by you.' What Trevelyan wanted was the
King's Speech, 'after the usual Foreign Office platitudes', to contain nothing
but provisions for dealing with the budget and the Lords. Before the budget
was sent to the Lords, a bill should be sent ahead destroying the Lords' right
to interfere with finance bills 'on the principle that we want redress of
grievances before granting supplies... I am inclined to think that the moral
effect of forcing the Lords to eat humble pie before they have to swallow the
Budget would be very great'.[53]
Trevelyan was in a fever of excitement at the prospect of the new
parliamentary session. 'Politics will be furiously interesting,' he told Molly.
'We may be out in a fortnight. But I think not. If we are not, the fortunes of
the party will be made for a generation. The Government are going to take a
very strong line.'[54] Like any good Radical, Trevelyan would have liked to see
the Lords replaced by an elected chamber. 'I am not certain,' he wrote to his

mother, 'that the audacity of such a policy might not compensate for [the Government's] lack of audacity in their strategy.'[55] But, he was prepared to recognise, as matters stood, this would lead to a hopeless *impasse* with the Lords. Relations between the two House would first have to be settled. By the end of April, when the Commons rose for the Easter recess, two conflicting plans faced each other. The Government had passed through the Commons three resolutions intended to weaken the power of the Lords. The Lords in their turn offered two resolutions intended to modify their composition. Asquith had introduced a bill to implement his resolutions — Rosebery, with Lansdowne's approval, intended to do the same for the Lords' resolutions. Deadlock could only be avoided by the King exercising his prerogative to create enough peers to swamp the Tory majority in the Lords. Meanwhile, the 1909 budget, with a few amendments, had been rushed through the Commons by 'squaring' the Irish and the ruthless use of the closure. The scene was now set for the final *dénouement* of the titanic struggle between the two Houses when Parliament reassembled in May. If then the Lords should refuse to yield to the Commons, the King's prerogative would have to be exercised. However, with his customary impeccable sense of timing, King Edward avoided the expected constitutional contretemps he had so long dreaded by dying on 6 May. The Tories, never backward in making political capital of any situation, implied that Asquith's Radicals had killed the King! Surely he did not intend to embarrass Edward's heir by ruthlessly pursuing the vendetta with the Lords? Behind the scenes Ministers bargained with Opposition leaders; commoners and peers worked for some compromise that might at least postpone the crisis. In the end it was agreed that there should be a conference between eight principals representing the two major parties. In vain, Irish and Labour members expostulated that they were being ignored. In July, Asquith announced that Parliament would suspend its meetings until November. Meanwhile, the worthy principals in conference continued their horse-trading.

Trevelyan did not believe the conference would produce anything worthwhile. In June he wrote, 'I utterly disbelieve in the conference... I don't see how we gain anything, and I fail to see what material concession we can make without abandoning our main position.'[56] In July he wrote that while most Liberals were 'suspicious and uneasy about the conference', they were not rebellious. 'Everybody is content to wait till the Autumn. The Tories are inactive.'[57]

On 10 November, it was officially announced that the Conference had failed. 'I have seen Lloyd George and Samuel,' wrote Trevelyan to his mother. 'I gather nothing is settled yet..., but, there will be no faltering now. Our headquarters consider themselves to be well prepared. I suppose that may precipitate an election.'[58] Lady Caroline replied that she had never 'believed it *possible*' that the Conference could have discovered a formula 'honourable to both sides... I hope Asquith will lead well now — so much depends upon that'.[59] Asquith received the private assurance of the King that, if necessary, he would create sufficient Liberal peers to allow the Government's bill to become law. The way was now clear for an election. Crewe announced the dissolution for 28 November. But for a fortnight debates in the House had been ill attended. All thoughts were concentrated upon the forthcoming election.

Trevelyan was quite happy about the general outlook of his party's fortunes. 'Wherever I go I find the Liberals in great heart. It does not look like our being beaten... Good trade has made Tariff Reform look foolish after the wailing in January.'[60] As to his own chances, he wrote to his father that while he thought it unlikely the Tories would allow him to be returned unopposed, he did not expect a very severe contest. 'Probably I shall have a carpet bagger.'[61] In the event, his opponent in the January election, G.T. Ramsden, having announced his retirement from the Tory candidature, reluctantly consented to stand again. The poll at Elland was to be declared on 8 December, but with only a week to go, Trevelyan told his mother that his constituents refused to get excited. 'I think they regard it as a formal election and a foregone conclusion.'[62] But on 3 December came a nasty jolt to his confidence when the Elland LRC called a conference of Trade Unionists, Socialists and members of the ILP, who agreed they would not support Trevelyan but abstain. This decision, the *Yorkshire Post* calculated, would cost Trevelyan more than five hundred votes. Labour dissatisfaction should not have suprised Trevelyan. Organised labour had been angered by the Osborne judgement.* Though Trevelyan had condemned this decision as 'a national disaster of the highest magnitude',[63] Labour supporters were angry with all Liberals because of the Government's response to this blow at Labour's fortunes.

Trevelyan's personal campaign was directed at one target only — the House of Lords. 'This is the simplest election of our time,' he told his constituents. 'You have simply to decide whether the Parliament Bill will be passed which the Lords have refused to discuss.'[64] Trevelyan's constituents responded to his 'forceful, lucid, effective, vigorous and thoughtful speeches. What further proof could be needed,' asked the *Brighouse Echo*, 'of his political acumen combined with great oratorical ability?'[65] When the poll was declared,

---

*On appeal to the House of Lords in the case of *The Amalgamated Soc. of Rly. Servants v Osborne*, it was held unanimously that Walter Osborne had correctly refused to pay a levy to his union for funds intended for the Labour party. Therefore, until reversed by statute, this judgment virtually removed all income from the Labour party. This in turn meant they were a great deal more dependent upon the Liberals. In the December 1910 election, Labour put up only 58 candidates, and of these, only 11 opposed Liberals. For many, it seemed the dream of an independent Labour party in Parliament had been doomed for ever by a judicial decision which the Liberals were only too anxious to see remaining in operation.

though he still retained a comfortable majority, Trevelyan's vote had fallen by almost nine hundred since the January election.

C.P. Trevelyan 6,613
G.T. Ramsden 4,549
Liberal majority 2,064

'Thank goodness now my part in the election is over,' wrote Trevelyan to his wife.

> I have made altogether fifty-six speeches, almost all of them at least half an hour in length... I hope I persuaded a few people to vote Liberal... What with the out voters, the old register and a pluviose providence, it is a wonder that we have done as well as we have.[66]

The Liberals had counted on gaining at least thirty seats, but the result was parity between Tory and Liberal with 272 members each. The Irish and Labour still retained the balance.

Asquith introduced the Parliament Bill in the Commons on 21 February. A few Tory stalwarts made sure that the bill moved slowly through the House. Early in April Trevelyan wrote to Lady Caroline that they were 'getting along very well now with the Bill'.

> The Tories are going very slackly and their amendments are grotesquely trivial. Balfour at present absents himself. I think he has made up his mind not to fight *very* hard. Our people are in very good heart and will back the government as soon as it chooses to take drastic measures.[67]

Despite this confident forecast, the Tories put up a sterner resistance than Trevelyan expected. It was not until 15 May that the Commons took its final vote on the Bill. The Lords, meanwhile, introduced their own bill of reform to the accompaniment of strident discord among its members. A temporary truce was called for the coronation of George V, but in July, after an overt threat by Lansdowne that the Tory peers would not accept the Parliament Bill as sent them by the Commons, Asquith informed Balfour by letter of the King's pledge to create sufficient peers to force the bill, if necessary, through the House. The responsible Tory leaders realistically could only counsel their followers to accept a *fait accompli*. The aged Lord Halsbury decided he would rather 'die in the ditch' with other like-minded peers. In the Commons, the Tories gave vent to their spleen and frustration by creating an uproar and shouting down the Prime Minister. Trevelyan described the scene to Molly.

> About twenty Tories, helped spasmodically by others, tried to shout down Asquith... It was a got up job and Hugh Cecil, Castlereagh, Remnant, Goulding, Cooper and Carson were primarily responsible. Balfour hadn't the courage or the decency to try and stop them... I am convinced that this ruffianism will alienate sympathy in the country, and I should not be sur-

prised if it leads to some Radical retaliation somewhere. We shall have crowds outside Palace Yard before long.[68]

To his parents Trevelyan wrote: 'This is a real revolution and Lord Hugh has at least done the service of impressing that ugly fact upon his party when they are already helpless to parry it.'[69] Trevelyan talked glibly of revolution; but the passion engendered by the fate of the Lords was scarce noticed outside the palace of St. Stephen's and the great houses of the land. 'Heat and the Lords are the only topics,' Trevelyan wrote to his wife on 9 August. 'The last act of the drama is come.'[70] The next evening, by a narrow majority, the Lords accepted the Parliament Bill. Society was in a turmoil. But the nation at large was supremely indifferent.

For all the bold propaganda, the extravagant claims, the way to social 'revolution' paved by the good intentions of Lloyd George and Churchill, had failed to capture the imagination and the sympathy of British workers. Their leaders, parliamentary and trade union, either did not seem to comprehend their plight, or appeared to ignore them altogether. Miners, cotton spinners, railwaymen and dockers; each in their turn struck for better conditions. They had enough of Parliament's panaceas. From the beginning of 1910 there was violence, arson, looting and riot. The middle classes trembled in anxious apprehension of danger to their persons and property. The workers pressed their demands ever more violently. The owners and shareholders remained intransigent, and Parliament raged over constitutional proprieties and procedural niceties! Tom Mann, the old labour leader, returned from Australia armed with the new Syndicalist gospel, spread the good news in a monthly journal he edited, *The Industrial Syndicalist.*

The Liberal Government tried to achieve a working compromise but 1911 was an even more violent year than 1910. Leaders talked, working men acted, and Winston Churchill despatched troops in all directions. In mid August, Trevelyan wrote to Molly:

> The labour agitation may produce almost anything. The news tonight is very bad — shooting in Liverpool — and a universal railway strike within hours... I fear there will be a serious situation before things get better. I think what has happened is this. A great wave of hope of a better kind of life has come over the mass of workers, of which the political success of our Government has been partly a cause and partly an evidence. On top of this feeling has come the success of several trades in London in getting immense increases of wages and shorter hours after a couple of days strike. The case of the carmen and the dockers was unanswerable. Everyone with a grievance everywhere says 'I will strike to win a little success.' Hence, the heather is on fire everywhere... So, we are now on the brink of a temporary overturn of society which may lead to very serious consequences. I hope, however, things may not get more serious.[71]

Here then was the threat of a real revolution, but not the kind of revolution that Trevelyan welcomed. In his political vocabulary 'revolution' was actually a synonym for 'change'. The instrument of revolution would be the workers certainly, but in harmony with the bourgeoisie, even as the progressive elements in the Labour and Liberal parties were in harmony! Parliament would implement the revolution by legislation. Only in that way could England become 'a green and pleasant land' for everyone. In 1909, after reading Prince Kropotkin's book on *The French Revolution*, he criticised Kropotkin's thesis. 'He wants to show that the bourgeois parties are no good and that the *sans-culottes* always do everything... The mob are necessary to the bourgeoisie, and the bourgeoisie to the mob in Revolution. Some kind of collaboration alone makes for success.'[72] But revolution in France or Russia was one thing. In England things would surely never come to such a pass?

> The Liverpool riots are very horrible, but it is a vile town with infinite poverty and unexhaustive religious bitterness hardening the feelings of the workers towards each other and to all men. I hope there are not too many towns where violence would blaze up so fiercely in so short a time.[73]

It is obvious that Trevelyan did not comprehend the root cause of labour's violent cry for help and understanding. He was not alone in his ignorance. It required too great a change of philosophy, too sudden a denial of long held opinions, to comprehend, to sympathise and to act, rather than ignore, make excuses or feel alienation. Josh. Wedgwood, who, like Trevelyan, allowed his political passions too often to be ruled by his heart rather than his head, was not intending to be cynical when he wrote in October 1911:

> Politics seem to me a little dull just now. What on earth ever made you go into politics at a time when Home Rule and Welsh Disestablishment were all you were allowed to talk of from a Liberal platform, I can't think. Have you noticed that it is almost indecent to mention strikes just now? It shocks my middle class constituents as though I was calling a spade a blooming shovel.[74]

The industrial unrest was a formidable embarrassment to those supporters of the Liberal Government who, for so long and with such certainty, had proclaimed that they were the workers' accredited representatives. 1912 began with a great miners' strike. Asquith tearfully explained to the Commons the reasonableness of the compromise solution he proposed. The miners remained unimpressed by the Prime Minister's lachrymose pleas. In contrast to 1911, this time there was no violence. The soldiers stood by at the ready: the workers sullenly ignored them. Tom Mann, for inciting the soldiers to make common cause with the workers, was imprisoned. Trevelyan, incensed by the Attorney-General's explanation of this action — 'not a word to show that he realised what a hole the Government is in; his whole argument left the situation as critical as ever'[75] — circulated a lengthy and detailed memorandum to Cabinet Ministers.

> I am very much impressed by the danger in which the Government is placing itself by the prosecution of the editor and printers of the *'Syndicalist'* and of Mr. Tom Mann. I hope you will excuse my placing my view before you, which is that of a very large number of Liberals. The immediate seriousness of the situation is that, so far from stopping appeals to soldiers not to shoot in case of strike troubles these prosecutions have at once challenged a repetition of them. It will not be only Victor Grayson who takes up the challenge. The *Labour Leader* has, at once announced its intention of making the same appeal. In today's *Times*, there is a quotation from Mr. Jowett MP, saying that 'it was the duty of soldiers not to shoot.' This statement was made at a meeting at which Mr. Ramsay MacDonald was present. So what the Government have really to decide is whether they will continue these prosecutions, which will lead as surely as the sun rises to the prosecution of Labour leaders in and out of Parliament. The suggestions which I press upon you are:-
>
> 1. This is not a matter which ought to be left any longer to the individual discretion of any Minister in or out of the Cabinet. It is a matter of vital policy.
> 2. That on grounds both of Liberal policy and expediency no more prosecutions should be undertaken from now onwards.
> 3. That the men already imprisoned should be amnestied as soon as the strike comes to an end.

The first point was a palpable hit at Churchill. Trevelyan then severely criticised the Attorney-General, Rufus Isaacs; condemned the Liberal Government's conduct as most likely to rouse the violent class feeling it was supposed to dampen; and ended by affirming that 'responsible labour leaders are put in gaol..., for expressing what at least half the Liberal party think they have a perfect right to say, however much they may disagree with it.'[76] From John Morley came an immediate retort.

> I have read and weighed your letter as carefully as I could... Liberals must take care not to kick overboard the ideas, instincts and principles of *Government*. For myself, I am not prepared to allow a mob to batter the police to pieces if I have a squadron of cavalry handy. And, if like Jowett, I thought the use of the Army in extreme civil disturbance wrong, I would censure the responsible Minister in Parliament. I should *not* say to soldiers they should mutiny. But, I'll hear what my colleagues say. About the press prosecutions — I *lean* your way, prima facie — only I never have been and never will be, for dealing in milk and water with Trade Union violence.[77]

The Government might bluster, but it could no longer ignore the *impasse* largely created by its own actions. With the connivance of the Opposition leadership, who on this issue did not wish to embarrass the Government any more than need be, a Minimum Wages Bill for the miners was rushed through Parliament in March. It embodied Asquith's earlier proposals that the men had rejected. How would they respond this time? Trevelyan wrote to the Bishop of Oxford:

> I am very much disappointed at the prospects with regards to the strike to-day. I feel quite certain that the men will be making a bad blunder and will alienate most public feeling from them if they do not accept what they have already won... This sort of stirring up of the people is all to the good, and what I am so sorry about is that the Labour men have not proclaimed upon the house tops the immense victory in principle which this short strike has won for them. It might have been a matter of twenty years without it.[78]

This letter might have served as a primer to the miners' leaders. Asked whether they accepted the provisions of the new Act, the miners voted to continue their strike. But on the technical point that there had not been a two thirds majority in favour of continuing strike action, the men's leaders accepted the Act, and then announced that they had won a great victory!

The Liberal Government staggered from one crisis to the next. The supreme quality of the Liberal leadership seemed to be its capacity to survive no matter what the odds. Lloyd George had salvaged something of a reputation as a peacemaker out of the industrial troubles, only to sully it in Radical eyes by a belligerent interference in foreign policy. His insurance scheme, of whose virtues only he seemed convinced, did nothing for Liberal fortunes. His oratory on Welsh Disestablishment lit a spark only in the Celtic fastness of Wales. With the Tories overtly preaching treason against Home Rule for Ireland, Liberal fortunes were at a very low ebb. To add to this sad equation, the Marconi Affair cast doubts upon the moral and financial probity of the Liberal Chancellor, Attorney-General and Chief Whip. A constant theme in Trevelyan's letters during this period was his dissatisfaction with politics in general and the Liberal leaders in particular. 'I am low about politics' became an often repeated refrain. In June 1913 he wrote about the Marconi Affair:

> Things go badly here. Elibank* investing party funds in the Marconis is shocking. He was a beastly gambler and intriguer. We paid too dearly for

*Alexander Murray, Master of Elibank, 1870-1920: Liberal Chief Whip, 1910-12. In March 1912 Samuel, the Post Master General, signed an agreement with the Marconi Co. The negotiations for Marconi had been conducted by Godfrey Isaacs, brother of the Attorney-General. Soon there were rumours of gambling in Marconi shares for personal gain using inside information that implicated Lloyd George, Isaacs and Elibank. There were debates in the Commons and Asquith was obliged to set up a Committee of Inquiry. Eventually, Samuel was found completely innocent, but the others, if not found guilty of corruption, had speculated unwisely. In the popular mind, the odour of corruption clung to the Liberal Ministers. The Marconi scandal was rarely out of the headlines for fifteen months and provided wonderful propaganda for those, like the Syndicalists, who had constantly maintained the moral bankruptcy of parliamentary politics.

his cleverness. There is nothing dishonest, but it is all not above-board. He knew it was a queer thing to do, or he wouldn't have concealed it. Another party scandal is coming along. Carr-Gomme is bringing a divorce suit against his wife, and the co-respondent is Crawshay-Williams. I understand that Crawshay-Williams' father was notorious for being 'the father of his people'... It appears to be an hereditary instinct.[79]

On the tenth anniversary of his marriage, Trevelyan wrote to Molly, 'My chief work and happiness lies at home... I now see the supreme and over-powering importance of the personal side of life. The world will in the main go the way it chooses without asking me. Not for that reason will I cease to importune it with speech and pen.' A secure, happy marriage; genuine concern for his growing family; his love for the Northumbrian countryside — these afforded the refuge from which increasingly Trevelyan sought to draw the strength to renew his enthusiasm for politics. The temptation to quit was strong when the Liberal Government seemed unable or unwilling to fashion policies that once more would capture the allegiance of the masses. He busied himself with routine duties at the Board of Education; he took an increasing interest in the problem of worsening Anglo-German relations; he continued his long campaign to win a positive response from the Liberal leaders to land taxation.

A delegation from the parliamentary Land Values Group had learned to their surprise and anger, that the land valuation started by the 1909 budget would not be completed until 1915. They supposed, and not without good reason, that the Liberal Government was dragging its feet. They argued the only certain specific that could rescue the party's fortunes with the electorate was if the Government enthusiastically adopted their policies. To make the point, they advertised E.G. Hemmerde's success in holding the marginal rural constituency of N.W. Norfolk. Land taxation had been the main plank in Hemmerde's by election platform. Perhaps even more significant was R.L. Outhwaite's victory in a by election at Hanley in July 1912 when he wrested the seat from Labour. For the land taxers, the nature of the victory they had won at Hanley was underlined by the defeat suffered by the Liberal candidate in a by election held a fortnight later at Crewe. They maintained the Liberal lost because he had not given sufficient prominence to land taxation.

Many influential Liberals, however, made no secret of their dislike for the land taxers and their infernal policy. A.C. Murray, the brother of the Liberal Chief Whip complained:

This group is running for all it is worth an extreme land policy, which in effect, although they deny it, amounts to a Single Tax on land values. The members of the group are becoming more arrogant every day, one of them having the audacity to say that there was no place in the Liberal party for anyone who did not accept their policy.[80]

What particularly concerned Murray, and other like-minded Liberals, was that Lloyd George, smarting from the personal and political rebuffs that he had recently suffered, in an attempt to restore his prestige among Radical Liberals, had delivered himself up as a hostage to the land taxers and now was intent upon prosecuting a ruthless campaign against landlords.

Trevelyan was not concerned about the opinion of Liberals like Murray. 'If a few rich Liberals are burned up into the bargain,' he wrote to Molly, 'who cares except the class to whom the rich Liberals belong. These poor men can only see personal spite in reform. Hence their hopelessness in resisting it.' [81] But even Trevelyan was concerned that Lloyd George was being driven on to the wrong track in concentrating his attention upon the land problem in rural rather than urban areas. The difference in priority attached by land tax reformers to the various measures they supported became wider as they competed for the Chancellor's favours. Those, like Trevelyan, who attached the greatest importance to urban rating reform, tried to exert the maximum pressure on Lloyd George. 'The Land Values Group are very persistent,' wrote E.T. John, the Welsh Liberal MP, to C.E. Breese. '[They] are almost as skilful in the manipulation of party machinery, as the socialists are among the trade unions.' [82] The extremists seemed to be winning. But how could one ever be sure about anything when it concerned Lloyd George? The Chancellor had appointed single taxers to his committee of inquiry, and then cheerfully told Murray he had no business to 'repudiate the Hemmerde group' because he was 'going to twist their necks himself'. [83]

By September 1913 Trevelyan appeared to have won a secure place of influence in the Chancellor's camp. Now, if ever, he could bring pressure to bear for local rating.

I had a most satisfactory breakfast with Lloyd George. He is going in general terms to bless Land Values in his speech opening the land campaign at Bedford on October 11th. I am going to propose the resolution and Masterman to second it, and to have twenty minutes to say what I want on the subject. The Land Values Group are delighted. It enables us to act now with official sanction in all our sayings. [84]

At Bedford and Swindon Lloyd George announced his agrarian programme; the latter speech coinciding with the publication of the Land Inquiry Committee Report. There was going to be a fixed legal wage for agricultural workers; there was going to be a Ministry of Land which would complete the revision of the land survey started by the 1909 budget. Lloyd George unfolded his Utopian vision — the workers would flock back to the countryside and there would be no more rural depopulation. It was all very fine, but the problems concerning urban and rural land were so very different. Was it realistic to suppose their solution could be combined in one huge reform? Lloyd George obviously thought so. But why had he said nothing about the rating question? Trevelyan wrote anxiously to Lloyd George:

> I see that you are going to speak at Middlesborough at the end of this week. I suppose that you intend to deal with the land question in urban districts. I want to urge you very strongly not to delay any longer declaring yourself in general terms at least in favour of land values as the proper basis of local rating... In a great many urban constituencies, this is what they mean by land reform. And, while quite ready to be interested in fair rents for farmers, fair treatment for shop keepers who hold under lease-hold, minimum wage for agricultural workers, what they have learnt to expect from land reform is the breaking of the land monopoly — i.e. — a system which will force the landlord to sell at reasonable prices... I can assure you that it is not only the aggressive Land Values Group in Parliament of whom I am thinking. Anxiety is being expressed to one from all sides as to whether you are going to shelve this question which is the thing which all the keen young town Liberals of Yorkshire, Northumberland and Scotland have been taught to understand. To masses of Liberals this is now an essential part of their creed... I hope that when you are coming into the region of Liberal strongholds you will recollect that in at least half the urban constituencies of the North, this is already a principal plank of the Liberal platform.[85]

The Chancellor, never a man for writing letters, answered Trevelyan's anxious promptings with his Middlesborough speech. The next day Trevelyan wrote to P.W.Raffan, a prominent land campaigner:

> The Middlesborough speech shows that he (Lloyd George)..., is beginning to realise fully the overpowering evil of the high prices of land. He has grasped as clearly as any of us the evil of rating on improvements... We have now to take his words and rub them in... At all costs our people have got to go forward with Lloyd George.[86]

Trevelyan was still concerned that some of his less politic fellow campaigners might, in their impatience, attempt to force the Chancellor's hand and damage their case. Raffan assured him that having read his letter to a meeting of the United Land Committee, 'it exercised a marked and salutary effect upon the discussion. Fels was all for revolt, and he naturally had some backing. Burt, Outhwaite and others expressed varying degrees of disappointment with the Chancellor's utterances, but we were able to prevent any adverse resolution being passed.'[87] Trevelyan's spirits lifted perceptibly. Everything seemed in train for the reform he had so long and passionately advocated. 'We were resolute before. Now we are confident and exultant,' he wrote to Molly. 'I have got Edgar Harper, the head of Land valuation to dine and talk tonight... Harper gives a very favourable account, both of Lloyd George's state of mind and of the progress of valuation.'[88] But time was

C.P. Trevelyan with Molly and their children, Pauline, George and Kitty, c. 1910

running out for the land tax campaigners. The shadow of more urgent problems lowered on the political horizon. European war was finally to destroy the hope of implementing any of Lloyd George's land schemes: but even before August 1914, the Liberal party was too busy wrestling with other problems to give much thought to the land.

In the week when Lloyd George made his Middlesborough speech Trevelyan, writing to Runciman, had admitted it was not land that was the immediate problem in politics giving him most cause for distress, but 'the mismanagement of the Dublin strike'.[89] The great campaign of strikes in England might have ceased temporarily, but in Ireland Jim Larkin caused so much concern by founding the Irish Transport Workers' Union that, when in August 1913 he provoked a strike among the Dublin tramworkers, he was arrested on a charge of 'criminal conspiracy'. Though released immediately, this was a signal for violence and disorder as the Dublin employers determined to counter-attack by refusing employment to any member of Larkin's union. Irish employers — Catholic and Protestant, Unionist and nationalist alike — combined against Larkin. The struggle lasted four months. Rioting was brutally suppressed by police and troops, and Larkin was once again jailed for using 'seditious language'. This 'persecution' of Larkin was, in Trevelyan's view, 'the height of political folly'.

> It is the kind of thing to make our relations with the Labour party impossible. The moderate Labour men are just as mad as the extremists at the present differentiation between Larkin and Carson. I know it is perfectly easy to find excuses for it, and that Larkin's methods may be intolerable. But most progressives think his main objects right and Carson's wrong. Yet he is imprisoned and Carson ramps about free...
>
> Remember this — you won't get through the Ulster affairs *unless you have organized Labour behind you.* You had better let Larkin out as soon as you can.*[90]

Though increasingly dissatisfied with the way the Liberal leaders acted, Trevelyan fortified his waning loyalty by comparing 'the irrational mixture of Whig aristocrats, industrialists, dissenters, reformers, trade unionists and quacks'[91] which was Liberalism in Parliament, with the Tories: a party that could consider 'an outbreak of cattle plague as vastly more important than overcrowding or infant mortality'.[92] Whatever their faults, the Liberal leadership could be weaned to sensible attitudes. In Ireland, in the sour depths of bigotry, the Tory party found both a situation to exploit and the

---

*Larkin was released. He crossed to England, talked with English Syndicalists and tried, unavailingly, to get the Parliamentary Committee of the TUC to declare a general strike in England in aid of the Irish strike. When this failed he asked British transport workers to refuse to handle Irish goods, but again he failed. The monarch of the Dublin proleteriat was singularly unsuccessful in getting anything from the English trade union movement save polite applause. The Irish strikers were finally defeated in January 1914.

allies to push their kind of revolution to its furthest limits.

With the House of Lords shorn of much of its power, Home Rule for Ireland became a certainty. That had been the price for the bargain between Asquith and Redmond, leader of the Irish party, for supporting Lloyd George's budget and the Parliament Bill. The initial stages of the Home Rule debate gave little hint of the troubles to come and Trevelyan was rash enough to suppose that the Tories had 'little real fight in them. Such a difference from 1893.'[93] Trevelyan wrote to Molly in January 1913:

> The 110 majority for Home Rule was a great success. Birrell made a quite magnificent speech. The Tories wanted to be noisy. But they were quite dominated by its elevated tone and its fine appeal to nobler instincts contrasting with Bonar Law's deplorable appeals to race hatred and religious violence.[94]

Of the Tories, he wrote to his mother, 'they are in very low water... I don't believe in them settling their differences by praising Bonar-Law... I prophesy that it will be quarrel and patch, quarrel and patch till the next election.'[95]

Victories in Parliament, however sweet, meant nothing in Ulster. In July, at a massive demonstration at Craigavon, the Ulster Volunteers were inaugurated. Increasingly alarmed by the obvious move towards bloody civil strife, Loreburn, in a letter to *The Times* suggested there must be a conference or direct communication between the leaders of the factions. Asquith rejected the idea of a formal conference, but in November entered into formal conversations with Bonar Law. They proved unavailing. In December, by proclamation, the importation or transport of arms to Ireland was forbidden.

The King's Speech at the opening of the 1914 parliamentary session spoke of 'danger', if the situation was not handled 'in a spirit of mutual concession'. Trevelyan admitted that both Liberal and Tory members were 'feeling uncomfortable, but the Tories most'.[96] The tension continued to mount. He wrote to his mother:

> The parties are like wrestlers at grips. There will be fearful rows before we have done, probably rioting in the House and murder outside. But it is rather fun living in what would have been rather a mild year in the period of history between Sulla and Augustus.[97]

On 9 March Asquith proposed a new initiative in the Commons which went some little way to accommodate the Ulstermen. Their only response was to demand further concessions. Asquith clearly stated that the Government had gone as far as it was prepared to go. Jack Seely, Minister for War, and Churchill at the Admiralty, began making plans for a campaign in Ireland. In the Commons, the debate reached new heights of fury.

Today in the House, Carson was violent in manner as well as words. More than one of us thought him a little unhinged. I think it is the strain of at last realising that he must either now let loose the passions he has been raising or allow them to tear him to pieces. They may do both. Bonar Law was in manner more subdued. Rebellion as it comes closer is a serious business.[98]

An unforeseen event precipitated the next stage of the crisis. Army officers at the Curragh, many of them Ulstermen, resigned rather than be involved in the strategic plans to put down any revolution in Northern Ireland. What could the Government do if the Army went on strike? General Gough, commander of the cavalry brigade in the Curragh, resigned. He was summoned to London and withdrew his resignation when given a written pledge by Seely that the Army would not be called upon to repress by force any resistance to Home Rule. When this was triumphantly announced by the Unionist press, Asquith denied the promise had been made. Seely resigned, and so did the Army Chief of Staff, Sir John French. Seely withdrew his resignation, then resigned again! With a courage that won him universal applause, Asquith took on the duties of Secretary of State for War. Trevelyan wrote of these events to his mother:

> The assumption of the two [offices] by Asquith, is the greatest coup of the whole of this remarkable business. The secret was very well kept. His Cabinet colleagues only knew of it ¼ hour before he announced it in the House... Harcourt I believe originated the idea. So unexpected was it that I have not heard anyone say he had thought of it before!... Now what is going on is that the front bench opposition are stupidly and obdurately unconciliatory... Behind them, every other speaker proposes peace in some form or another. Their rank and file know that they must come to terms.[99]

The King, anxiously concerned with the political *impasse* that brought ever nearer the possibility of civil strife, in July summoned a conference of eight members: two Liberals, two Tories, two Ulstermen and two Irish Nationalists. The chair would be taken by Mr. Speaker. To Labour and most of the Liberal press it seemed the King, like the Army, was interfering with the prerogatives of Parliament. 'This is a serious business,' wrote Trevelyan to Molly,

> If Asquith didn't supervise it, it is grossly unconstitutional and partisan. If he did, he is responsible for allowing the King to justify the conduct of the disloyalists. The only advantage is that it will lead to outspoken protests by the Labour and Radical sections and a turning of the politics of working men towards republicanism.[100]

The conference proved fruitless. 'So much for the King's interference. Larn him to be a toad,'[101] wrote Trevelyan unfairly. The King's action had been dictated by his desire *not* to have to assert his authority and thus reveal the breakdown of parliamentary government.

The Ulster loyalists had openly scoffed at the December proclamation banning the importation of arms. They already possessed sufficient arms and ammunition. The opposing Irish Volunteers, not so happily equipped, on 26 July received a consignment of 25,000 rifles together with ammunition from a yacht that put in at Howth, near Dublin. The Volunteers intended to make a triumphant entry into the city, but were met *en route* by a British regiment that put them to flight. The troops, returning to Dublin, were greeted by angry crowds. In a panic the troops opened fire. Three people died and there were a number of other casualties. Trevelyan was furious.

> You will see that the Dublin trouble arose for unjustifiable interference..., unsanctioned by government. That is how you are served in Ireland by officials who date from the Ascendancy. This bloody business in Dublin will raise such a sense of injustice that our people will be lashed to fury. However, the course is straight now till the end of the session, that the only result will be a grimmer determination to compensate Ireland by Home Rule at once.[102]

But in Catholic Ireland the moral of the Dublin shootings was clear, and not at all to the credit of the Liberal Government. To the Irish Volulnteers it was plain that while the Government had suffered the Ulster Volunteers brazenly to flout the law, it had ordered the soldiers to shoot down their innocent women and children in cold blood when, in self defence, they had chosen to arm themselves. So myths are made, and the bloody affray in Dublin, born of panic, became a triumph for the glory of the Irish Nationalist martyrs. As Irish leader at Westminster, Redmond was in a very difficult position. Was he to remain the accomplice of a Government of 'murderers', or lead the insurrection that would crush Carson's forces and establish a free and united Ireland? Yet, even as Ireland trembled on the verge of civil war, the first notes sounded calling all men to a greater war in Europe. Truly the world seemed then 'a mad and bad place'.[103] On 30 July 1914, Trevelyan wrote to Molly, 'I have ceased to care about Ireland. The bigger question overshadows it completely.'[104] What mattered a sordid squabble in Ireland when the great Powers of Europe were about to hurl themselves at each other in mortal combat that would embrace almost all the nations and peoples of the world?

RESIGNATION:

1914

On 3 August 1914, having heard Sir Edward Grey tell the Commons that Britain was set upon a course that would lead almost immediately to war with Germany, Trevelyan wrote to the Prime Minister resigning his junior post in the Government. 'I have not felt justified in troubling you at such a time with an expression of my opinions. But the difference I'm afraid is fundamental and concerns our whole relations with France and Germany.'[1] Even as he wrote, Trevelyan must have heard the distant muffled cheers of members as most unreservedly pledged themselves and the nation to war. Why had he, unlike most Liberals, refused to support the Government? Why had not his reservations been overborne by Grey's statement which had won the acclamation and agreement of Parliament?

Trevelyan's letter of resignation had not been a matter of hasty passion or pique later to be regretted. For the past few days he had thought of little else. He had consulted with men whose experience and judgment he could trust — Lord Bryce, E.D. Morel, Geoffrey Young, and his brother, George. They all had approved his action. He had been in constant communication with Walter Runciman who, as a Cabinet Minister, had passed on the changing news of loyalties and strategems, of doubts and hopes that until the last moment had plagued the Government. Runciman had not himself chosen to resign. 'That one is miserable beyond measure is natural enough, but in our view that is not in itself sufficient to justify us in handing over policy and control to the Tories.'[2] This explanation did not touch Trevelyan; such an argument was little more than 'sticking plaster for a broken leg'.[3] Trevelyan's anger and disillusionment was directed neither against his party, nor the halting excuses of his Cabinet colleagues, but against the perfidy of one man.

Trevelyan had chosen to trust Sir Edward Grey. When the Foreign Secretary had said that England was under no obligation to support France in arms, he had believed the Minister implicitly. Now Grey, who ceaselessly had advertised his love of peace, in the name of *conscience* and *honour* had inveigled Britain into a war which was not her concern; it was Grey who, by his promises in the past, and presently by his words, had crushed out all hope of England remaining neutral. The responsibility for the country's commitment to Armageddon was Grey's. He had betrayed his country's, his friends' and his party's interests, and compounded his infamy by an appeal to the basest passions.

> He gave not a single argument why we should support France. But he showed us he had all along been leading her to expect our support, and appealed to us as bound in *honour*... The Tories shouted with delight.

Trevelyan, like most Liberal members who gave the Government its majority in the 1906 Parliament, had no particular expertise or interest in foreign affairs. After a Tory government, the first priority for Liberals was an attack upon the mountain of too long neglected domestic problems. In his election address, the only reference to foreign policy made by Trevelyan was tucked away in a short paragraph on the need for economy. The times, it boldly declared, were propitious for peace, but only 'if we cultivate our present good relations with France, if we foster our growing friendliness with America, if we use our strength to enforce peace, if we recognise that the power of the dangerously aggressive bureaucracy of Russia has been crippled, probably for ever'.[5] Trevelyan did not spell out in detail specific remedies or attitudes towards foreign policy for all was contained within the policy of Free Trade. He championed Free Trade, not upon economic grounds alone, but because it taught the sovereign truth of the interdependence of nations. Some Radical Liberals foolishly supposed him suspect on foreign affairs because he called himself a Liberal Imperialist. They thought there must be an inevitable dichotomy between his loyalties as a 'Limp' and the 'advanced' opinions he proudly advertised on domestic matters. Trevelyan admitted no such dichotomy. The '*Manchester Guardian* Liberals', as he dubbed the anti-Imperialist section of his party, were men of sincerity and good purpose. But if carefully examined their theories were often quite unrealistic. In a short essay written in 1907 — *England & Peace* — Trevelyan had dealt less kindly with the pacifist element in Liberal and Labour ranks, than with the Tory leaders, Balfour and Lansdowne. If some Tories were jingoes, no one could doubt that Balfour and Lansdowne were men of peace. Many Radicals and Socialists in England, no matter what they claimed to the contrary, were

> not to any real extent international. They are for peace in the main. But they have no logical or complete anti-militarist policy. They are content at present with a policy of reduction of armaments, the encouragement of

arbitration and a persistently friendly attitude towards other Powers.

It was an impertinence for them to suppose that Liberal Imperialists were any less enthusiastic in their espousal of peace than 'publicists and politicians who presume a cosmopolitan knowledge that few can rightly claim'. Of the two Liberal leaders chiefly concerned with foreign policy, Sir Henry Campbell-Bannerman was a Radical; Sir Edward Grey, a Liberal Imperialist.

> Both are men of peace. They have behind them a party whose first demand is peace. When all rulers in all the nations of the world have as little will to quarrel as ours have now, as complete a faith that discussion and arbitration are the only completely rational methods of settling disputes, war will begin to cease.[6]

Trevelyan's was neither a compelling nor a sophisticated view of international problems. He was content to leave foreign policy to the Foreign Office 'experts' who could be trusted — a totally different view from that held by many of his friends. Certainly, before 1914, he did not consider the Labour party, despite its frequent and loudly advertised claims to the contrary, to be better fitted than the Liberals to pursue the path of peace. The Labour party in Parliament was no more than a group of ill-organised, uninfluential, Radical sheep that donned the wolf's clothes of Marxism only for emotional junkets like the International, or for rabble-rousing at street corner meetings where excess was excused in the name of vision. They could never be more than useful lieutenants in the pursuit of peace by the Liberals. Why devise a new litany when the old could be sung so well in unison? The conduct of relations between great nations was too serious an issue for experiment. Experience was the premium, and Liberalism the proven champion of reason and justice in international politics.

Trevelyan hated war but he was no pacifist. He shared with many Liberals a sentimental attachment to the ideal of peace, extolled the virtues of arbitration, and thought that expenditure on armaments should be limited so that scarce resources could be concentrated upon improving the conditions of the poor. He was a founder member of the National Peace Council, the most important and influential of Britain's peace organisations. He was never convinced, however, that the traditional pacifist agencies were equipped to exercise any significant influence upon the conduct of nations. In private, he was always quick to point a jesting finger at their more ridiculous aspects and to dismiss their more utopian claims. In November 1913, having addressed an important pacifist meeting, he admitted in a letter to his wife, that his companions had been 'a funny crowd. There were even people..., who thought we ought to disarm altogether'.[7] Such people, for all their fine words and undoubted good intentions, were not remotely equipped to insure the advent of a new world of peace and good will among men. He much preferred the arguments of Norman Angell with their frank appeal to self-will and sound economics. Idealism and nobility were all very well, but to Trevelyan much pacifist propaganda seemed bizarre.

Trevelyan was interested in naval and military affairs. *The Nation*, a Radical weekly, might assert that 'army reorganisation... [was], no special problem of Liberalism', but like Sir Charles Dilke, Trevelyan thought of himself as something of an expert in such matters. He never supposed that debates on the Army Estimates were either a bore or a waste of valuable time, an attitude that many Liberals affected. He considered that Haldane's tenure of the War Office was an unmixed blessing. He always retained a warm place in his affections for 'Pussy' Haldane from those early days when they had intrigued together, with little art and even less effect. Most Radical Liberals distrusted Haldane 'the one-time standard bearer of Lord Rosebery', but Trevelyan 'understood Haldane', or so he professed, a claim few would have made when exposed to the Minister for War's diffuse oratorical style with its rivers of rhetoric that 'flowed on for ever'. In the parliamentary diary that he kept for a few weeks in 1907, Trevelyan recorded that when Haldane introduced his scheme for Army reform 'he spoke for three and a quarter hours, longer than he needed, but very clear throughout'.[8] The measure of Haldane's scheme, as Trevelyan saw it, was that it afforded much the best solution that had been offered the country for the reorganisation of the Army, a task which was long overdue. Nor were the reforms an affront to Liberal ideals as some claimed. They were the embodiment of two fundamental principles — the strengthening of the voluntary element and the securing of value for money. Radicals might pretend they were advertising 'true' Liberalism, but all they were doing was indulging their anti-militaristic prejudice. Petulant assertions that time and money were being wasted on War Office reform were nonsense. The demands of national defence could not be ignored. He supported Haldane's measures for the same reason that had won over Sir Henry Campbell-Bannerman to 'Schopenhauer's case in the Cabinet: the reforms were the best guarantee for defeating the claims of the conscriptionists. Here was a theme to which Trevelyan returned in 1913 when Haldane had left the Ministry of War for the Woolsack.

Radical Liberals, so Trevelyan thought, had paid insufficient attention to Haldane's not entirely unsuccessful attempts to meet the demands of the 'economists' in his party to trim his estimates. The same could not be said of the naval estimates, whoever was First Lord — Tweedmouth, McKenna, or Churchill. 'The main difficulty there,' Trevelyan assured his mother, 'is Jacky Fisher and his sea dogs, who want impossibilities and have to be thumped by the Cabinet.'[9] Up to the outbreak of war in 1914, while deprecating the need for constant increases, Trevelyan believed that Liberal First Lords (with the possible exception of Churchill) were intent upon securing the best value for the smallest expenditure in consonance with the paramount consideration that the nation's security should never be endangered. Trevelyan never doubted that England's navy should remain the most powerful in the world, and the price of such supremacy could never be less than that asked of Parliament by a *Liberal* Government. In a speech to his constituents during the 1909 naval panic, when England doubled her Dreadnought building programme in response to a supposed acceleration by the Germans, Trevelyan maintained that the Goverment's demands were reasonable. He saw no inconsistency between the Liberal Government's annually increasing demands for maintaining the navy, and a sincere wish to reduce the burden of armament expenditure.

> The Government has made attempts, both by example and negotiation, to induce other countries to reduce their armaments... There was never a saner and more pacific Government in office, and there was never a saner man at the head of foreign affairs than Sir Edward Grey from whom we have never heard one single word of bravado. What we have to do is see that the nation is secure in the event of any deplorable struggle, and to that end we can place our trust in the business-like men at the head of the Government. We can be confident that sufficient preparations will be made without doing anything that is likely to provoke those with whom we are now on terms of friendship.[10]

'Trust' is the key word in this speech. It explains much about Trevelyan's general attitude to questions of foreign policy and armaments. In particular, there was his trust in Sir Edward Grey. Just prior to his appointment as Under Secretary at the Board of Education, it had been rumoured that Trevelyan might go to the Foreign Office as Grey's Under Secretary. Trevelyan told his father that 'it would not have been an impossible position because I have a profound confidence in his general policy and studious labours for peace'. There was but one possible area of disagreement between Grey and Trevelyan. 'Grey would necessarily have felt that he could not have had my full approval in some of his dealings with Russia. Consequently he would probably have been inclined to leave as little as possible to me.'[11]

In the attitude Trevelyan adopted towards Russia, there was always to be a considerable element of the politics of romance. For him, nothing less than the expulsion of the Russian Government and Tsar beyond the pale of human society was fit reward for their black iniquities. Sentimentalism invested the Duma, the Russian parliament, with a significance that in terms of practical politics it never merited. Trevelyan's concern for Russia's fate was shared by most English Radicals and their Labour allies. A letter from A.D. Sanger received by Trevelyan some months before the signing of the Anglo-Russian Convention in 1907, baldly states the case for refusing to consort with the Tsar.

I write to you because you have always vigorously taken the side of liberty and righteousness in your parliamentary career... It is very hard to see anything but evil in the entente between Russia and England. We must surely be doing something to strengthen the Russian Government in exchange for the assurances she is giving us. It is much easier to trust Sir Edward Grey and the Liberal Government — but even they may consider material advantages..., of more importance than the evil of helping the party of reaction in Russia. If we are doing this it seems to me we are committing a stupendous crime... Can you, and will you do something? If we are really allying ourselves with the present Russian Government, I can see nothing to excuse it — and no evil is so great as selling our birthright for a mess of pottage.[12]

Grey derided the critics of his Russian policy. He thought, as did Campbell-Bannerman, that to demonstrate against the Tsar's Government was only to injure the cause of Liberalism in Russia by playing straight into the hands of the reactionaries. Trevelyan saw the Anglo-Russian problem in terms of a duty owed by Westminster, to succour nascent democracy in Russia. The Liberal championship of freedom would be hopelessly compromised should their Government associate with the organisers and apologists of massacre, the Russian Government. Whatever the international considerations, Grey's policy appeared to be pandering to Russian despotism. Conscience dictated that Trevelyan should pursue Grey for some explanation. A Russian Committee was formed, of MPs, academics and journalists, to collect and publicise information. Trevelyan was chosen as chairman. His espousal of the anti Anglo-Russian Convention cause won him praise from many of his friends.

It would have been a pity to have left to the Labs the whole honour of voicing the best traditions of Liberal foreign policy... Honesty, after all, is the best policy, and we should pay as heavily in after years with the Russian Constitutional State for any temporary advantage we gain now by countenancing the present authorities.[13]

George Young's letter to Trevelyan was emotional, and the claims exaggerated, but it was typical of the general opinion in Radical circles that nothing could ever justify a Liberal Government consorting with 'murderers'.

When, in June 1906, it had been announced that the British fleet, as part of its Baltic cruise, would pay a complimentary visit to Kronstadt, Trevelyan was eager to question the Foreign Secretary about this dubious diplomatic manoeuvre. Grey, who always hated answering questions in the Commons, and whenever possible preferred a private arrangement, wrote to Trevelyan:

Could you not put off your question about the fleet? I do not think you can realise what the effect of these questions is likely to be. I should like to have the opportunity of explaining what I believe is the true situation to you first... You could then decide, as you thought right, about putting the question.[14]

Trevelyan, as he would do often in the future, acceded to Grey's request, but sent the Minister a trenchant letter criticising the Government's policy towards Russia.

> The cause [in Russia]..., is the biggest at issue in the world. And some of us care nothing for diplomatic custom where the freedom of the people is hanging in a very nice balance. We hate the Russian Government so we cannot be silent. I write freely to you now in order that you may know my general impression.[15]

The letter must have infuriated Grey. Nevertheless, Trevelyan was always quick to accept Grey's proffered explanations and he believed when the Foreign Secretary put his finger to his lips and extolled the virtues of silence, it was not for Liberal members to press him for explanations. Grey could, and *must* be trusted.

Grey was as much concerned as any of his Radical critics when the Tsar dissolved the first, and then the second Duma, and the existence of the third and fourth Dumas plainly was maintained at the price of total subservience to the wishes of the Tsar's ministers. Some measure of success for the reform movement in Russia was always Grey's best argument for obtaining support for his policy of rapprochement. News of the first Duma's suspension had reached London the day Campbell-Bannerman was to address a meeting of the Interparliamentary Union where, for the first time, Russian delegates would be present. The Prime Minister had delighted almost all Liberal opinion by proclaiming, 'La Douma est morte; vive la Douma.' Trevelyan wrote to his wife:

> Russia is horrible and exciting... C-B's 'Vive la Douma' has caused great excitement. I wonder what Edward Rex thinks of it? Rumour has it that the German Ambassador at once called on Grey. I wish all the Kaisers would huddle together. We may then have the chance of seeing all their heads chopped off at one blow instead of just Nicholas the Last's. What a commentary on Grey. I have argued with him that he would only find himself in a desperate hole if something like this happened.[16]

But Campbell-Bannerman's trite slogan had been sufficiently ambiguous to allow Grey to wriggle out of a diplomatic contretemps with the Russians. Then, to Grey's further embarrassment, he learned that a deputation would be sent from Westminster with a message to the late Duma's President. Grey was able to stop this wild scheme, but in Trevelyan's papers there remains the handwritten message he had drafted to be sent, which captures exactly his attitude:

Believing from our own long experience that constitutional parliamentary government is the only certain security for peace, order and freedom in a nation [we] welcomed your meeting as the birth of parliamentary institutions and the promise of a new era of popular liberty and good government for the people of Russia. We desire to express our profound conviction that the cause, of which you are the custodians in Russia, is bound eventually to triumph.[17]

Russia was but one of many problems that continued to harass Grey throughout his tenure of the Foreign Office. Another issue, in which Trevelyan played an important if not a leading part, concerned the Congo. Appalled by the exploitation of the native population in the Congo, E.D. Morel formed the Congo Reform Association designed to expose the iniquities perpetrated by the Belgians upon the hapless Congolese.

In the course of the 1906 election campaign, Trevelyan had criticised his Tory opponent, Sir Thomas Brooke-Hitching, for speeches favouring King Leopold's policies in the Congo made when visiting Brussels. Threatened with a libel action, Trevelyan anxiously telegraphed Morel for information which he thought necessary for his defence and that Brooke-Hitching's lawyers might not make available. The threatened action was settled, but, more important, friendship was established between Morel — always anxious to recruit new parliamentary support for his crusade — and Trevelyan. Trevelyan became one of the select band who repeatedly advertised in the Commons the scandals and iniquities of Leopold's rule in the Congo. Morel became a frequent visitor to Trevelyan's London home where, over dinner, they would devise strategy with other sympathisers.

Grey moved with far too much circumspection in dealing with the Congo question to satisfy Morel. He suspected Grey's motives. Grey frequently expressed the fear that, if the British Government took a decisive step to solve the problem, it might lead to unwanted European complications. Morel thought the truth was that Grey's hands were tied by a secret treaty with France which the public neither knew about nor would have approved. Trevelyan, however, defended the Foreign Secretary. In March 1908 he wrote to Morel, 'Parker, MacDonald and I saw Grey today. He is taking action, and we are all of us entirely satisfied with what he told us.' And again, a week later, 'After seeing Grey I do not know what more can be done. Belgium knows our national views because Grey has expressed them in his speech. What else can Grey do? Are we to go to war?'[18] Trevelyan's overt championship of the Congo Reform Association ended with his appointment to the Board of Education in October 1908. Morel, congratulating Trevelyan, added, 'I wish your new appointment had been at the Foreign Office... I hope you will not lose all interest in the Congo: You will be a great loss from among the stalwarts in the House.'[19] Trevelyan maintained his interest in the fortunes of Morel's Association until, to his entire satisfaction, its aims were eventually realised with the transfer of the Belgian Congo to the Belgian State. 'I attended the last of the Congo meetings,' wrote Trevelyan to Molly in June 1913, 'where Morel broke his wand like a Prospero or a Cobden.'[20] The most important feature of the friendship for Trevelyan in the pre-war years was that Morel, by his assertions concerning Grey's good faith, first sowed the seeds of doubt in Trevelyan's mind about the Foreign Secretary's policies.

Trevelyan did not need convincing that the most practical step the Liberal Government could take to ensure peace in Europe was to develop closer ties with Germany. Why should not the entente policy embrace Germany if it could accommodate Russia? But, unlike many of his friends, Trevelyan remained convinced that Grey was well disposed towards Germany. That relations between the two countries were less than amicable was not the fault of policy decisions by the two governments, but because of the atmosphere of mutual suspicion and fear created by yellow press vapourings and the evil intentions of certain chauvinistic groups. In particular, unscrupulous elements in the·Tory party were prepared to manipulate the people's prejudices in the sordid hope of gaining some electoral advantage. The way these Tories engineered the various anti-German scares was little short of a national crime.[21] But Trevelyan could find no evidence to suppose the *Liberal* Government was other than sincere in its desire for good relations with Germany.

In May 1911, after riots in Morocco, the French government sent a military expedition to relieve their forces in the Moroccan capital. The French claimed this was necessary to protect foreign interests in Fez. On 1 July the German government despatched a gunboat, *The Panther*, to Agadir, ostensibly to protect German merchants. The actual point at issue between France and Germany was that a German request for compensation under the terms of the Algeciras Act,* was ignored by the French. Most Englishmen, if they had noticed the events at all, would have dismissed them as yet another example of the way greedy European Powers bargained over their real estate rights in Africa, and consequently, as of no particular concern to them. The whole situation, however, was suddenly and dramatically altered when Lloyd George, made a speech at the Mansion House containing a warning to Germany that was little less than a contingent declaration of war. At the time, British politicians were furiously engaged in the final stages of the Parliament Bill. If Trevelyan thought that the Chancellor's remarks were ill-advised, it was because Lloyd George 'already had enough on his hands without taking on the German Emperor'.[22] The menace of war had been

---

*The Algeciras Act signed between Germany and France in 1906 was intended to delineate the rights and spheres of influence of the two Powers in North Africa.

dismissed as mid-Summer madness. Therefore it was with surprise that on the last day of August Trevelyan received a note from Walter Runciman marked *Most Secret*, warning that German action in Morocco might lead to most unfortunate circumstances for Britain. 'Runciman thinks,' wrote Trevelyan to Molly, 'that the situation is very explosive and that we may easily be involved if Germany and France come to blows.'[23] But within a fortnight Runciman wrote to say that the future course of events in Morocco was 'likely to be more tedious than dangerous, unless Germany springs an ultimatum out of the blue which I cannot believe'.[24]

Trevelyan asked Runciman to supply him with 'a good account of the origins of the first troubles in Morocco, of the Algeciras Treaty, and of the difficulties which have now arisen'.[25] Morel was soon to publish an account, *Morocco in Diplomacy*, which gave a particular interpretation of the diplomatic antecedents to the Agadir troubles. Morel's thesis was that Britain had been involved because Grey had been misinformed by his Foreign Office advisers, and was so dominated by his fear of Germany that he had allowed Britain to be tied to France's chariot wheels. If Trevelyan thought this idea exaggerated, Morel was quick to point out that 'none of the facts in my book have ever been contested.'[26] Germany, Morel argued, had a good case in law for her action in Morocco; France was not the injured innocent she pretended to be; and Lloyd George's speech had been an indefensible provocation. England should beware of the way she was being drawn by Grey and France into European entanglements that must sooner or later lead to war with Germany. Such a war would be for the sake and at the behest of the French.

Until the Summer of 1911, Trevelyan had obviously taken little interest in the Moroccan situation. There was to be more than enough copy in the Radical press on the subject in the next few months. The National Peace Council called loudly and incessantly for a campaign of Anglo-German understanding. Leading Radicals in the Liberal Party, Lord Courtney, Sir John Brunner and Arthur Ponsonby, busied themselves with the organisation of committees designed to examine, in general, the problems of democratic control of foreign policy, and in particular, Britain's policy towards Germany. Trevelyan appears to have been almost unaffected by these passionate protests which were directed particularly against Grey. In November, Grey was obliged to defend his policies in the Commons against the incessant attacks of his own party members who maintained that he was responsible for the disastrous estrangement between Britain and Germany. He had perverted the Anglo-French entente, by an unauthorised revival of the doctrine of the balance of power, into an anti-German alliance.

Grey's reply to his critics, in Asquith's word, 'torpedoed' them. Some, however, remained unrepentant. Trevelyan was almost certain that Grey had refuted the case made against him. His speech had been 'good' though there still remained one doubt. 'I don't think that I was absolutely convinced that there need have been all the fuss there was in July. It certainly rose out of suspicion of Germany which her ultimate action did not justify.'[27] From now on, Trevelyan would listen with less scepticism to the charges brought against Sir Edward by Radical and Labour members.

In February 1912, Haldane was sent to Berlin on a special mission. Grey's critics had long maintained that if a capable and unprejudiced British negotiator approached the Germans directly, a settlement of the outstanding difficulties separating the two countries would swiftly follow. Haldane's mission, however, was not the success the Radicals had confidently predicted. They blamed Grey for his less than enthusiastic support of the mission; and Churchill who, while Haldane was in Berlin, had chosen to make an intemperate speech about the German navy.

In July 1912, while Ludwig Stein, a leading German pacifist, was staying in England, Trevelyan invited him to dine with him at his London home. Trevelyan would have liked to have written something for Stein's journal, *Nord und Sud*, but 'it is not easy to see what to say as a member of the Government'.[28] In this last admission lies the key to understanding why Trevelyan was so reluctant openly to avow any suspicion of Grey, or his growing disenchantment with Anglo-German relations. He was convinced, above *all* other considerations, it was his duty to maintain his support of the Government. Possibly the memory of how he had been passed over for office until the end of 1908 exaggerated his concern that he should be seen by his party's leaders to be a loyal and responsible supporter. By any scale of practical, political priorities, it was madness to place as hostage to a conscience troubled by no more than suspicions, those domestic reforms that only a Liberal Government could be expected to promote. Trevelyan's dilemma was shared by all those Liberals who had reservations about the Government's conduct of foreign policy. The party's leaders were not unaware of this and they worked assiduously to undermine any tendency to revolt among their supporters by raising the convenient spectre of the alternative of a Tory Government. Nevertheless, if slowly and reluctantly, Trevelyan was weaned to a position where he was prepared to admit to those closest to him that he questioned the wisdom of Grey's actions.

In October 1912, Trevelyan dined with his brother George and Professor Edward Granville Browne, 'the anarchist friend of Persia', as Trevelyan described him. The meeting was to prove a further significant step in the development of Trevelyan's suspicions concerning Grey's policies. Browne, a distinguished scholar and authority on Persia, was also an avowed opponent of the Anglo-Russian Convention. He was vice chairman of the Radical Persian Committee, a group which constantly scourged Grey. Browne argued that to please France, Grey had destroyed Morocco; to please Russia, he threatened to destroy Persia. He had lowered both international morality and British prestige by pursuing an unceasing feud with Germany giving rise to perpetual war scares and increasing expenditure upon armaments. The Foreign Secretary was as impatient of parliamentary criticism as he was contemptuous of public opinion. The only reason that Grey continued to pursue his contemptible course was because he could always count upon the support of the official Liberals as well as the great majority of the Unionists. Trevelyan would not have enjoyed hearing an indictment that coupled members of the Liberal Government, like himself, with the Tories. But Browne's vigorous advocacy roused him to admit, at least to his wife, that he could no longer afford to grant the Government's foreign policy his blind and unquestioning loyalty.

> I am afraid I am becoming more and more definitely opposed to Grey and his whole outlook and policy, his reticence and his sympathies. However, there is nothing sufficiently tangible to quarrel with openly. But I have practically made up my mind that if we begin verging towards war, or seriously quarreling to uphold either the Russian or French alliance, I will not be party to it.

Even then, hope tempered bold resolution. 'However, the chances are, that may never come.'[29]

Trevelyan salved his troubled conscience by attacking Lord Roberts and the National Service League's campaign for conscription. 'It was right for someone to speak out,' wrote Trevelyan's mother, 'and you have performed a good service to Liberalism in doing so.' Sir George added his congratulations. Roberts' campaign was 'detestable... It is the most wicked thing I almost ever remember'.[30] Trevelyan had spoken on the same platform as Runciman, and his friend had complemented his anti-conscriptionist speech with one concerning peace and Anglo-German relations. 'It was splendid,' reported Trevelyan to his wife, 'and indeed the very first outspoken statement by a Cabinet Minister. I am amazed the papers have not paid more attention to it than they have done.'[31]

In the Spring of 1912 Trevelyan paid a short visit to Germany. With German labour leaders and editors he discussed the problem of misunderstanding and suspicion that haunted relations between their two countries. He thought to dispel the notion that Britain's policy was the encirclement of Germany. Though France and Russia stood armed and hostile upon Germany's borders, the Germans suspected that it was England which was behind the scheme. Bessermann, the leader of the National Liberal party in the Reichstag, had expressed this universal German fear when he claimed, 'England is everywhere.' Trevelyan confided in Molly, 'I am more and more troubled about Germany. This naval competition is terrible. However, the forces are so big that all one can do is preach peace and appeal to the general sense of men.'[32] This was neither a counsel of hope nor action. For a few weeks following his German visit, Trevelyan frequently mentioned his concern for Anglo-German relations. But the siren call of home life after a difficult parliamentary session, the prospect of returning to his beloved Northumberland after London, impinged upon, then banished, uncomfortable thoughts about armaments and foreign policy. He wrote to Molly, 'I am weary of London; I am weary of Germany; I am weary of the Navy. Yet, can life be so bad when you are always there in the background?'[33]

In the Spring of 1913, by a strange twist of fate, the problem of Anglo-German relations in general, and Grey's attitude towards Germany in particular, suddenly appeared to be resolved by the successful cooperation between the German and British Foreign Offices over the wars in the Balkans. Even those who had been Grey's most vociferous critics now recanted their opinions. The very real threat of a European war arising out of the Balkan imbroglio had been averted, and the credit for this, they maintained, belonged in equal parts to the Kaiser and Sir Edward Grey! German and British Ministers talked of each other's countries in considerate and conciliatory tones. Publicists busied themselves with much talk of Anglo-German rapprochement. In March, Asquith, while extolling to the Commons the cooperative efforts for peace made by the Great Powers, silenced a difficult Tory critic by asserting categorically that Britain had no military obligations toward France, official or otherwise. The Prime Minister could not have made a more unequivocal statement that Britain, despite the claims of critics, retained a 'free hand'. The Germans could forget their suspicions that Britain was committed to a military alliance with France against them. If they retained any doubts upon that score, Asquith's repetition of the same denial only a fortnight later should have quelled all doubts. Trevelyan was delighted. Clearly Grey's critics had been wrong and the uncomfortable suspicions in his own mind could now safely be discarded. Should Trevelyan still have retained any doubts, a long letter from the British newspaper correspondent, Dudley Ward, confirmed his own opinion.

> No other interpretation is possible that we are under no obligation whatever may happen (whether a war is defensive or offensive) to tender military aid to France... The main point that has been gained is that we have removed all reason for Germany to think that France is being encouraged by the certainty of our support into undertaking a war of aggression. However foolish this may appear to be, many people here have believed it, and Asquith's assurance has caused a very real feeling of relief. By far the greatest number of newspapers here were thoroughly enthusiastic... It is the most significant step towards Anglo-German understanding that has yet been taken.[34]

Morel, the sternest public critic of Grey's 'Germanophobia', sent Trevelyan an article he had written for the *Daily News* that declared Anglo-German relations were now better than they had been for a decade. If this happy state of affairs was to be retained, however, lovers of peace would do well to recognise that in France and England there were still powerful influences at work intent upon wrecking this new found accord. Chauvinists in France — Clemenceau was merely the arch villain — were determined upon a policy of *revanche* and would be only too eager to involve Britain in their unworthy designs. In Britain, the evil influences were less obvious but no less insidious. In particular there had been a remarkable growth of propaganda and support for conscription. Lord Roberts' National Service League, aided and abetted by the usual irresponsible Tory jingoes, was a worthy object of attack by any Liberal politician. Morel urged Trevelyan to, 'Fight strongly against any threat of compulsory service and smite the deep-seated, insidious, poisonous propaganda of the National Service League.'[35]

For months Trevelyan had been seeking a way in which he might actively serve the cause of peace without embarrassing the Government. He had written to Norman Angell urgently seeking 'some suggestions for a practical parliamentary platform for pacifism'.[36] The Tories in the Commons were busily engaged in canvassing the case for conscription. They maintained that Britain's Expeditionary Force was intended to support the French in a possible European war, rather than act as the 'police force of the Empire', which when he had formed it was how Haldane had described the Force's function. Trevelyan had written to Morel in February stating his determination 'to enter upon a vigorous *private* campaign' to refute Tory claims that were responsible for 'keeping the Germans from the best relations with us'.   There was urgent need for a new statement of the anti-conscriptionist case and this was a task Trevelyan was well fitted to undertake. It was as much in accord with his own sympathies as with the best Liberal traditions.

Trevelyan's case against conscription rested mainly on the assumption that Britain's navy was sufficient safeguard for her security. He must have recognised the Germans had to maintain massive armies that could be adequately supplied only by conscription, in order to repel any possible invasion by the French or Russians poised manacingly on their borders.* The German Socialist programme always had coupled reference of international disputes to arbitration with 'the training for universal capacity to bear arms'. They were no more aware of any paradox in this than were British Radicals in their professions of peace coupled with a pride and determination to maintain

*By 1913, Germans of all political parties recognised that their country's future existence in an armed Europe depended upon the maintenance of her armies at peak strength and efficiency. A *Weltpolitik*, based upon a huge navy intended to challenge British naval supremacy, was no longer realistic. Thus, there was now in Germany a much more favourable climate for *détente* with Britain. This did not, however, imply any lessening of intent to maintain her armies by conscription.

British world naval supremacy.* Though there was trouble enough to secure material for his pamphlet, Trevelyan also experienced difficulties in getting it published. His intention had been to give it to the Liberal Publication Department, but they refused to publish. In bewilderment, Trevelyan wrote to Runciman, 'I don't know what unorthodoxy they have found in it... I feel certain from what two or three people have said to whom I have shown it, that it is "wanted".'[38] Eventually it was agreed that the Young Liberals would publish the pamphlet, but that Trevelyan would have to bear the cost. The first issue was rapidly sold out and there were requests for a reprint. In Liberal circles, the pamphlet generally met with approval. Runciman wrote that in his opinion it was 'quite the best statement of the Liberal view yet written'.[39] Richard Holt's comment was typical of many Trevelyan received.

> Your pamphlet on conscription is capital. But, we have got to take our Admiralty and War Office severely in hand, and when Home Rule is out of the way some of us ought to put anti-militarism first. Winston's speeches are disgraceful.[40]

Trevelyan would have been among the first Liberals to welcome a cut in the prodigal expenditure upon armaments. But he had never seen the same sinister significance in that burden as had the Liberal party's Radical disarmament group who were noisier and more active than ever when, in the Autumn of 1913, they learned that once more Churchill was preparing another extravagant set of naval estimates. Nor were they cheered by the words of the Prime Minister who, addressing the National Liberal Federation meeting at Leeds in November, said he saw no hope of any substantial relief. *The Nation* commented;

> While the Liberal party has at last awakened to the question of armaments with zeal and passion, the Prime Minister has virtually accepted..., the fatalistic formula..., that while other Powers do nothing, we can do nothing either.[41]

On 1 January 1914 Lloyd George, in an interview in the *Daily Chronicle*, reviewed the 'organized insanity' of 'the overwhelming extravagance of our expenditure upon armaments'. The Chancellor was obviously seeking public support for the cause of economy for which he stood against Churchill in a divided Cabinet. Trevelyan responded eagerly to the appeal.

> I hope you will allow me to say how glad I am to see that you have declared yourself against the huge armament increases in terms which imply that you expect action may be taken by us to reduce them. I don't think it is a moment too soon for I have been for some time in doubt whether even the necessity of carrying Home Rule would get us over the next session unless some prospect of reduction were tendered to our party. The feeling in the

*The British Navy, they would have argued, was a 'defensive' and not an 'offensive' force.

country is stronger about this than anything else at present. It is not confined to Liberals and it will grow steadily. I am extremely glad that you have made this declaration.[42]

Trevelyan's objection to increased naval expenditure was based, not upon any moral imperative but primarily upon party calculation. An approaching election was a better scourge of conscience than appeals to pacifist sentiment. Again, in letters Trevelyan exchanged with Walter Runciman concerning the forthcoming naval estimates, their calculations were about the need to maintain a united and successful Liberal party.

At the beginning of January, Runciman wrote to Trevelyan:

> It is now clear that George and Winston have drifted further apart. This has been apparent for some time to everyone who could watch their tendencies from within; George drawing closer to his old Liberal associates..., leaning more and more on the main body of Radical opinion, while Winston has..., been living incessantly with his Tory friends... His real blood feeling and early training have shown themselves mainly in his speeches on armaments and to armament audiences which were his sincere, instinctive, unembarrassed declarations of faith as well as of policy. Our decision will be recorded about January 22 or 23 when he will go. There will be a scare which we must face. Already the Tory papers are at work, and George raps in with his *Daily Chronicle* interview... So all looks set fair for a united Liberal party minus Winston. It will be a signal for a storm which no doubt we shall weather, and then we shall settle down to holding the fort with Winston added to our assailants... This brilliant, unreliable Churchill who has been a guest in our party for eight and a half years.[43]

At the same time as Runciman was writing this letter to Trevelyan, Sir John Simon was urging Asquith to drop Churchill, a loss that might be 'regrettable', but '*not* by any means a splitting of the party'.[44] Many members of the Cabinet felt a personal antipathy towards Churchill, but Trevelyan retained a certain affection for the brilliant if erratic First Lord. If Winston rejoined the Tories then it would be 'a very serious addition to their fighting strength in the House'.

> If he succeeded in gaining the leadership of the Tory party, I am not sure that I should deeply regret it. He is no more likely to deliberately encompass war than the present gang are to blunder into it fecklessly. And on public grounds I am bound to say I prefer a real free trader and a man with a sound contempt for crusted Toryism as leader of a revised Conservative party.

For Trevelyan, however, the most important and immediate consideration remained, not Churchill's political future, but the fortunes of the .Liberal party.

To allow Winston to go in order to take a first step to the checking of the armaments furore will immensely consolidate our party. The strongest, spontaneous feeling at the present time..., is alarm at the growth of the fleet with less than no prospect of the pace steadying or decreasing. But if Winston does go, it is Asquith who must bow him to the door and not Lloyd George. It will not be to anyone's interest that the public should say that it is a fratch between the two competitors for the Liberal leadership, and that Churchill leaves because Lloyd George has outdistanced him.[45]

Churchill was not to be 'bowed to the door' either by Asquith or Lloyd George. He stayed, and his estimates were accepted by the Cabinet and the Liberal party because consciences were overtaken by political actualities. Increases in the cost of the navy were not to be measured in the scales of morality but by the need, at any cost, to maintain a united party. In the circumstances, it was convenient for those Liberals who deplored Churchill's success, to hide their impotence by claiming they had acceded to his estimates because of the Ulster troubles. But no one was really convinced by this excuse.

With Churchill's naval estimates out of the way, most Liberals adopted a complacent attitude towards problems of armaments and foreign policy. Domestic issues dominated politics. Lloyd George told his Guildhall audience in July 1914 that he was more concerned with the prospect of civil strife in Ulster and the threatened strike by the 'Triple Alliance' of railwaymen, miners and transport workers, than any foreseeable troubles in Europe because a crazed Bosnian student had murdered an Austrian Archduke and his wife. A week later, the Chancellor was telling the Commons that relations between Germany and Britain were better than ever. The next day Austria delivered her ultimatum to Serbia.

Trevelyan would not have argued with Lloyd George's estimate of foreign affairs. On 27 July he wrote to his wife:

I am tired and bored beyond any expression. It is chiefly the strained uncertainty of the political situation. I have no doubt most other people are equally restless. The next fortnight will be very critical.[46]

Trevelyan was referring to the Ulster situation, and it was not until a week before he resigned from the Government, that he first mentioned the European scene.

As to Europe, I think there will be a great war. But I do not think that we will be drawn in. At any rate, all my energies will have to be devoted to urging my Cabinet friends not to let ourselves be involved in the smallest degree.[47]

It was with amazement and shock that most Liberals suddenly realised the imminence of a European war. The Radical press insisted that it was the duty of the Government to proclaim England's neutrality. The Tory press countered that Britain, by the terms of the *entente*, was obliged to join France against Germany. Trevelyan was not unduly concerned by what *The Times* and the rest of the Tory press might have to say. As long as there remained a 'real peace party in the Cabinet', then it was 'most unlikely that we shall allow ourselves to be dragged in even if there is Armageddon'.[48]   Nor was he prepared to believe, as at one point his father feared, that there had been a deal made with the Tories over Home Rule as the price of entering a European war. 'I cannot believe it is quite as bad as that,' he wrote to his mother.[49] Quite simply, Liberal members *had* to trust their Government's often repeated determination to keep the peace. If there was a problem it was whether Grey would prove to be strong enough in these difficult and dangerous circumstances. Trevelyan had met the Foreign Secretary casually in the lobby of the House and naturally had asked him whether there was any news.

> I said something quite politely about the matter concerning us not at all, and that I presumed we should be strictly neutral. He replied in an extra-ordinarily hard unsympathetic way. He seemed to be coldly angry with me.[50]

Later that same day, Trevelyan wrote to his wife:

> I find at the bottom of my heart I distrust Grey, though I am sure he will do his best to keep the peace... A man is not to be trusted who does not at least say *to himself*, whatever others may do we cannot go to war... If Russia goes to war, if then Germany goes to war with her, it will be our duty to say that we will on no account take part in the struggle.[51]

Trevelyan already had decided who should be cast as the villains in the tragedy now playing out its final act upon the European stage. Russia was the only nation anxious to fight. If Britain should enter the war then it would be Grey's fault, for the man would 'not see the utter wickedness of [Britain] being drawn in under any conditions, and therefore we may get dragged along by circumstances'.[52] It was not that he believed Grey wanted war; the trouble was that 'he will not say we won't go to war'.[53]

It was not Trevelyan's nature to wait idly upon events. He recognised there was little the individual could do, but he determined at least some kind of public organisation ought to be started to secure Britain's neutrality. 'I am so disgusted,' he told his wife, 'at the inactivity of the mass of people who do not want war, that I am staying in London to try and manufacture a larger system of protest... We shall see what can be done.'[54] He was joined in this enterprise by his brother George, and on 1 August, Trevelyan gave an account of their joint efforts to his wife.

> We have been occupied most of the day in getting a Neutrality Committee started. It will be useful if war begins on the Continent and there is a

period here of violent agitation for a war. A curious case of nothing ever being done unless you do it yourself. I hope it will now go all right. I shall leave it to Norman Angell, Graham Wallas etc.[55]

Trevelyan still believed that Britain would not be involved. News the next day from Runciman that the Cabinet had decided that the Expeditionary Force would not be despatched to France further persuaded him that at the least 'we are not going to war at once'.[56] However, events now moved so swiftly that in another letter written later that same day, Trevelyan revealed he was now much less hopeful of Britain's chances of remaining neutral.

Everything is as bad as can be, except that our Government are trying to keep out of the war if they can... The single great point of danger is Belgium. Germany is almost certain to violate Belgian neutrality by passing through Belgium to attack France. She may do more and try to conquer Belgium. In the second case it would be a position of unparalleled difficulty for a British Government however anxious to avoid a collision.[57]

For many Liberals, as anxious as Trevelyan that Britain should remain neutral, Belgium was to prove the stumbling block. Richard Holt, an anti-war Liberal, hoped until the last minute that Britain could keep out of the war. But, as he recorded in his diary, 'when Germany decided upon an unprovoked attack upon Belgium..., it seemed impossible for us to stand by'.[58] Why did Trevelyan not adopt the same attitude? On the morning of 3 August he was still undecided as to the action he should take.

It looks very bad... Unless the Prime Minister gives a satisfactory account of what they are doing, I shall have to resign. But I am unable to tell at all yet, and there is no use discussing it. Everything is the decision of an hour... George and Morel are here, but we shall know nothing until this afternoon.[59]

A little after three o'clock in the afternoon, Grey rose to speak to a crowded and expectant Commons. Everyone knew that *this* was the decisive moment in the crisis. 'Let every man,' the Foreign Secretary advised, 'look into his own heart, his own feelings, and construe the extent of the obligation for himself.'[60] Grey's appeal won the acclaim and agreement of all but a handful of his audience. His speech crushed any hope there may have been that Britain now would stay out of the war. For Trevelyan, the time of doubt was over. He would resign. Grey might have spoken of honour — 'a hateful mediaeval survival' — and of England's interests. He had spoken too of obligations owed to France, obligations that on previous occasions the Foreign Secretary and the Prime Minister, publicly and expressly had denied. The reason why England was now committed to war against Germany was patent. 'I never was clearer in all my life... We have gone to war from a sentimental attachment to the French and hatred of Germany.'[61] As a Liberal, Trevelyan refused to be party to such infamy.

WARRIOR FOR PEACE:
1914-18

In any political crisis it was Trevelyan's custom to explain his views and actions to his constituents. Resignation from the Government was to be no exception to that rule. John Burns, the only other member of the Commons to resign office, refused to account for his action to the House. Trevelyan, though he regretted the decision, in deference to his senior colleague did the same. Therefore, he considered his letter of explanation to his constituents particularly important as 'a public record of some of the reasons against this miserable business'.[1] The letter did not receive wide-spread national press coverage — only the *Manchester Guardian* carried the full text — and, save favourable comment from *The Nation* and more qualified approval from the *New Statesman*, the rest of the press for the moment remained silent.

In his letter Trevelyan rehearsed his criticisms of Grey's *entente* policy, rejecting the Foreign Secretary's appeal to 'honour' as worthless. 'We had chosen our side already. We ought to have no side in this quarrel except the one overwhelming interest of our people. That interest is peace.' He 'disapproved as heartily as anyone' of Germany's invasion of Belgium, but 'if France had committed the offence, I think we would have found some protest sufficient short of plunging our country into war'. Trevelyan questioned Grey's dubious assertion that Britain would suffer little more by her engagement in the war than if she had stood aside.

However overwhelming the victory of our navy, our commerce will suffer terribly. In war too, the first productive energies of the whole people have to be devoted to armaments. Cannon are a poor industrial exchange for cotton. We shall suffer a steady impoverishment as the character of our work changes... All this I felt so strongly that I cannot count the cause adequate which is to lead to this misery. So I have resigned.

Trevelyan ended his letter with a short paragraph that it would have been as well if many of those who soon were to revile him as a traitor had read and noted.

> But now, having made good my protest, let me say to those who agree with me and to those who do not, this is no time for mere words or continued recrimination. The time will come later when we shall debate the origins of the disaster. Blunder or no blunder the war is here. That is the terrible present. And our simple common duty is to help our country.[2]

The immediate response to Trevelyan's resignation was sympathetic and understanding. Kate Courtney wrote that 'because he had so much to lose', Trevelyan's action had been 'unexpectedly fine'.[3] Somewhat to his surprise he found that in Parliament 'no one is other than very nice to me, though as a matter of fact I have hardly talked to any Tories'. Richard Holt, for instance, though strongly supporting the Government's intervention because of Belgium, was 'very agreeable'. And even Asquith, so Trevelyan was told, had spoken of him nicely.[4] Gulland, a junior Liberal whip, wrote to Molly the day after war was declared:

> I am sorrier than I can say that Charles has resigned. His friends here are just as proud as you are of the high motives that have induced him to take such action. I congratulate you on having a husband that dares to take so courageous a course.[5]

Until the public announcement of his resignation, Trevelyan did not attend the Commons. But as soon as that was over, he went to a meeting of the handful of Liberals who were prepared to work with the Labour party for peace. When Trevelyan entered the committee room he was greeted with loud cheers. 'Poor fellows,' he wrote to his wife. 'They have been deserted by almost everyone. I am quite famous.'[6] This hysterically enthusiastic welcome was repeated the following evening when Trevelyan dined with Norman Angell and a group of Angell's 'young men'. Their wild enthusiasm was a manifestation of what Bertrand Russell was later to describe as 'a herd instinct stimulated by fear' among the opponents of the war. In many ways, the first weeks of hostilities were to prove the most difficult in which to steer a determined anti-war course. Before the battle of the Marne in September and the development of the war of attrition in the trenches of the Western front, the Germans advanced towards Paris and the coast with alarming speed. There were widespread rumours — apparently officially authenticated — of atrocities perpetrated by the Germans on the hapless Belgians. In the resultant highly charged emotional atmosphere not to share with the majority of their countrymen a hatred of Germany suggested they were denying instinct. The pitifully few pacifists motivated in their opposition to the war by a legion of disparate reasons huddled together for mutual comfort. Years later Russell recalled, 'When we were all together we felt warm and easy and forgot what an insignificant minority we were.'[7] For his part, Trevelyan had no illusions about the situation. He was well aware that the hysterical atmosphere was inimical to intelligent planning. 'Fear and anxiety,' he told his wife, 'are ill bed-fellows for reason.'

In those early days of hostilities it must have seemed to many opponents of the war that the only realistic attitude was to suppose 'further action for peace [was] hopeless for a season'.[8]   Keir Hardie admitted that Labour's anti-war demonstrations, speeches and resolutions 'all alike had been futile. We simply do not count.'[9] Those who for years had warned against war with Germany, who had fought for disarmament and the settlement of international disputes by arbitration, and who had averred that Britain would always remain neutral in any European war, now, almost without exception, seemed prepared to admit defeat. Their broken spirit was summed up in *The Nation's* defeatist comment, 'We have no criticism to offer.'[10]   And the 'patriotic' press gloated at the discomfort of the 'idealists' who had 'refused to look reality in the face' and who preferred 'to be deceived and to deceive their followers.'[11]

Trevelyan, in those last hectic days before Britain's entry into the war, had done what little he could to organise and encourage neutralist opinion. It was he who had financed the British Neutrality Committee set up by Graham Wallas. Sadly, that — like Angell's more elaborate and costly campaign — had been a complete failure. Undeterred by these initial set-backs Trevelyan had continued to rally support for peace wherever it could be found. He maintained that in a desperate situation recruitment of sympathetic opinion was more important than any party political consideration. He wrote to the Socialist, George Lansbury:

> I hope my friend that both the passionate impatient ones like you and the slower ones like me who do not hope for such quick realization may be less critical of each other than we have been. For this fearful common enemy has overwhelmed all we care about.[12]

But Lansbury showed little passion or impatience in dealing with this urgent overture. It was not until October that Trevelyan received a reply.

> I send you this line to say that I agree we must unite in spirit and not on cut and dried formulae... I haven't anything to propose only I like to meet with those whose faith is mine too as I believe in the communion of Man & Woman as well as of saints and in these dark days we all need the strength that comes from fellowship.[13]

Trevelyan, however, placed more faith in practical rather than mystic strength, and to this end had already turned to E.D. Morel.

On the evening of 5 August, Trevelyan met with Arthur Ponsonby, leader of the Liberal Foreign Affairs Committee, a group that unavailingly had tried to influence the Government to remain neutral; Ramsay MacDonald, then still leader of the Labour party; and Arthur Henderson, Labour member and secretary of the British International. It was after this meeting that Trevelyan wrote to Morel:

> There is a body of Liberal members united on common action on the war question, trying to establish connection with the Labour party. Ponsonby, Morrell and Rowntree inspire it. I think it more than likely that it may be an organisation which could connect with outside efforts and groups.[14]

Morel responded eagerly to Trevelyan's overture, but there was an immediate setback. Trevelyan had been elected chairman of the parliamentary group of Radicals. The committee's intention to seek closer ties with Labour was frustrated when Labour members, until then united in their opposition to the war, began to quarrel among themselves. Still undeterred — though he admitted to his wife that for the moment they were 'quite powerless' and could expect 'nothing but a disagreeable time'[15] — Trevelyan met with Angell and some fifteen supporters at the Salisbury Hotel, where, 'in the course of an evening I completely altered their plans for them and arranged that they should turn *War & Peace*** into the brains of the new movement which we should now have to start for the future'.[16] This new movement was soon to become the Union of Democratic Control, the single most important agency of opposition to Government policy during the war. Despite his typical assertion in a letter to Morel that others than himself inspired the movement, it had been Trevelyan who, straightway after his resignation, hastily composed on the back of an envelope a rough draft of the Union's objects. This draft was headed by two titles; British Democratic League, and British League for Uniting the Democracies of Europe.

A definite group now began to emerge: Angell, MacDonald, E.D. Morel, Ponsonby, Arnold Rowntree the Quaker MP, Bertrand Russell, and Trevelyan. Initially they met at the home of Philip Morrell the Liberal MP. Russell was to recall in his *Autobiography* that the politicians seemed more concerned with the problem of who should be the leader of the anti-war movement rather than with actual suggestions for the work they might undertake against war.[17] But the real divide within the fledgling organisation was not over who should lead but between the more cautious spirits who were anxious not to antagonise possible future support by over-hasty initiatives, and those who were all for pushing ahead at the earliest possible moment. Trevelyan had already drafted a letter proposing three objectives: the prevention of secret diplomacy by parliamentary control of foreign policy; negotiations after the

---

* *War & Peace*, the monthly journal of Angell's pre-war organisation had begun publication in October 1913. Morel, Ponsonby and MacDonald had been among its earliest contributors.

war for an international understanding that would depend, not upon governments but popular parties; and that the peace terms should neither humiliate the defeated nations nor rearrange national frontiers so as to provide cause for future friction between nations. This draft was approved, signed by MacDonald, Trevelyan, Angell and Morel, and circulated privately to likely sympathisers.

It had been Trevelyan's hope that the Union would prove attractive to those 'progressive' Liberals who had been the keenest advocates of radical social reform before the war. They might be expected to view the war as the ruin of their schemes, and thus more readily support the Union. Replies to the initiative began to come in. They were approving, but cautious. 'I think your letter is good,' wrote Arnold Rowntree, 'but..., it is at present *most* important to keep it private and just use it for quietly mobilising the peace forces.'[18]   Bryce advised that, while it was sensible to consider what ultimately might be achieved, for the present they should do nothing publicly.[19] MacDonald and Morel were opposed to these cautionary counsels. Believing that the Government should be criticised immediately for involving Britain in an 'unnecessary' war, MacDonald published a violent attack against Grey in the *Labour Leader*. Morel meanwhile, installed as secretary of the group in temporary offices in Trevelyan's London house, was busily completing a pamphlet that argued the war could have been localised, if not averted, had the Germans been given by the Foreign Secretary a prompt and unambiguous statement of British policy towards Belgium. Morel was uncompromisingly critical of Grey's secret *entente* policy. If published, the pamphlet was certain to alienate most Liberals.

Trevelyan's immediate response to Morel's draft had been that it was 'admirable... I hope this week to get it in order and in type. Next week we shall be issuing it in thousands... '[20] But Morel's squib was never to appear in its original form. Cautionary counsels were too influential to be ignored, and none more so than C.P. Scott's. His advice carried much weight on two counts: his editorship of the *Manchester Guardian*, and his belief that Lloyd George, the 'pacifist' Chancellor of the Exchequer was 'an unattached member' of Asquith's Cabinet, 'and sits very lightly'.[21]   Temporary silence was obviously a worthwhile price to pay if it meant capturing Lloyd George for their cause. With the Welshman's support they could be assured of a great addition to their strength from the left wing of the Liberal party. Scott wrote to Trevelyan:

> ... it would be expedient to hold back the pamphlet. The war is at present going badly against us and any day may bring more serious news. I suppose that as soon as the Germans have time to turn their attention to us we may expect to see their big guns mounted on the other side of the Channel and their Zeppelins flying over Dover and perhaps London. People will be

wholly impatient of any sort of criticism of policy at such a time and I am afraid that premature action now might destroy any hope of usefulness for your organization later. The original policy was to wait and prepare and I feel sure that it is the right one. I saw Angell and Ramsay MacDonald yesterday afternoon and found that they had come to the same conclusion.[22]

While this news of Angell's attitude would not have surprised Trevelyan, that of MacDonald's change of mind was unexpected. But a few days earlier MacDonald had urged the holding of a conference to capture public opinion by criticising the Government's pre-war policy. Trevelyan was not altogether convinced that caution was either the better or wiser part to play, but he was prepared to defer to the majority view. Ponsonby, increasingly now playing a more influential role in the affairs of the nascent organisation, remained 'more firmly convinced than ever that... it will be wiser to wait... *I feel this very strongly.*'[23] Trevelyan compromised to the extent that he agreed to have Morel's revised pamphlet (some suggested changes by Ponsonby had been incorporated) set up in type so that it could be brought out within a week. Trevelyan wanted no unnecessary delay that would allow their opponents further to strengthen their hold upon public opinion. He was busy also, recruiting writers for other possible pamphlets. 'I hope to have a whole series ready in a few weeks,'[24] he wrote to Molly. Helped by his brother Robert, Trevelyan was gathering material for a paper on the Belgian 'atrocities' he intended to write himself. 'It is quite shocking the way people believe every invention or rumour.'[25]

On 10 September, the Tory *Morning Post* published the original letter that had been circulated privately among potential supporters. The *Post's* disclosure[26] was the signal for a vicious attack upon the Union by the 'patriotic' press with the *Daily Express* in the van. T.E. Harvey, the Quaker MP, had warned Trevelyan that if a single copy of the letter 'got into the hands of our opponents' it would be 'a serious danger'.[27] Now they had been betrayed, there seemed no reason any longer to delay publication of Morel's pamphlet. As Trevelyan wrote to Scott, 'The Tory press is beginning to say that the movement is secret. Of course, they say we are pro German. That is necessary. But we had better not let it be supposed that we are afraid of coming out into the open.'[28] A few days earlier MacDonald had written to Trevelyan that despite Scott's opposition he had been persuaded it would be better to publish Morel's pamphlet. 'We cannot afford to offend Scott, but if public opinion is left to be controlled by the influences now alone playing on it, it will be impossible for us to do anything with it before long. I have also hinted,' concluded MacDonald, 'that the little Welshman is slim.'[29] This conjecture as to Lloyd George's loyalties was soon confirmed. In a speech at Queen's Hall on 19 September, the 'pacifist' Chancellor cast his lot with the war party, extolling 'the everlasting things that matter for a nation — the high peaks we have forgotten, of Honour, Duty, Patriotism, and, clad in glittering white, the great pinnacle of Sacrifice, pointing like a rugged finger to Heaven.'[30] Losing 'the little Welshman' meant that now there was small hope of recruiting those Liberals Ponsonby had described as 'the sort of people who will drift towards us eventually' provided that their sensibilities were not unduly offended by 'exaggerating Grey's responsibility for previous policy', or by attaching any blame to England rather than Germany for the catastrophe of war.[31] Scott was also lost. 'I agree with your objects,' he told Morel, 'but I should be apt to part company with you as to methods. So I am better out of it.'[32] Many Liberals now were equally anxious to desert the cause of peace even before it was properly born. Harvey, Rowntree and Morrell, who at the beginning would have been counted among the leaders; Graham Wallas, who thought the causes of the war better debated by historians in the future than by present protagonists; and Leonard Courtney, who would not have Grey's integrity impugned; all, to some extent refused to stand and be counted in public as members of the UDC, considering party loyalty more important than the expression of dissent.

Morel's pamphlet was not published immediately. Persuaded by the 'arguments' of the *Daily Express*, the printer refused to print Morel's critique. 'It would be against my conscience and what I conceive to be my duty to the State,'[33] he wrote to Trevelyan. It was a desperate moment. Even Trevelyan's eternal optimism was badly shaken. He confided to Molly, 'all around me men are funking..., men who are afraid they may be wrong, afraid they may be thought impracticable, afraid of something and nothing... As far as I am concerned, I am simply working on faith. There is almost nothing to encourage.'[34] But, whatever his private doubts and sorrows, to his colleagues Trevelyan maintained a resolute face. To Ponsonby he insisted it was now imperative their case should be stated openly so that the public might judge. If they did not confront the public with their criticisms of the policies that had led to war, then there was no likelihood of there ever being a public opinion that would insist on democratic control of foreign affairs. 'We shall end up by being classed with those who approve the war.'[35] Eventually it was agreed that a second circular should be sent to potential supporters, and a letter published to rebut the attacks made upon them by the Tory press.

The letter insisted there could be no satisfactory solution after the war unless certain essential conditions were satisfied. These were: no transfer of one province to another without a plebiscite; no treaties without Parliament's knowledge and sanction; no more 'Balance of Power' notions but instead a British policy directed in future to the establishment of a 'European Concert'; and finally, a drastic reduction of armaments and the nationalisation of the armament industry. All these conditions essentially were negative, echoing

Cobden's classic Radical plea, 'No foreign politics'.[36] The letter ended:

> It is the purpose of keeping these essential conditions of lasting peace before the British people that the Union of Democratic Control..., is in the process of formation. You will note that there is no question of this association embodying a "stop-the-war" movement of any kind... The whole emphasis of our effort is laid upon indicating clearly the fundamental principles which must mark the final terms of peace if the general policy for which the present Government presumably stands..., is finally to be vindicated.[37]

Of the letter's five signatories — Ponsonby's name was now added to the original quartet of Trevelyan, MacDonald, Angell and Morel — Trevelyan fairly could have claimed that it had been his efforts, his money, his astute immediate selection of Morel as secretary and full-time organiser for the movement, the neat balancing act he had effected between comforting Angell, encouraging Ponsonby's resolution and tempering MacDonald's intemperate early enthusiasm, made him the single most important contributor to the Union's birth. Trevelyan's efforts had ensured that there was now 'a sympathetic centre..., supported by an organisation' to which those who opposed the war could attach themselves 'to find relief in a terrible situation'.[38] Others might have talked, but it had been Trevelyan who had acted. Nevertheless, initially the less scrupulous elements of the 'patriotic' press supposed that Trevelyan had been captured by the other members of the UDC executive as a respectable 'front' man for their nefarious activities. Cecil Chesterton, hysterically revealing 'The Pacifist Plot' to readers of the *New Witness*, noted that Macdonald — 'a very astute intriguer who has surpassed all his contemporaries in the difficult art of obtaining positions of trust from persons who do not trust him' — Angell — 'who has eclipsed Lord Northcliffe in the profession of self-advertisement' — and Morel — 'who ran the Liverpool gin peoples' crusade against Belgium' — had been 'acute enough to see the advantage of obtaining the aid of one entirely honest man whose name will also give them the entrée to the governing class'.[39] Horatio Bottomley's scurrilous weekly, *John Bull*, in an article on the UDC entitled 'The Treason Mongers', censured Trevelyan for making common cause with 'quasi-traitors'. A 'former Minister' had no business 'associating himself with pernicious propaganda', or with men like Arthur Ponsonby whose 'manifold heresies often enough in the past strained the allegiance of the hard-headed constituents of the Stirling Burghs'.

> The Union of Democratic Control suggests a measure of popular support which, in point of fact, is conspicuously absent. This misconception will be helped in no small measure by the signature of an ex-Minister which will doubtless impose upon many persons to whom the vapourings of an Angell or a MacDonald would make but scant appeal.[40]

These delusions concerning Trevelyan's true role and influence within the UDC were not confined to the lucubrations of journalists like Bottomley and Chesterton. Even when Trevelyan advertised his position of authority and leadership with a slashing response to St. Loe Strachey's assertion in *The Spectator* that the UDC was financed by German money — a letter Trevelyan admitted was 'rather too strong', even for a 'maligning, scurrilous scoundrel like St. Loe'[41] — long-standing friends in the Liberal party would not or could not bring themselves to believe that Trevelyan's new associates were his by choice. Gerald France wrote to Trevelyan advising him to show that same courage that had prompted his resignation, and 'come right out from these associates before it is too late and incalculable harm has been done'.

> Every time I see your name associated with theirs it gives me a stab of pain. It matters to me nothing what they say about Ramsay MacDonald. I do not believe he is a straight man or a brave man... Ponsonby too doesn't matter to me since his unfortunate lapse into vulgar abuse on August 3rd.* Angell has been proved a false prophet as to one half of his thesis and Morel is, as far as I know, a good man with a natural bias against the name of Belgium, but you my friend are worth something better than to be wasting your time and opportunities and name with men of this stamp... I only write because I have greatly valued your friendship. If I did not and wished you harm I would urge you to continue.[42]

But Trevelyan was set upon a new path with new friends, and there was to be no turning back. The penalties and pains for that decision were to be harsh.

On Trevelyan's eightieth birthday in October 1950, a friend wrote:

> In the first half of your career you made the very best of the luck of your birth, brought up in the surroundings of a distinguished family, educated in the height of fashion of the time, established as a promising politician, a junior minister for the party that had been your father's, married to a handsome and brilliant woman. That was the distinction of the first forty years; but the real courage and enterprise emerged in the second half... Your absolute conviction of the fault of the war policy in 1914 in the face of universal support... Anyone who knows you appreciates that you made your policy from your own reasoning and whatever the inconvenience and unpopularity you act unflinchingly and conscientiously to work out your own policy. You know what you think you should do, and you do it.[43]

In his reply Trevelyan agreed with this assessment. Until the outbreak of war in 1914, he had been 'accepted by and accepted the Liberal tradition. I was definitely a Radical, but never outside the limit of party and conventional

*Presumably a reference to Ponsonby's speech in the Commons attacking Grey and referring *inter alia* to 'a group of half-drunken youths waving flags..., outside a great club in St. James's Street being encouraged by members of the club from the balcony... And that is what is called patriotism.'

independence. Then I was thrown on my own resources. [I was] as lonely as ever could be in opposition to the first war and my criticism of the Government for not trying for a settlement.'[44]

The really bitter sense of isolation that Trevelyan suffered sprang from severing, not party ties, but the leading reins of family tradition and sympathy which often in the past, though they offered comfortable reassurance, had cabinned the natural impulses of a more wayward spirit in the name of caution, loyalty and discretion. The harshest immediate price Trevelyan paid for his freedom was estrangement from his youngest brother George. He admired his brother's intellectual gifts and George had been his most valued advisor outside Parliament. George's support and advice had been vital to Trevelyan in those anxious days before Britain entered the war and he had resigned office. But then George's certainty and bold resolution had evaporated and when his eldest brother pressed him to identify himself more closely with the fortunes of the anti-war group, he refused. 'I will give you as much private advice as I am capable of,' he wrote to Trevelyan, 'but I am not a politician or a public man, and I will not be drawn into it in any responsible manner.'[45] A little more than a month after the beginning of war, Trevelyan was writing to his brother Robert that George, like their father, had 'gone over bag and baggage' to the pro-war party. He added, more in hope than certainty, 'I dare say they will slide back.'[46] But even of this ill-warranted hope, Trevelyan was very soon disabused. Sir George Trevelyan made no secret of his belief that Grey had done all that he could to avert the war, that England's involvement was a burden that in honour she could not have rejected and of which all true Englishmen ought to have been proud.[47] Estrangement from his father Trevelyan accepted much more readily than George's desertion. He wrote despairingly to Molly:

> I know that wisdom may begin to come to poor human beings through misery. But even that I doubt when I see people like George carried away by shallow fears and ill-informed hatreds... It shows how absurdly far we are from brotherly feeling to foreigners when even in him it is a shallow veneer. He like all the rest wants to hate the Germans.[48]

Trevelyan later admitted to his wife that at the bottom of his heart the only thing he personally minded about the war was George's disagreement. 'I am more discouraged by it than anything because it shows the helplessness of intellect before national passion.'[49]

To compensate for the loss of George's support, Trevelyan developed closer links with his brother Robert. Two cousins, Phil and Robin Price, and his formidable Aunt Anna, gave Trevelyan what support they could. Yet it remained that he had chosen to follow a course that differed radically from that of the two members of his family who had exercised the most influence upon his political career before August 1914. This division within the family ranks, though it never led to any overt personal rancour, made Trevelyan's isolation much more real and apparent than otherwise it would have been. The press in his constituency gleefully seized the opportunity to make effective if crude propaganda.

> All Mr. Trevelyan's near relatives and also those of his wife, are at present engaged in doing what they can to support the Government and further the cause of the Allies. There is unanimity of word and action on their part... Sir George Trevelyan... loses no opportunity of using his pen to indicate his approval of the policy adopted by His Majesty's advisers. Mr. G.M. Trevelyan is supporting his friends the Italians who are united in the Grand Alliance. Sir Hugh Bell is indefatigable in his efforts to promote recruiting: Major Bell is with his regiment facing the enemy; Miss Bell is nursing the sick and wounded. They could hardly do more. Mr. Trevelyan on the other hand, talks about peace — that is all.[50]

Before his resignation from the Government, Trevelyan had enjoyed particularly close and friendly relations with his constituency executive as with many of his constituents. But his letter explaining why he had resigned from the Government received a very cool reception. Within a month it was patent that among his constituents sympathy for his act had almost totally evaporated.[51] However, as long as Trevelyan took no initiative concerning his status as Liberal member for Elland, the constituency organisation seemed loath to do anything, particularly as national Liberal leaders continued to speak in sympathetic accents of their genuine regret that Trevelyan had chosen to resign. Doubts as to what action they should take were reinforced for the Elland Liberal Council by the obvious fury of local Tories. In the circumstances, for the moment it seemed much the best to wait upon a statement of intention from their member.

Trevelyan realised that a personal appearance before his Association could not be delayed for long. He confided in Ponsonby that it was 'not a particularly pleasant prospect but I do not consider it altogether hopeless'. [52] In the last week of November 1914, Trevelyan addressed his constituency Association.

> About 200 came. They were certainly very sad and anxious; most of them, of course, support the war, and they did not know what to do about me. They were all personally friendly. My speech had a profound effect..., it disturbed the conscience of a lot of them. They had never heard the case against Grey before and then questions afterwards showed how surprised they were... It was an amazingly interesting afternoon because we all showed perfect good temper and perfect mutual respect.[53]

As a result of this meeting, the Association decided their best course was to do nothing save maintain a watching brief. This was not because they had been persuaded by Trevelyan's advocacy; rather they feared that should they demand his resignation and he complied, then they would simply 'be placing the constituency in the hands of the hereditary enemy'.[54] All things considered, they, like Asquith, would prefer to 'wait and see'.

The situation was unsatisfactory and Trevelyan realised it could not be maintained indefinitely. It is clear, however, from the counsel he gave his cousin Philips Price, he did not judge it the time to take any hasty initiative.

> There will probably be no election until after the war. If there is it will be under the auspices of a party truce. If it does not come until after the war, he would be a bold man who would prophesy what kind of opinion would then be in favour with our population. The proper thing will be to do nothing of any sort.[55]

Trevelyan's public involvement and leading role in the fortunes of the UDC, and more importantly, the distorted press coverage of those activities, increased the hostility Elland Liberals felt towards their member. And the 'patriotic' press did its best to fuel their discontent. It was the considered editorial opinion of the *Daily Sketch*, for example, that:

> With a man of Mr. Trevelyan's views Elland should be in Prussia. Trevelyan would then have a very congenial atmosphere — in the Reichstag... England nor Elland has no place now for men of the Trevelyan stamp. We have no time to listen to his foolish and pernicious talk. It is a scandal that he should be in Parliament when he continues to preach these pro-German and utterly impracticable pacifist doctrines. Trevelyan must go.[56]

Eventually, in April 1915, the Divisional Executive Council called a meeting of delegates. Reports from the local Associations were unanimous in their demand that Trevelyan's services as their parliamentary representative should be dispensed with. A general resolution, passed unanimously, declared 'the futility of again adopting as their candidate their present member'.[57] A special committee was appointed to find a suitable successor. Effectively, Trevelyan had been dismissed by the constituency Association.

There were the expected letters of commiseration from friends, and George Lansbury's *Herald*, unlike the rest of the press that noticed the event, provided a tearful paragraph on the theme that battlefields were not the only place of sacrifice. 'He must have known when he resigned that he was giving the death blow to his career, and the courage which compels such a step is not to be distinguished from the courage of a soldier who falls in battle.'[58] If friend and foe alike thought him finished, Trevelyan had quite other ideas on the subject. Despite its eminently reasonable tone, the reply he gave the Elland Association was not calculated to please. While they might go ahead with their plan to choose another candidate, Trevelyan had no intention of resigning.

The present time I consider to be unsuitable for the discussion of the long course of policy which involved Great Britain in the war... The questions arising out of this war will dominate politics for the next generation. And I have no doubt that as it becomes apparent that Liberal and Democratic policy is more than ever needed during and after the war it will appear also that we shall not have ceased to share many common opinions even though you have chosen this moment to sever our close political connections.[59]

Naturally the Association were perplexed as to what to do next. Effectively, there was little they could do if Trevelyan insisted on remaining as their member. The Association's hotter heads, with the less than disinterested encouragement of Mr. Harry Dawson of Huddersfield — the new Liberal champion — pressed for more extreme action. A Mr. Thornton, for example, reviled Trevelyan as a 'pro-German and traitor', and sponsored a resolution, accepted with scarcely a dissenting voice, that 'Trevelyan be taken out and shot'.[60] In public, at least, Trevelyan appeared unmoved by these violent denunciations from erstwhile supporters. Indeed, from time to time he received letters from constituents who initially had attacked his stand against the Government but since then had been persuaded to examine more dispassionately his case. One such constituent, for example, wrote:

You will perhaps remember correspondence between us shortly after the outbreak of war, wherein I censured your disapproval of the Government... Then I considered your attitude unpatriotic and ruinous to Liberalism in the Elland Division. Much has happened since to change the perspective of one's outlook and now my differences from you seem small by comparison with the great democratic causes which you and a few others are upholding... I therefore think I ought to inform you that, if at the next Election you contest the Elland division, even as an Independent Liberal or as a Socialist, I shall vote for you.[61]

Trevelyan felt his estrangement keenly. When he reviewed the crisis of August 1914, and the early months of the war, he could admit to his wife that for the first time he was grateful his political career had not been more successful. Had he been a Cabinet Minister he could not claim that he would have seen 'the right course to take... I might have been blinded as so many of those good men have been by their nearness to the business and their sense of importance to the country. Thank God I have no responsibility for the ghastly business is my chief feeling now.'[62]

It is no paradox to say that, of the UDC leaders, Morel not excepted, Trevelyan was a warrior for peace. His pacifism was not born of a gentle, yielding nature, nor was his crusade for that cause ever less than uncompromising, aggressive and unflinching. Churchill, sensible of Trevelyan's stubborn pugnacity and his natural abilities as a leader of other men — traits he shared with Jos Wedgwood — offered both men, despite their public disavowal of the war, commissions. Jos, in time, accepted his, and received public recognition for his gallantry in battle. Trevelyan refused — 'I said I would ask for it when I wanted it'[63] — and earned the jeers of press and public that vilified him, along with so many other brave men and women, as 'traitor', 'pro-German' and 'coward'. The wounds earned in the battle of conscience were no less difficult to sustain than those suffered in Flanders' mud or on the beaches of the Dardanelles. It was not Trevelyan's disposition to hide from trouble; rather, his instinctive reaction to any threatening situation was to confront it boldly. For a cause he believed in, he would never admit defeat. Many for a time were deceived into believing otherwise by a press campaign of lies, slander and defamation represented as the 'patriotic truth'. Wedgwood was to write to Morel of the UDC and its leaders in September 1915, 'You have become a "hands-upper" organisation. If that is your Union it is not for me... I am not going to help you discuss the terms of peace till the Junkers are beaten to a frazzle.'[64] But little more than six months later Wedgwood again wrote to Morel: 'When you see Trevelyan tell him to keep on keeping on. All over the country he is converting people who are too cross to admit they are converted.'[65]

It was not Trevelyan's stubborn persistence in his difficult crusade that alone aroused Wedgwood's admiration. Rather it was the essentially aggressive spirit that underlay it, that revealed itself occasionally in response to constant provocation. Though words and actions were to be guarded carefully in public, it was sometimes possible in private to relax and admit, as in a letter to his brother Robert, that nothing would give him greater pleasure than 'to discharge two barrels into Blumenfeld's backside at thirty yards',[66] for that editor's constant persecution of the UDC in the columns of the *Express*. Or, after constant importuning by a former political friend that he should abandon MacDonald and Morel, to admit that it would have been much more to his liking 'to spend my whole time at Cambo teaching the youth to shoot and acting as a special constable under some bridge of the NER', than, 'playing the public part I now take'.[67] It needed real courage and resolution in the face of a persistently unfriendly fortune to resist the temptation to succumb to the blandishments of former friends, colleagues, even family, to take the easy and popular course, retire to his beloved Northumberland for the duration of the war and wash his hands of the UDC. Perhaps of all his relatives, Trevelyan's young cousin Robin best comprehended the price that had to be paid for espousing the cause of peace. He had enlisted as a gunner at the outbreak of war. 'Certainly,' he wrote in May 1915, 'the act of enlisting..., was simply the following of the least line of resistance. Those who did were mostly afraid of doing anything else.'[68] In his letters to Trevelyan, Robin Price frequently returned to this theme. Recovering from wounds in November 1917, he wrote, 'I often think of you

Charles and wonder how you stick it. Give me shells any day rather than abuse.'[69] Once Trevelyan wrote to Ponsonby, 'You are a good man to go tiger hunting with.'[70] Ponsonby, Morel, MacDonald, or any member of the UDC, would have affirmed the same of Trevelyan.

Apart from the work that kept him in London — attendance at Westminster and administrative duties in the central UDC office — Trevelyan made a particular contribution to the welfare of the Union of Democratic Control in two fields. It was due to his efforts that much of the money that financed UDC activities was raised. Early in November 1914, on one of his frequent financial forays, Trevelyan wrote to Molly of how kind and generous the Cadburys had proved to be. 'The old man is so friendly and enthusiastic about all we are doing. We and the Labour leaders are his one light and hope. He has given me £250 at a blow.' Trevelyan found fund raising 'a particularly hard row to hoe. Often and often,' he told his wife, 'I feel inclined to say let us go to Cambo and live retired there until this horror is over and nobility has again some chance and reason some place in this mad world.' When such despairing feelings were particularly strong Trevelyan admitted how glad he was that he had 'burnt [his] boats at the start by creating the UDC to prevent that cowardly retreat.'[71]

Much more conducive to Trevelyan's temperament than drumming up funds was addressing groups of possible supporters. Such speeches were a much more demanding test of his skills as an orator than the friendly meetings with constituents that he had addressed before the war. From the first he had been determined to speak 'in all the principal places in the country. It will take much time and it will be very slow work,' he wrote to Molly, 'as we are beginning from nothing in apparently hopeless circumstances... That, however, does not trouble me much.'[72] On 5 November 1914, he addressed a meeting of the Birmingham branch of the UDC which, so he claimed, was 'quite successful'. Of the one hundred and fifty present there had been 'few influential people, but a great many of the ILP. It is slow work..., but those who come are first rate.'[73] The next day Trevelyan was at Tibberton in Gloucestershire, sharing the platform at the Liberal Club with his cousin, Phil Price. The audience was a mixture of Liberal and Labour supporters. 'The old Liberals,' wrote Trevelyan, 'were hopeless, all anti-German mad. More and more it is clear that the young men alone who have faith and hope in human nature can see beyond the present hatreds. It is a very interesting sign.'[74]

The dozens of speeches Trevelyan delivered at these meetings in the first year of the war, differed little in their content. He was always anxious to stress that the philosophy of the UDC was not one of despair or hopelessness as the jingo press would have had people believe.

This war is more favourable than any other for rousing new forces in our and other countries, forces that are necessary to combat and overpower old ideas of the value of war that are so destructive, sanguinary, horrible and useless... Our policy deals not only with peace but that which will make peace permanent. Why begin now? Some say we are not only unpopular but useless. But, it is a general principle of political action that it is never too early to begin. And we already know that we are right.

Speaking of the other UDC leaders, Trevelyan insisted that none of them cared about their own political fortunes. 'The war has taken away our reputations as it has done our careers. Our wish is to build up democratic opinion so that such another war will be impossible. Whether *we* do it is immaterial. We are only determined that it shall be done.' Unless the people asserted their right to control their own destiny by the intelligent understanding of foreign relations then the future prospects for the fate of mankind were indeed grim — 'a vista of scientific wars down the coming generations ever more terrible and destructive'.[75]

Wherever and whenever he was asked to speak for the UDC, Trevelyan never spared himself to meet the demand. But the war was more than a year old before he was invited to speak on the subject nearest his heart to a group of his own constituents. He started on rather a melancholic, even dispirited note. 'Most of the old things about which you and I have agreed have been blown to the winds by this disaster. The better sort of world which I had hoped to help to build in England is not to be in my generation.' However, when he talked of the role of ordinary people in ordering the foreign relations of their country, he roused his audience of more than five hundred to shout their fervid agreement.

> I tell you straight that I do not trust statesmen and diplomatists unaided by public opinion, to pursue a policy which will make peace a permanence. Everything in history leads me to distrust them. The ruling classes today nourish the conviction that national hatreds and rivalries are inevitable. I turn for hope away from the great and learned and rich who have had the making of this war, to the common men and women whose only responsibility is that they left the war to others to settle... It is only by democracy beginning to think for itself by the putting into operation of the principles of human brotherhood that anything can be made out of the present deplorable embroilment but unutterable and permanent human disaster.[76]

This appeal to the collective wisdom of ordinary people as the future arbiters of their foreign policy rather than 'the intriguers of the upper class', was not an exercise in demagogy designed to achieve cheap and easy acclamation. Rather, it was an utterly sincere expression of Trevelyan's faith in the virtues and the common sense of the common people. Trevelyan shrugged off Courtney's gentle remonstrance that 'amongst the proletariat as much as among the peerage, the right thinkers are a sad minority'.[77]

To take their message to the people required much physical as well as moral courage. In the van of the 'patriotic' press, the *Daily Express* made the Union its particular target. It spared no lies in whipping up a mood of hostility and overtly encouraged bully boys to break up pacific meetings. After a particularly violent incident at Kingston in which Arthur Ponsonby had been manhandled, he wrote to Trevelyan, 'I don't want such an experience..., again in my life.' To complain, as Ponsonby did to the Commons, merely invited further abuse. 'The monstrous thing is that their organized movement of bands of drunken ruffians is made by the newspapers to mean adverse opinion to UDC policy. The *Times* yesterday was outrageous saying I had not spoken the truth in House. I have written to them, but I doubt if they put in my letter.'[78] A meeting between Simon, the Home Secretary, and Trevelyan proved fruitless. The UDC executive decided that the best way of protecting themselves was to concentrate on meetings where a large Labour contingent could be expected to form the greater part of the audience. So, an unforeseen consequence of the scurrilous campaign against the UDC by the 'patriotic' press was to drive its Liberal leadership into an even closer alliance with the Left.

Encouraged by the apparent success of its campaign of intimidation, the press continued to promote violence, concentrating in particular upon a meeting to be held at Farringdon Street. 'Is Germany,' inquired the *Daily Express* in bold headlines, 'to hear the wail of the peace cranks from the city of Empire?' Trevelyan wrote to Simon:

>...it might be as well for the police to be informed of the threat [to break up the meeting]. During the whole year in the many meetings we have held throughout the country, with the audience now regularly running into hundreds and sometimes thousands..., there has not been a single case of spontaneous disturbance of a meeting. In the..., meetings where the disturbance was serious, the *Daily Express* had carefully engineered it.[79]

The police attended the meeting, but stood idly by as one group of soldiers in the audience attacked the platform party, while others discouraged likely UDC supporters from even entering the hall.[80] Trevelyan, his wife and the rest of the speakers, were forced to barricade themselves in a back room until eventually the rowdies departed. Such incidents, the danger to life and limb apart, made it difficult for the Union to hire halls for their mass meetings. Yet the leaders refused to give up and stuck to their self-appointed task. In time this became easier as war-weariness persuaded people that there might be some substance to the UDC message despite the hostile claim that they were a 'pro-German', 'treasonous conspiracy'. Writing to his brother Robert in June 1918 of meetings in Elland, Trevelyan claimed that he had enjoyed:

>a very remarkable time... I spoke at eleven out-door meetings in seven

days. I was listened to with close attention everywhere by large crowds. I calculated that I addressed six thousand five hundred people in all, as many as nearly one tenth of the constituency. No disturbances. A good deal of complete agreement, but mostly profound anxiety and desire to find a way out of war.[81]

To address meetings in the country was one thing; to speak in Parliament another. Until Asquith formed his coalition government with the Tories in May 1915, Trevelyan like Ponsonby had been reluctant to attack the Liberals, considering it both a better and more profitable exercise to exert influence upon former colleagues by moderate opposition rather than by an all out parliamentary attack. The formation of an alliance between the Liberals and the Tories suggested that this frail hope of influence by stealth could be abandoned. What could be hoped of men who for short term political gains would readily sacrifice friends of a lifetime? As Trevelyan wrote to his mother:

The throwing over of Haldane by Asquith and Grey to the Tory wolves is the dirtiest political thing that has occurred in my political life, except the lie which those same two gentlemen told the nation that we were bound to fight for France when we were in fact bound in their opinions.[82]

In truth, the Coalition Ministry was a less efficient instrument for securing the nation's fortunes in war than had been its predecessor.

The substitution of Balfour for Churchill seems to me to be an insanity. I daresay Churchill may be too gambling a strategist. But he has done well in the nett result and he is resourceful, fearless and ready to change men. Balfour doesn't get up till 12 o'clock and is a portent of casual inefficiency to every Liberal and most Tories. If I didn't think our way absolutely supreme in hands however bad, and the war certain to end in stalemate however good the strategy, I should be desperately angry.[83]

However, of more immediate concern to their fortunes, as Trevelyan told Ponsonby, was the formation of the Coalition. This meant there now was:

no effective party in the Cabinet anxious for an early peace. Pease, Samuel Beauchamp, who all held that we were fighting for Belgium are gone, and Simon and Harcourt who may hold the same view (even if supported for opportunistic reasons by Lloyd George) will be helpless before a solid force of Tories...[84]

Possibly now was the time for a change of tactics and they need no longer remain silent in the House. An 'attack on the new Coalition will not be resented,' declared Ponsonby, 'but welcomed by many Liberals, if it is judicious and can be shown to be really patriotic. Should we therefore continue to be silent?'[85]

There remained the problem of deciding the right moment to express their critical views to the House. A letter Ponsonby wrote to Trevelyan in June 1915 reflects this particular dilemma.

> I have been rather wretched. I sat through the debate yesterday feeling we might have got in as time went on. Then after a night's reflection I felt more strongly that I ought to speak and could say something useful and unprovocative. But Ramsay, Adamson, Jowett were all against it so the debate has ended and I have been silent. Perhaps it is as well, but I feel a wretched coward... It is true of course that in the extremely gloomy state of public opinion silence is the best policy but it must not continue. We must come out soon or else we shall be swamped.[86]

How could the UDC leaders expect to be listened to when the military situation continued to be so unsatisfactory? Who would admit that 'Peace by negotiation' — the Union's policy — was a practicable or even an attractive proposition? Such calculations, however, were not in tune with Morel's disposition. What price parliamentary tactics when 'heart and brain united strike a deeper human note'? He wrote to Trevelyan:

> If only you and AP (Ponsonby) would, for the nonce, be less humble minded and forget utterly that you are politicians, remembering only that you are men who *feel* the atrocious and senseless tragedy.
> *You* have sacrificed your position in the Government and have risked your seat..., you have both cheerfully faced heaps of public and social un-pleasantness. But for what? Surely not to wait until the tragedy is consummated; to remain silent in the national council chamber when the situation demands above all things, an act of courage which will wrench men's minds back to realities, and tear aside the veil of untruth which blinds their eyes?
> It is not the politician's art which is required at this moment but the naked soul of man bursting the fetters of make-believe... Feeling as you do, neither of you can *possibly* be ineffective if you remember that all through the country there are masses of men waiting for just this call to stir in them, emotions, only slumbering after all, and needing the live touch to become sentiment in their poor muddled minds.[87]

Trevelyan was not the man to ignore such an appeal. People might talk of a 'fight to the finish', and conscription (an affront to any Liberal conscience) was only a few months away. Yet, underneath the apparently uncompromising surface of the nation one could not fail but detect the 'growing yearning for peace'.[88] Now was the time to speak out boldly in Parliament. In November 1915, Courtney and Loreburn in the Lords, Ponsonby and Trevelyan in the Commons, spoke of the need for a negotiated peace. They did not divide the House — they were too tiny and ineffective a minority for that. Nevertheless, the Commons listened, attentive if disapproving. Ponsonby wrote to Molly of her husband's speech:

After waiting for three days Charles got in last night... It was of course, a most difficult thing to do and for his first few sentences he was unsettled but gradually he got the ear of the House... He made his points well and when he sat down some around (in absolute disagreement) said that it was a 'first rate speech anyhow'... The point is his speech came off. It came at a good moment and must draw attention. I haven't seen the newspapers yet. There will be plenty of abuse but I am sure there will be a good response. Why mine, which was not reported hardly anywhere..., has produced letters from strangers.[89]

Such were the frail straws at which Ponsonby and Trevelyan were obliged to grasp. There were letters enough for Trevelyan's parliamentary performance. One, among many similar, from James Hoggan, a grand nephew of Thomas Carlyle.

I hear[d] from the gallery the brave and eloquent speech which you made..., and it needed all my self-restraint to prevent me rising and applauding you. I am sure you are too wise to be discouraged by the vulgar and ignorant clamour which you and the brave men who think like you are now being subjected to.[90]

But, save abuse, the parliamentary pleas of the UDC leaders were boycotted by the national press. They were to speak again to the Commons: three times in 1916, and again in February 1917, each time without seeking a division. But when they did, on four occasions in 1917, and once in 1918, they could muster only an insignificant handful of supporters in the division lobby. In October 1916 Trevelyan had written to C.P. Scott, 'When I spoke in the House I found that there was a universal interest in what I had said, and a great deal more approval expressed afterwards than I dared to expect from many Liberal quarters... For the first time those who do not hold our views can descend to argue.'[91] From these early hopes, the slide to despondency and hopelessness was, if slow, inevitable. The bravest spirit would have shrunk in the face of such unyielding indifference, much harder to support than hostility. In August 1918, Trevelyan admitted to Ponsonby that 'the utter uselessness of hoping to rouse the House of Commons has very much come home to me'.[92]

Where did the fault lie for the ineffectiveness of their parliamentary campaign? Could it have been 'the infernal confusion of creeds in the Opposition' as George Bernard Shaw supposed? Would Trevelyan have done better not to have attached himself to any organisation, and thus have kept clear of 'the motley crowd of Pillars of Fire at one extreme and blood-thirsty anti-Imperialists on the other with whom you have to struggle'?[93] Shaw, with the presumed innocence of one inexperienced in the ways of Parliament, suggested that Trevelyan should be bold enough to make 'a definite bid for the Leadership of the House'. Though this idea was far-fetched, his letter does give a clear picture of the parliamentary scene.

The situation at present is that England has no respectable spokesman with modern ideas. Why is Holt so absurdly taken in by Hertling and Czernin? Simply because they speak like liberally educated gentlemen, and our people reply like Jingo commercial travellers so grossly ignorant of history... Lansdowne and Balfour know better, but they are not democrats and it is not their speeches that give our tone to the world but the vapourings of George, Carson, Northcliffe, Clemenceau, Pichon &c, who produce nothing but manifestoes of brigands which disgrace a case. The result is a horrid confusion of mind in which..., you and MacDonald are held up as pacifists of the Pillars of Fire order, whilst funksters who are being driven to frantic military activity by mere terror are paraded as Napoleons.

... Between you and the Front Bench there is, to put it bluntly a crowd of blackguards, uneducated, illiterate and financially desperate even when they are spending £50,000 a year or pretending to. In a big business like this, small distinctions disappear. Bottomley will comprise us no more than George, nor George less than Bottomley. There is no use in remaining disgustedly in the background waiting for your turn: they will never make way for you. You must shove through to the front. You have great advantages: you have an unassailable social and financial position, intellectual integrity and historical consciousness, character, personality, good looks, style, conviction, everything they lack except cinema sentiment and vulgarity. If you feel equal to a deliberate assumption of responsibility it is clear to me that you..., can very soon become the visible alternative nucleus to the George gang and the Asquith ruin... I have been lately saying on occasion, 'What about Trevelyan?' and the only objection is that you seem to have specialised too much as a Pacifist.[94]

Trevelyan was both flattered and pleased that Shaw should think it worth his while to encourage and advise him. But he refused to entertain any illusions about his political prospects, though not, he added hastily, 'by modesty or pride', or 'fear of responsibility'.

I have not got political versatility or House of Common ways, and am much more of a political preacher than a politician. Rightly or wrongly also I have a disbelief in shoving. I agree that the public won't come and fetch me out. But that is because they don't want the kind of view which I represent, not because I don't hustle in the ways usually adopted to attract their notice.[95]

This reply met with a typical Shavian rejoinder.

It is time to find a policy and form an alternative ministry. A Prime Minister without political versatility or House of Commons ways: that is to say one who is neither an Opportunist-Adventurer, nor a liar and a blackguard, nor a light comedian tickled into mimicry like Robert Harcourt, is just what is wanted... You must come in and supply what the Labor Movement cannot and Webb will not: a new diplomacy.[96]

This correspondence between Shaw and Trevelyan had been triggered off by a letter Trevelyan had published in *The Nation* early in February 1918. Although since the beginning of the war there had been little enough to encourage Trevelyan in his desire for peace, 1917 had provided some measure for hope. There had been the Russian revolution in March which Trevelyan had welcomed ecstatically. Then the American President, Woodrow Wilson, had added further fuel to the campaign for a negotiated peace with his 'fourteen points'. Arthur Henderson's dismissal from the Lloyd George government meant that in future Labour would officially oppose the Government's war policies. This was a great stroke of fortune for the UDC as they would no longer be alone in Parliament. 'The Labour decision,' Trevelyan wrote to Ponsonby, 'is so great an event that it may be better to let them make the running now.'[97] In December 1917, a special Labour conference approved a *Memorandum on War Aims*. This, in almost all particulars, matched the policies promoted by the UDC and the Independent Labour Party. Henderson seemed determined that the Labour party should attract the Radical members of the UDC, and sharing, as they now did, common views on foreign policy and thus subject to the same violent jingo attacks both in the press and Parliament, the two groups were drawn closer together. A change in the Labour party's constitution in February 1918, and the publication of *Labour and the New Social Order* — their domestic programme which was much in accord with the ideas of the Progressive Liberals — hastened the process of assimilation between the Radicals and Labour.

In November 1917, Trevelyan had written to his brother, Robert: 'I am interested to hear you have joined the ILP. If I were in your [position] I probably should do the same. We are discussing the situation very fully in London.'[98] For Trevelyan, the publication of Labour's *Memorandum on War Aims* cleared the political ground of most of his doubts and reservations. In January he wrote to Massingham, the editor of *The Nation*:

> I enclose a copy of the letter which I wish to publish. It is rather of the nature of a manifesto to challenge discussion... It is the first expression I think in public by a Liberal member of the view that the Liberal leaders cannot lead democracy in the next stage and that the leadership has so far passed to Labour that we ought in some way to either cooperate with it as comrades, or associate with it as open allies. I am therefore anxious to have as wide attention paid to it as possible.[99]

The letter was published in the next issue of *The Nation* under the heading, 'Can Socialism and Radicalism Unite?' His 'manifesto left little doubt in readers' minds how Trevelyan would answer that question.

...Hitherto the British Labor Party has played a secondary part as a force of discontent driving Governments into progressive courses. It has now become a directing force, stepping in to divert the world from ruin where the old parties are impotent to shape a policy.

The new situation arouses in an immediate and acute form the question which is disturbing the minds of so many men and women as to where in the new epoch they owe political allegiance... The Liberal Party today has no voice except through its leaders. But in this tremendous crisis they have been conspicuously unable either to prevent the world conflagration, to conduct the war successfully, or prepare the way for an honorable democratic peace. In fact they have failed to lead in action and thought. What likelihood is there that they will lead effectively when the world has to be rebuilt on the ruins caused by the war?

Many Radicals are already openly joining the Labor Party. Others are hesitating, uncertain whether the reconstruction of the Labor Party means only a finer electioneering machine for registering discontent and class irritation in Parliament, or a much bigger thing — *i.e.* the force, which, utilising the best intellect of the country, will rally men of all classes to a broad policy of internationalism and economic revolution through law...

The chief note of new policy must be thoroughness. For the time of compromise, of the slow and patient evolution to a better social condition, has passed with the war. No reversion to pre-war programmes..., will satisfy the new demands. Our lives have been spoilt by compromise, because we tolerated armament firms and secret diplomacy and the rule of wealth. The world war has revealed the real meaning of our social system. As imperialism, militarism and irresponsible wealth are everywhere trying to crush democracy today, so democracy must treat these forces without mercy. The root of all evil is economic privilege. The personal problem which faces so many of us is that we cannot waste the rest or our lives in half-measures against it. Where shall we find the political combination which will offer us resource in its strategy, coherence in its policy, and fearlessness in its proposals?[100]

Trevelyan knew that his letter would stir a hornets' nest about his ears, especially from those who thought that he was playing traitor to his class. 'Do you,' wrote one old Harrovian furiously, 'in the utter tosh you write at a time critical for our country, wish to turn Europe into a commune with Lenin as Prime Minister and Ramsay MacDonald as deputy? Do you wish to introduce us to the luxuries of Bolshevikism, murder, rapine and pillage, or do you merely wish to see your own country ruined? Really your friends ought to look after you... Yours pityingly.'[101] Not for a moment did Trevelyan believe that England would ever suffer the extremes of the Russian revolution. 'Very large numbers of men here, who would in Russia, or many other countries, form part of the unthinking reactionary parties, are ready to contemplate quite fundamental revolution through law.' If this were not so, then, 'the temper of the returned soldiers and the munition workers generally, would make violent revolution an absolute certainty within a year or two'. As to the more important, real and immediate problem of the Liberal party's future, to Trevelyan it seemed obvious it had allowed itself 'to be left behind because it does not recognise the intellectual changes brought about by the war'.[102]

Nevertheless, there was a very natural reluctance among many who had been Radical members of the Liberal party finally to sever their connection with Liberalism and attach themselves to Labour. Despite Lloyd George's chicanery, his opportunism to maintain, whatever the cost, his personal power, and the deplorable weakness of Asquith's statements during the critical months at the beginning of 1918, a majority of the Radical group in the House of Commons decided they would continue to act with the Liberal party. As C.H. Wilson wrote, after a meeting of the Yorkshire Radicals in March 1918, they were 'disappointed at the decision'. However, they remained wary of throwing in their hand completely with Labour. 'How far,' asked Wilson of Trevelyan, 'will joining that party cripple our individual liberty whether as private citizens or public representatives?'[103] Added to this, any prominent Radical-Liberal contemplating the move to Labour was confronted by a tangle of constitutional problems and proprieties. Of these Ponsonby wrote feelingly, if not without humour, to Trevelyan, after a constituency meeting:

> Really, the Labour Party's constitutional problems are beyond me. They seem constantly tied up by all the technical formalities. There are the local ILP, the NAC of the ILP, the Labour party with its new constitution, the Miners Federation, the local branch of the Miners Federation, the LRC for the country and the constituency, and I don't know if that even comprises all the different organizations.[104]

Of the Radicals among the leaders of the UDC, E.D. Morel was the first to join the ILP shortly after his release from prison on 30 January 1918. It was not until November that Trevelyan publicly announced that he had joined Labour. In the 'coupon election' at the end of that year, Trevelyan stood as an independent. There was even an offical Labour candidate standing against him. He had delayed the announcement of his change of allegiance for too long for it to profit him at the hustings. His commitment to joining the ILP had not been conditioned by selfish calculations in a profit and loss ledger of votes. He admitted he had been 'slow in coming to the decision', for 'old political attachments are strong' and for 'nineteen years' he had been 'Member for Liberalism'. But 'it is clear to me now where I must inevitably find myself. If elected... I must work with the men I agree with — [the] leaders of the ILP.'[105]

The public announcement that, for the future, he was joining with Labour, brought a cool note from Trevelyan's mother:

Your decision..., is, of course, a trouble to us. I hope you will get on with your new friends and not let them lead you into deep waters. It will make a considerable difference to you and your family but you have doubtless considered everything. I had hoped that after the war we might find ourselves all more in sympathy on public affairs.[106]

Trevelyan was not surprised by this expected response from his parents. His reply was swift and unbending, but did not conceal his hurt.

I of course knew that you would regret my leaving the Liberal party; but there is nothing unnatural, sudden or surprising about it. You talk of my 'new friends'. In the first place I have worked in close comradeship with several of the leaders of the Labour party for four years... But beyond that at least half of my Liberal friends are either joining the Labour party now or are on the verge of joining it. At least thirty Liberal members have been discussing the pros and cons of it for the last eighteen months... Any amount of my private friends of the same education, and, if that matters, social position as myself, are joining now. So little is it a matter of surprise or concern by those that know me well that many friends who have not yet actually taken the step say I am right... I want you to understand, so far from being an outcast, I am only doing what most of my friends about whose opinion I have ever cared must have expected me to do, and what a large section of them are doing themselves.[107]

Seizing the initiative afforded by the sudden ending of the war, Lloyd George called a General Election. Coalition candidates proclaimed the gospel of peace and the new order — 'Hang the Kaiser', 'Make Germany pay'. There was little hope for a candidate who continued to preach that the war had been an avoidable catastrophe; who suggested that those who had fought had been misled by their political leaders, and that those who had died had been the unwitting victims of a vain sacrifice. Trevelyan's was not a popular stand to take, and to prejudice even further his chances of being re-elected, in a four cornered fight he stood without the benefit of official party backing. His coalition opponent was G.T. Ramsden, now *Lieutenant* Ramsden. Harry Dawson stood for the Liberal interest, and D. Hardaker was the official Labour nominee.

With the help of a handful of friends, Trevelyan boldly put his case to an electorate that, at least, listened politely to what he had to say. Molly, Trevelyan's constant companion in this his hardest parliamentary campaign, wrote proudly of how her husband,

stands up so straight and fearlessly, and with his wonderful ringing voice pours forth great rolling sentences spoken from the bottom of his heart. He is gaining ground enormously, almost entirely because of his power of eloquent speaking, but also because people know that they can trust him. They fear him because he is so sternly honest and so unbendingly, uncompromisingly outspoken. [108]

The campaign, even polling day itself, was so untypical of anything Trevelyan had ever before experienced that to the last moment he had 'not the ghost of a notion who ha[d] won'. One thing only was certain. There had been a particularly heavy poll.

There were no colours, no cars, no shouting, simply a refusal to say who they were voting for. My meetings were the only ones that were decently attended... But I have not the remotest idea whether all this quiet voting means voting against me regretfully because of my views on the war, or a landslide to Labour by a constituency desperately puzzled to choose between the Labour candidates. I never heard an offensive word at my meetings, in the streets or anywhere. I never knew people half so cordial. I strongly incline to the view that I shall be out by a big vote..., but I have never enjoyed an election half so much before. For I have fought this entirely my self, without organization, big-wigs, speakers or anything to help me but my own capacities and a handful of friends.[109]

To the end Trevelyan supposed that he was converting people to his way of thinking. But it was not to be a victory against all the odds.

Lt. G.T., Ramsden (Unionist-Coalition) 8,917
Harry Dawson (Liberal) 7,028
D. Hardaker (Labour) 5,923
C.P. Trevelyan (Independent) 1,286

Though he had been crushingly defeated Trevelyan was not unduly depressed for, entirely by his own efforts, he had done as well as several of the Liberal leaders with party backing. 'If I had been the official Labour candidate,' he wrote to his mother, 'I should have run Ramsden very close. In any case, there doesn't seem a place for any free man in Lloyd George's tied house.'[110]

Defeat strengthened Trevelyan's conviction that he had been right to join Labour. He wrote to his brother Robert:

The Liberals are absolutely hopeless. Even George [Trevelyan] has been writing the most beastly jingoism on behalf of his dear Italians in the *Manchester Guardian*. The fact that not even peace can restore *his* balance shows how hopeless the mass of Liberal intelligentsia must be everywhere.[111]

The immediate reward Trevelyan earned for his courageous stand for peace against war was rejection by the constituency he had served for almost twenty years, and the quiet, though no less real opposition of most of his family to those ideas he most prized. The latter, though he would have been the last to admit it, was undoubtedly the harsher penalty to accept. 'His stand and his sacrifice will sow seeds which will flourish when the pantaloons of the day have disappeared,' wrote Morel to Molly. 'Courage and consistency are worth infinitely more than what he loses for a time.'[112]

FROM LIBERALISM
TO LABOUR:
1919-24

A generation had been sacrificed on the altar of war to the incompetence of military leaders and to satisfy the vainglory of politicians and kings. But the peace in Europe did not give Trevelyan and those that thought like him much relief. Trevelyan's daughter, Katherine, in her autobiography recalled a simple domestic incident that catches, with the child's direct vision, the measure of her father's disillusionment.

> On November 12th, the day after the Armistice was signed, I went and bought Father a green tie, as he had been wearing a black tie all the war in protest against political villainy. After wearing it for a week he returned to his black one.
> I asked Mother: 'Why doesn't Father wear my tie?'
> 'Your father doesn't think it a good peace,' she answered; and it wasn't.[1]

In Paris the victors had produced, not a moderate settlement as the UDC wished, but a vindictive exercise; militarily, economically, morally and territorially unfair to Germany. The reorganisation of boundaries in the Balkans and Eastern Europe violated the sacred Radical principle of nationality. Intervention in Russia was merely the crowning example of the moral and political turpitude of the victors. Even President Wilson, of whom so many had hoped so much, in the event proved a sad disappointment. The ending of war was not to be the prelude to an era of amity, reconciliation and reconstruction, but a confirmation of hatred, mean-minded spite and vengeance.

A personal problem added to Trevelyan's burdens during the early days of peace. Immediately after his election defeat at Elland, Trevelyan sought new employment for his energies. His father, now eighty years of age, was no longer able to supervise his estates, yet he stubbornly refused his eldest son's request to play a larger part in their management, a task for which he was particularly well suited. Early in January 1919, Trevelyan wrote to his father:

> I have now if I am wise, to act on the assumption that I shall not return to politics as my chief occupation. I am nearly fifty. I don't propose to idle. But whatever I do must offer some prospect of permanent activity. The whole bent of my interests is rather towards business and administration. I know by now what my capacities are. I am a very good administrator. That does not mean that I believe I have any proved ability for launching new schemes involving large expenditure or change; but I have capacity for controlling an organisation and for managing and getting on with men.[2]

The tone was trimmed so that his father might not suppose his intention was to embark upon a revolutionary reorganisation of the estates. But for Sir George, the prospect of his restless eldest son taking a greater part in the administration of the Wallington estate was not one he would countenance in any circumstances. Lady Caroline Trevelyan pleaded with her husband; George appealed on behalf of his brother; but all in vain. The old man refused to be moved.

The engagement between father and son was brief but bitter; the distance between them exaggerated by Sir George's refusal to see Trevelyan. 'Father has refused to accede to your proposals because he was sure it would lead to constant cross purposes and scenes. And after this last affair,' added George, 'whosoever the fault mainly may be, I am bound to say that that is exceedingly likely.'[3] Trevelyan handsomely conceded to his father.

> My bitter disappointment at finding not only that the avenue was closed but that it was quite impossible even to discuss it with you, made my manner towards you disrespectful. I am extremely sorry to have given you pain for I repeat that I am constantly sensible of your great kindness to me in other ways.[4]

Trevelyan's exclusion from the management of his father's estates meant that he was obliged to think more seriously than he otherwise would have about his political future.

The General Election that had returned Lloyd George to power at the head of an enormous coalition majority swept away the entire UDC representation in the House. The new Commons meeting in January 1919 was as different from any of its predecessors as that of 1906. 'Was there ever anything like it?' asked Ponsonby of Trevelyan. 'It is so bad that it makes me shout with laughter and, as my wife says, it is a compliment not to be elected to such a Parliament... The absence of any decent opposition in the House, of any men of weight and experience is very serious... But of course, the thing cannot last because it is a sham.'[5]

Sham or no, the UDC leaders — Ponsonby, MacDonald, Morel and

Trevelyan — had now to set about arranging their political affairs so that at the next contest they might be better suited. The prospect of Trevelyan fighting a successful campaign in Elland was remote. 'Dear Comrade,' one of his Labour supporters had written immediately after the election, 'I don't know your intentions but I expect you will try your fortunes elsewhere. Prejudice here will take long years to die down and searching for better luck in another constituency will not have the handicap of such ignorance to fight and face down.'[6] Trevelyan needed a new constituency but he was determined it should be a North country seat.

In June 1919, members of the Newcastle Independent Labour Party met to choose their candidates for the next election. Replying to a request that he be nominated, Trevelyan wrote:

> I am ready, if a favourable opportunity offers itself, to stand for Parliament... I do not yet know the circumstances of the Newcastle seats and I could give no *final* reply without knowing which seat was in contemplation... But, if a strong wish for me to accept nomination is expressed I should hope to find that I could comply with that desire. Even at this stage I must express my keen appreciation of the honour done me by those comrades who wish to put my name forward for consideration.[7]

These expressions of enthusiasm for the 'honour' done him, and the salutation and conclusion of the letter 'Dear Comrade', and 'Yours fraternally' — were not insincere gestures, the 'great man' demonstrating his 'common touch'. Trevelyan was genuinely excited and involved by his adoption into the Labour movement. As he wrote to a friend, Eleanor Acland, 'I find the ILP quite enormously the most congenial organisation I have ever worked with — more camaraderie and less jealousy.' His desire to be elected to Parliament as a Labour member contained nothing of condescension. He did not suppose — as many another ex-Liberal did — that in joining Labour he could, by heredity, education and experience, supply a superior leadership that by common consent it presently lacked. Labour might want for leaders, but then, so did all the other parties. 'They have proved themselves totally incapable of leadership during the war and are worse still after it. It is only by the growth of a new conscience and policy *from below* that partial righteousness may be restored to the world.' As far as Trevelyan was concerned, hope for the future lay not in great leaders but 'the common people..., and they will use the Labour party'. Labour, like the other parties suffered from poor leaders. But for Trevelyan ultimately that was of little significance, 'since the party is democratic'. And to prove the point, Trevelyan quoted 'some amusing evidence of this I have just had'.

This afternoon [24 May 1919] I went to a Labour Conference in Newcastle

— one thousand delegated from the Tyne TU Adamson* came down and made, as he would, a stupid speech wearying them with irrelevance and feebleness. No one, except himself, regarded him as a leader. They were frankly bored. The moment his back was turned they went to business in a good series of vigorous speeches and a sharp discussion on 'direct action', and whether there ought to be a strike against the Russian War and Conscription.[8]

In June, Trevelyan received a letter from W.E. Moll, chairman of the Labour Party for the Central division of Newcastle.

With you as candidate for Central, we should have an added advantage that you would be able to make an appeal to the small business ward, St. Nicholas, which a Trade Unionist candidate could not do, as well as securing the working class vote in the three larger wards... The Liberals did not fight the division at the last election and if you were known to be in the field I do not think they would intervene.[9]

Arrangements moved smoothly to the desired conclusion. In July Trevelyan was unanimously elected a member of the Central Branch of Newcastle ILP. In September, by 66 votes to 28, he was nominated Labour candidate for Newcastle Central.

Trevelyan might well have taken the rest from national and international political issues that his labours during the war had earned. But release from his parliamentary duties meant he could give more time to other activities. He travelled in Europe, frequently in Germany and France, talking with the people as much as to professional politicians, seeing for himself the havoc wrought by war and the political chaos engendered by the peace settlement. He continued his work for the UDC, acting as editor for the Union's monthly journal, *Foreign Affairs*, whenever Morel was absent. And always, there was a vast private correspondence to conduct with friends and acquaintances. During the war it had been his task to help banish the uncertainties and misgivings of long-serving Liberals who could not readily admit the possibility that their party leaders might be wrong. Despite his own inclinations in the matter — 'I am not making any special effort to drag my friends over at once into the Labour party'[10] — inevitably he was obliged to explain why he of all people, born, reared and educated in the Liberal tradition, twenty years a Liberal MP, and perhaps most significantly, a leading member of the land owning class, should have chosen to join the Labour party.

When Trevelyan set himself the task of explaining to a wider public the reasons for his conversion, the book he wrote was in no sense an apologia. The

*When Arthur Henderson resigned from the leadership of the parliamentary Labour party to devote his energies to reorganising the party machine, William Adamson of the Scottish Miners was elected Chairman and leader in Henderson's place. With Henderson's defeat in the election, the innocuous Adamson retained his place until succeeded by J.R. Clynes in February 1921.

spirit in which *From Liberalism to Labour* was conceived and written, is contained in the very first sentence. 'My appeal is to those who can expect great changes without apprehension.' Should anyone question the need for change, Trevelyan spelled it out and explained why change would succeed. 'Great experiments are possible in a society where the existing order is patently bankrupt.'[11] His criticisms of the failures of Liberalism were not designed to win converts to Labour by persuasion or patient argument so much as by main force. Liberalism had been abandoned during the war; Asquith had surrendered Free Trade; conscription had been introduced without consultation, the ancient liberties of speech and person had not been defended but made questions of Government toleration. In its foreign policy, Liberalism was indistinguishable from reactionary Imperialism. At least for this part of his thesis Trevelyan won the support of Lord Loreburn.

> The older 'Liberal' party to which I belonged, is hopelessly destroyed and fit only to be burnt out of existence... Our opinions have been betrayed by Asquith, Grey and Haldane... The one thing needed at present is to expose and ruin the chances of these imposters to get into power again... So, I wholly sympathise with your leaving the so called 'Liberal' party.

But for Loreburn as with many another Liberal, it was one thing to deny the Liberal party, quite another (because their view was essentially negative) to suppose it was wise to join the Labour party.

> It is in the main sound on foreign policy. But it has no men of high educa-tion and ideals to lead it, and the Labour members have been, as a whole, also defective in practical wisdom. They are as much responsible as anyone for the triumph of Imperialism. They are like Thomas and Henderson, will-ing to shout with the noisiest crowd. And their domestic policy is idiotic. Merely a copy of the old nihilist and Bolshevik creed, which would mean civil war on top of our other misfortunes. There is not one, except perhaps Smillie and Snowden who would shrink at any degree of Communism if the asses and sheep of the rank and file make enough noise. They are de-voted to their imaginary class interests as are the propertied classes to theirs.[12]

Loreburn's sentiments were very familiar. Trevelyan was often accused by former political associates that his joining Labour was 'really changing sides in a social war. If either side is victorious in that war,' wrote Sir John Fry, 'it can only be at a great loss. Surely, there must be some other way...?'[13] But Trevelyan was quite unmoved by any thought of 'the great privation, even ruin, for individuals of his class', when 'the present system caused even greater privation and a greater ruin to the people. Vague aspirations are not the slightest use unless materialised in a reforming policy. Perfectly selfish standards now control the world. The question which everyone has to face is whether these standards will not continue to control the world as long as the basis of industry is self seeking and not cooperation.'[14]

What kind of domestic policy was Trevelyan proposing that would institute the 'great transition to the cooperative commonwealth' where 'the class and economic inequalities that had ceased to be tolerable to an educated proletariat' would be eradicated? He proposed the nationalisation of the land, the railways and the mines, a capital levy to remove the burden of the war debt, free secondary education and free access for all classes to the universities. This he described as a 'minimum' Socialist programme. It was hardly a manifesto to conjure visions of revolution, or make timid individuals fear for their lives or their investments. Why then the exaggerated opposition of those who claimed Trevelyan was playing Judas to his class and England's fortunes? Trevelyan claimed that he had done no more than recognise an inevitable historical tide that others, for selfish reasons, refused to acknowledge. Many of the middle class failed to see because they were 'too ill-instructed and had been taught not to think during the war. The terrible failure of the Liberal leaders,' he wrote to Eleanor Acland, 'is that they have been the direct agents of this obscuring of the political intellect and conscience of our people instead of the enlightening guides to a democratic policy... As a doubtful generalisation I should say that the mass conscience of the upper and middle class has vanished altogether for the time.'[15] A few years later, in the preface to Harold Langshaw's book, *Socialism and the historic function of Liberalism,* he wrote:

> Liberalism..., has never dared to lead fearlessly against modern industrial society. It stammers, and has stammered all my political life. I never could get in the Liberal party a full-blooded condemnation of our economic system and the direct intention to replace it by another... The Labour party exists to reorganise economic society. The Liberal party does it against the grain. That is why all social reformers are all bound to gravitate, as I have done, to Labour.[16]

Examine Trevelyan's claim and even without indulging in the benefits of hind-sight, it is clear that his political metamorphosis had required him to shed little of his Liberalism save that party's name, and loyalty to a leadership that had betrayed its trust. 'Faith in Democracy, belief in Free Trade, love of personal freedom, respect for national liberties, are all part of the Labour creed. The Labour party is, indeed, the safest custodian of these cherished Liberal principles.' The conclusion to the argument was obvious. 'As there is no fundamental antagonism between a Radical and a Socialist, the process of cooperation will continue. I believe that ordinary Englishmen care very little under what name they get the article which they require.' [17]

This last was typical of Trevelyan. Strip his writing of the obvious party polemics and it remains futile to seek sophisticated arguments. He wrote from the heart to the heart. The strength of his arguments lay not in any subtle dialectic but a simple (one might say without injustice, naïve), unselfish honesty of purpose. Most interestingly, though his vision was of the future, he sought justification for it by reaching back — as one would expect of a Radical — to W ̣E. Gladstone! It was no accident that the repeated refrain in *From Liberalism to Labour*, was the paramount need, 'by bold and necessary strokes to again let loose the moral forces of the world', a theme he best illustrated by his criticism of British policy towards Ireland and Russia.

For Trevelyan, Ireland's misery was because it had been left to the mercy of British reactionaries, to pine more hopeless than ever before under military repression. The Irish had not been granted Home Rule, yet 'the men on whom Gladstone's mantle had fallen uttered no single protest against Ireland having been denied the right of self-determination'. In effect, Trevelyan believed the Government had sponsored violence and imposed on the Irish a 'White Terror'. The first act of any Labour Government would be to remove the Army and the hated Black and Tans. They were a menace, not only to civil order in Ireland, but to the rest of the United Kingdom, for they were 'practiced in all the arts of suppressing a civilian population'. Socialists alone would make self-determination a reality in Ireland, and thus expose 'the failure of British Imperialism; hundreds of years of racial coercion culminating in chaos and brutality after the long farce of killing Home Rule with kindness'. There was no reason, save the greed and brutality of the British Government, why Ireland should not be 'free and friendly, unarmed and under the protection of the League of Nations'. This 'bold stroke' (as without exaggeration, Trevelyan described it), would 'proclaim to the world that a new spirit had come into the greatest of democracies'.

Much more controversial than his view of the Irish situation was Trevelyan's notorious sympathy for Soviet Russia. Of all Trevelyan's political infatuations, his love of Russia and his exaggerated expectations of that country's revolution in terms of world peace as well as political and economic freedom for the Russian people, caused his former political allies to pour opprobrium upon his ideas, and accuse him of wanting to destroy Britain in the holocaust of revolution. They completely misunderstood Trevelyan's conception because they tested his ideas against their own prejuduces and apprehensions. At Versailles, in Ireland, in its attitude to the Russian revolutionaries, Trevelyan perceived common manifestations of the British Government's shameless and relentless will to serve the forces of reaction. Far from being bent on encouraging civil strife and revolution in England, Trevelyan believed that only by re-cognising the new Russia could the forces of reaction be routed peaceably in Britain. And more, 'such a policy would reverse the whole of the Versailles Treaty'. That Russia's fortunes were central to Trevelyan's total view of the European political situation may be judged from a letter he wrote to his friend, Prince Max of Baden, early in 1922:

The middle class in England are not recovering the political standards or capacity for moral indignation which they showed in Gladstone's time, and the Liberal leaders are not the men to arouse it. They fail to stop the unspeakable atrocities of our present oppression of Ireland, which rivals Radetsky's performances in Italy. Far less are they capable of remedying the more distant and complicated atrocities of the peace treaties and the economic oppression of central Europe. The power in Great Britain is and will at present remain in the hands of the militarist sections who have no mercy and who are chiefly bent on the suppression of Russia. That is why the emancipation of Germany depends on the complete defeat of the anti-Soviet Crusade... The defeat of the Russian policy of the Allies, complete peace with Russia, the recognition that every country may do exactly what it likes with its own internal economy is the condition precedent of any improvement in the general situation. *The bullies of Germany and the bullies of Russia are in France and Britain the same people.*[18]

Trevelyan was never a Communist. He did not suppose that the Communist analysis of the ills of society was accurate or its remedies relevant. A determinist theory, or for that matter, any theory that did not recognise England's particular character, needs and disposition, had no appeal for him. If others chose to believe him a revolutionary, a Bolshevik; supposed that his internationalism precluded a deep love for England and much that was peculiarly English, then that was their mistake not his. He really could not be bothered to refute the wilder assertions of 'retired majors and the worst sort of product of the public school system'. As to Communists in the Labour party, he clearly indicated his attitude in letters to his wife during the ILP conference in 1921 when the proposal to join the Third International had been turned down by an 'immense majority'. He then wrote of the Communists;

> ... they are being obstructive. It is very interesting to see how the revolutionary spirit works. My own feeling is that, though they are extremist wreckers of the type of the French Revolution, they don't make much impression on the British character. I feel certain that whatever harm they may do to the smooth working of the Labour movement they will never dominate it, nor indeed get a great deal of power in England. The patience of British people is very great. It is a practical quality of superlative value.[19]

His attitude had undergone no fundamental change from that shown during the Syndicalist troubles a decade earlier. He interpreted the Communist failure in 1921 as an expression of British Labour's intention;

> (1) to work out our own salvation in our own way and not at the dictation of Lenin as to our methods; (2) that we do not intend to spend our time talking about preparing civil war instead of persuading people to become Socialists. The Communists will probably break off and most of them won't be a very great loss.[20]

Since his adoption as Labour candidate for Newcastle Central, Trevelyan had fretted to be back once more near the centre of the nation's affairs at Westminster. In September and October 1922, Lloyd George and his associates, hopelessly misconstruing a problem of middle-eastern politics, sought to fight a general election on a coalition ticket. This plan was frustrated by the obduracy and suspicion felt for Lloyd George, not by the leaders of the Conservative party, but its backbenchers, and in particular, the then little known Stanley Baldwin. The Conservatives, meeting at the Carlton Club, determined they would fight the election as a separate party. Lloyd George was done for. He resigned, never again to hold office. Andrew Bonar Law was elected Tory Leader and Prime Minister. He promised tranquillity to the people of Britain. But with Lloyd George and his followers bent upon revenge for their injuries; the Asquithian Liberals, rejoicing at the Welshman's downfall yet intent on pulling down the Tories; and Labour vociferous as ever in its claim for recognition, for politicians at least, Law's assumption of office was a prelude to increased conflict.

Trevelyan could look forward with some confidence to his own electoral contest. It would be a three cornered fight, but there had been considerable dissension within the Liberal camp. Many Liberals declared their intention to vote for Trevelyan. Trevelyan's agent, Walter Percival, had geared the constituency organisation to the highest pitch of readiness. 'We are in great fettle here,' wrote Trevelyan with obvious pride. 'My people are working and we had a magnificent start off.'[21] In the poorest quarters of his constituency, along the steep banks of the Tyne and where the houses tumbled one above the other in the sloping, mean streets below Scotswood Road, they were Trevelyan supporters to a man. They roared for 'Wor Charlie' and for his 'missus', who canvassed if not so noisily, just as energetically as her husband. Central Division was the cockpit of Newcastle politics, and in the Labour Committee rooms in Diana Street they were convinced they had the best candidate, the best candidate's wife, and the best agent. Such confidence was not to be denied. When the poll was declared, Trevelyan was a clear winner and Central Newcastle was a Labour gain.

> C.P. Trevelyan 13,709
> Sir G. Redwick (Con). 8,639
> J. Dodd (Lib) 2,923
> Labour majority over Conservative 5,070

Trevelyan's pride and pleasure in the Labour party's achievement, lit a note he sent his brother Robert a few days later.

It was a glorious win smashing both Toryism and Liberalism. On the Tyne, Liberalism is dead. In Northumberland and Durham, *not one seat*. Yet in 1906, 1910, 1910, there was no Tory seat in Northumberland, I think 6

Liberal and 2 Labour (both by leave of the Liberals). Now there are 6 Labour and 4 Conservative. Runciman, Barnes and Denman, three first class candidates, absolutely nowhere. A new power has arisen. You should have seen the drive of the new force. 22 men canvassing every night for a fortnight. I never saw anything like it at Elland.[22]

The election had given Bonar Law and the Tories with 345 seats, a comfortable majority over the two Liberal groups and Labour combined. With 142 members and a 30 per cent share of the total votes cast, Labour became the major opposition party. Within the parliamentary Labour party, to Trevelyan's particular satisfaction, the ILP group had immeasurably increased its influence. Trevelyan was more than content to be back in the Commons which, perhaps because of the number of Labour colleagues, appeared altogether more friendly and attractive than it had done but a few years earlier. 'I have,' he told his mother, 'quite a different feeling about the House now to what I had. Perhaps I am no longer in awe of it?... I am not nearly as bored as I used to be with the prospect of the long months in London.'[23]

Bonar Law's period as Prime Minister was soon cut short by his fatal illness. In May 1923 Stanley Baldwin, raised from comparative obscurity but a few months earlier, became Tory leader and Prime Minister. Baldwin's inheritance from Law was no political sinecure. In the face of chronic problems; in Europe, the vexed question of German reparations; at home, the worsening unemployment situation; Baldwin decided there could be no other remedy than Tariff Reform. The ghost of Joseph Chamberlain once more was given substance. In November, Baldwin requested that Parliament be dissolved for yet another election, and the King reluctantly acceded. To Trevelyan, like many another 'progressive', Baldwin's move seemed a manoeuvre designed to take advantage of the unemployed; nothing more than a 'stunt' to strengthen the manufacturers more easily to fleece the home consumer. 'It is a clever dodge,' Trevelyan wrote to his father, 'to score before the people are ready. But clever dodges are seldom finally profitable.'[24] Perhaps the most significant fact of Baldwin's announcement was that the two wings of the Liberal party rushed into reunion. The prospect of power was certainly a wonderful incentive to that particular marriage of convenience, though inevitably the hasty consummation was given the requisite polite moral overtones.

For Trevelyan, the Liberal threat to divide the 'progressive' vote which had been of little significance in his constituency in the previous election, this time was altogether removed. It was to be a straight fight between himself and a Tory candidate, F.M.B. Fisher. The campaign was fought with a commendable restraint on both sides to eschew personalities and concentrate upon policies. At the count, it soon became clear that Trevelyan's handsome majority of the year before had been seriously eroded. Molly, standing anxiously watching, was approached by Fisher. He declared in a blasé manner, 'Well, I think it's a majority of about five hundred.' She dared not ask him on which side the majority lay.[25]　In fact, though Trevelyan's vote fell by more than a thousand, and the Tory vote rose by almost three thousand, labour retained the seat.

> C.P. Trevelyan 12,447
> F.M.B. Fisher 11,260
> Labour majority 1,187

Though the Labour Party increased its vote in the 1923 General Election by little more than 100,000, Labour MPs in the Commons rose from 144 to 191. Labour was the second party in the House, for, while the Liberals polled an almost identical number of votes, they received 158 seats. The Tories, with 258 seats remained the single largest party. In these circumstances, it was the Liberal choice either to keep the Tories in power, or defeat them and offer Labour a first opportunity to form an Administration. In a letter written during the election, Trevelyan had asked MacDonald whether he would contemplate a coalition with the Liberals, a course Trevelyan did not favour. MacDonald affirmed there was no question of a coalition, adding, 'We shall certainly take office if the opportunity presents itself.'[26]

Baldwin did not choose to resign immediately after the election, but met the House and was defeated on a Labour censure motion that the Liberals supported. The next day, 22 January 1924, the King summoned MacDonald to the Palace. He was sworn of the Privy Council and requested to form a Government. MacDonald assured the King that all his colleagues fully realised the great responsibility they were about to assume. Though they might be inexperienced in governing, nevertheless, they were honest and sincere men. The King was not to upset himself because of George Lansbury's public reminder of the unfortunate fate that had befallen Charles I; nor would the Labour Government's diplomatic recognition of Russia be allowed to cause His Majesty undue offence. Thus mollified, and somewhat reassured that his Government would not be a collection of raging Bolsheviks and republicans, the King wrote in his diary '[MacDonald] wishes to do the right thing'.[27]

During December, in a period of comparative calm and isolation at Lossiemouth, MacDonald had considered those whom he should, and more importantly, could invite to form an Administration. He alone of the Labour leadership at that time had the capacity to create a Government; only he had the contacts allowing him to call on the services of Liberals, and even Tories, to buttress and complete an agglomeration of working class trade unionists, middle class intellectuals, and upper class idealists. Even more than in the making of most Cabinets, there had been the wildest speculation (as much among likely contenders for office as in the press) concerning MacDonald's final choice of colleagues. While confidently expecting an offer of some sort, Trevelyan had no idea what he would be given. He had no prejudice as to the disposition of posts, save grave concern at the rumour, retailed to him by Ponsonby, that Jimmy Thomas would be offered the Foreign Office. Like Trevelyan's fears for his own fate, — the offer of the 'dull' Presidency of the Board of Trade, or worse to be fobbed off with the Governorship of some Colony — this rumour proved unfounded. After a meeting with MacDonald he was able to report to Molly, 'Well, I no longer have only six children — I have six million.' He was to be President of the Board of Education with a seat in the Cabinet, 'the place he wanted above all others'.[28]

While MacDonald was at audience with the King, Trevelyan and his new colleagues waited upon the Prime Minister in his room at the Commons. Trevelyan did not record in the note he made at the time, what an unusual congéries they were. Their almost total inexperience of office excepted, they had so little in common that only the historical accident of the need to form a Labour Administration could have accounted for their association. The eagerness with which these first ministers engaged themselves in the endless intricacies and confusions attendant upon ceremonial and court etiquette; their tortured, conscience stricken resolution of sartorial conundrums (whether or not they ought to wear knee breeches) perhaps better than anything else in those first days indicated that their intent was to exist, to be respectable and accepted, rather than advertise themselves as the harbingers of a new order that would plant a revolutionary, red Jerusalem in England's green and pleasant land. But the cautious subscription to policies that would not offend tradition was, in practical political terms, the essence of their leader's singular conception of Socialism.

In the early years of his joining Labour, the euphoria induced by a real feeling of comradeship caused Trevelyan to discard his usual circumspection, and he allowed MacDonald a place in his pantheon of political heroes. In July 1923, comparing Stanley Baldwin, for whom he always retained a high personal regard, with MacDonald, he wrote:

> I am beginning to think we have now got the finest men heading the two main political parties that there have been in my time. Baldwin is simple, MacDonald subtle. But they both say the very genuine things they think instead of hedging and concealing. It is such a comfort after the disingenuousness of Lloyd George, the indifference of Balfour and the insipid precision of Asquith.[29]

Experience of MacDonald as Prime Minister was to temper, then alter that first impression. Trevelyan might have been more cautious in his estimate had he thought more of his war time experience of MacDonald in the Union of Democratic Control. Then, there always had been difficulties in getting

MacDonald to move on any issue. Usually others had to prepare everything beforehand and, at the last moment, shove MacDonald into the final act of execution.[30] It remained Trevelyan's opinion, however, long after his denunciation of MacDonald to the parliamentary Labour party, that only MacDonald could have formed the first Labour Administration. In 1924, MacDonald's 'intense dislike of doing anything unpleasant or decisive' was not immediately so important as were 'his few prejudices in regard to people' and 'his wide circle of friends'. These qualities, plus his being 'such a fine speaker..., well suited him for his task'. His 'fundamental inertia — an unwillingness to do anything unless forced to', matched the designated role of the minority Labour Government; 'the object of the exercise above all else was to demonstrate that Labour could carry on a Government'.[31]

From the beginning there were grumbles from sections of the Labour back benches. These criticisms arose from a confused mixture of thwarted idealism and an inability, because of their lack of parliamentary experience, to appreciate either long term stratagems or how much their leaders were in thrall to the Liberals. They were directed at the moderation and caution of Labour's legislative programme. Like their leaders, the back benchers found themselves without power. For them, however, there was not the compensation of office.

Trevelyan's appointment as a Minister had particularly pleased his father. Pride in his son's enhancement of a family tradition of high public office helped him to ignore, if not entirely forget, that his eldest son's allegiance to Labour's cause had been at the cost of 'deserting' Liberalism. There was another consideration to the elder man's advantage. He now had an ideal opportunity to indulge fully a constitutional disposition to play Nestor. Though wise enough not to give political advice to his eldest son, nevertheless he could draw without reserve, and often to some point, upon his vast store of parliamentary anecdotes, retelling stories from a past that to him was almost more real that the present. On receiving news of Trevelyan's appointment he wrote:

It is a very great advantage indeed in any genuine and important office, to go to a department the working of which you familiarly know. It is a saving to time, and a source of confidence and comfort, which no one can imagine who has not experienced it, and likewise experienced its opposite. To be the one man in a great office who knows nothing about the processes and the one man who has to make the decisions, is a most bewildering business. My father, even, felt it, and said that in his first fortnight at the Treasury he saw the snakes coming out of the papers in his dreams at night. Well, you have as long a family tradition of official work to keep up as George has of book-writing, and I have no doubt you will do it worthily.[32]

Not only was Trevelyan familiar with the routines of the Board of Education, but born into the traditional ruling class, educated and trained for a political career, unlike many another member of the Government, he was never in awe of his civil servants. He was fortunate, however, that his advisors proved, without exception, enthusiastic and cooperative. In short, after many frustrations and disappointments in his past political fortunes, Trevelyan found office a delight. That pleasure more than compensated for the arduous duties and the necessarily long periods when he was separated from his family and his beloved Northumberland. In his daily letters to Molly the constant refrain without complaint became, 'I am enormously busy.'[33]

To have charge of the Board of Education gave Trevelyan a particular advantage over almost all his Cabinet colleagues. The party counted education among its highest priorities. The improvement of educational standards and opportunities was not only a moral obligation, but had considerable electoral implications for the future. As Haldane informed readers of *The Encyclopaedia of the Labour Movement*, the party

> ... must be content with nothing short of a high level in mental training and it must take..., such interest as a Party in the effort to reach that level as to ensure that it is going to work without rest if without haste. Unless it does this, it will in the end be judged hardly by that public opinion which it desires to win to its side.[34]

The Fabian cadences of this statement by the Labour Lord Chancellor reflected the opinions he had held consistently for more than a quarter of a century. Similarly, Trevelyan as a Labour Minister did not need to make any particular change in his attitudes from those he had shown when a junior minister at the Board in the Liberal Administration before the war. In 1910, supporting J.H. Whitehouse, he had argued that poor parents should have the same opportunities as those of the upper classes to insist on their children's continued education by keeping them at school.[35] In 1926, Trevelyan was writing that the essence of Labour's educational policies was to claim 'as good a chance for the children of the workers as for the children of the well-to-do'.[36]

Secondary Education for All, written by R.H. Tawney, was published by the Labour Party in 1922. Beatrice Webb claimed that Trevelyan's policies were largely made for him by Tawney, but there is no direct evidence to support this.[37] Tawney's book proposed the expansion of secondary education, the abolition of fee paying and the raising of the school leaving age. All this was to be a gradual but certain process so that 'what [was] weak in the higher education of the country should be strengthened, and what [was] already excellent would be made accessible to all'.[38] Statutory powers already existed to achieve most of these aims. The provisions of the Fisher Education Act of 1918 had been halted not revoked by the 'Geddes Axe'. In his ten months as

Minister, Trevelyan relaxed the conditions for the payment of state grants; restored state scholarships; increased the proportion of free places in secondary schools; increased maintenance allowances for pupils at secondary schools; tripled the adult education grant; and local authorities were encouraged and empowered to raise the school leaving age to fifteen. There would have been more, certainly a national scheme for raising the school leaving age, had there been time, and had there been the money.

Two examples illustrate the kind of problem Trevelyan faced in this period of office. Raising the school leaving age was an almost total failure. Only a few local authorities were bold enough to submit schemes for approval and implementation. This was understandable as many authorities who otherwise might have raised the leaving age, refused to do so fearing they might deprive their children of work which would be taken by fourteen year olds from neighbouring, less progressive, areas. Trevelyan did not need the Association of Education Committees to tell him that his piecemeal proposal was unsatisfactory. But, as the lack of money made a national scheme impossible, the alternative was to encourage local authorities to act upon their own initiative. One important lesson was learnt from this abortive exercise: Labour would be effective in the field of education only when it controlled local as well as central government.

Trevelyan's proposals concerning the introduction and extension of grammar school places proved the only subject that roused the other political parties to censure him. Eustace Percy for the Tories, and H.A.L. Fisher for the Liberals, castigated Trevelyan for a mistaken sense of priorities. Fisher argued that the payment of fees gave parents the satisfaction of feeling that they had a stake in the fortunes of their child's school. Percy claimed that the abolition of fees would divert funds from the more necessary and urgent task of increasing the number of secondary school places. In fact, Trevelyan's scheme was a watered down version of the proposal made by his party's advisory committee on education that had asked for an immediate increase in free grammar school places from twenty five to forty per cent. To encourage more free places, after prolonged discussions with the Treasury, Trevelyan had managed to establish that any free place above the twenty five per cent minimum would attract a special government grant of £3. It did not matter how strongly Trevelyan favoured any particular scheme, or the enthusiasm and the weight of argument with which he was urged to action by his advisory committee; the hurdle that had first to be surmounted was Treasury approval. If Trevelyan had charge of the nation's education, Philip Snowden controlled the nation's purse strings, and the Chancellor would always have the final say.

If not in physical stature, by disposition Snowden was a 'Gladstonian' Chancellor of the Exchequer. The policy of social reforms he had preached throughout his life, he was determined would rest on the foundation of a

C.P. Trevelyan, President of the Board of Education, c. 1930

balanced budget and a rigorously controlled economy. Trevelyan considered Snowden 'probably the ablest man in the Government', 'admirable to do business with', as he was 'always prepared to listen to suggestions and give a clear and prompt decision upon them'. Because of his personal disposition to be as generous towards education as he counted financially prudent, Snowden 'agreed to expenditure on education probably more easily than on almost any other item'.[39] An advantage Trevelyan's plans shared with John Wheatley's for housing, was the expenditure would be spread over a period of years. But in public Trevelyan wished to give the impression that his plans were lavish. A rather too enthusiastic account in the *Labour Magazine* not only set the press 'considerably agog about [his] policy', but made Snowden 'a little alarmed' at Trevelyan's advertisement of what seemed excessive spending. The facts were very different, as Trevelyan recorded in a letter to his wife. 'I pointed out..., that he [Snowden] had sanctioned everything. He said he thought that the collective effect gave an impression of immense expenditure. I said I was sorry but that he must forgive the rhetoric.'[40]

Trevelyan scarce put a foot wrong in his first period as President of the Board of Education. After his unhappy experience during the war, and then the period out of the Commons, it took almost five years before he could claim he had 'ceased entirely to be afraid of speaking'[41] to the House. He admitted that for a long time, addressing the Commons was a 'fearful event', rather than the 'cheerful exertion' Rosebery had claimed the 'ordeal' to be. [42] Nevertheless, his first speech as Minister was a considerable success, and won a hard earned accolade from his father.

We had a very warm and fraternal letter of satisfaction from George this morning. He says it is held to be the best performance from the Ministerial bench this Session. The *first* speech in Parliament is an ordeal and a terror to the speaker, but the House almost likes a certain sort of failure, which it regards as something of a compliment to its own terrors. But the first, first-class speech from a leading Minister is the most vital event of his career. It fixes on him, and ought to fix, a certain received character which the House accepts, and which dominates all his relations to Parliament from that time forward, and cannot be changed except by something of a moral miracle on his part, or a political convulsion around him.[43]

Trevelyan's success was not limited to the House. He had always enjoyed public speaking outside Westminster, and, despite the pressure of his work as a Minister, he was much in demand and rarely refused the opportunity to address audiences anywhere in the country. He was the first President of the Board to speak at the annual conference of the National Union of Teachers creating as much good will by his presence as by his announcement that the economies imposed by Geddes were to be ended. He wrote to Molly of his'

... triumphant time with the NUT... There was a huge meeting of about 2000 or more, all teachers. They all stood up and clapped and cheered when I got up. They cheered again when I sat down. It was a remarkable ovation. They were entirely pleased with my speech... There never has been a Pres. of the Bd. there before. So it was a great and unique event, apart from the odour of sanctity in which I exist at present. [44]

Two days later, Trevelyan enjoyed an equally enthusiastic reception at the ILP congress. His speech, he told Molly, gave him as much as his audience 'great satisfaction'. [45]

Molly, who really enjoyed her new position as a Minister's wife, whenever possible accompanied Trevelyan to public functions. During the Parliamentary session they had always entertained on an extensive scale. In July 1923, for instance, Trevelyan calculated that in the course of a year they had given 134 dinners; 85 lunches; 131 teas; 248 parties making a grand total of 598'. [46] Now, to Molly's delight if not her husband's, their formal entertaining considerably increased. Shortly after Trevelyan became a Minister, however, Molly was taken seriously ill, and her necessarily long convalescence did not end much before the fall of the Labour Government. It was a cruel blow to her ambitious social plans for which she more than compensated during Trevelyan's second period in office. Trevelyan valued their dinners and parties for the opportunity afforded to encourage younger politicians. As one of the relatively few Labour members who was a seasoned Commons campaigner, he was always ready, if asked, to give advice on the peculiar ways of the House. Thus, he did much to increase the morale and enhance the effectiveness of many young, inexperienced recruits to Labour's parliamentary ranks. [47]

Trevelyan, Wheatley and Jowett formed a triumvirate within the Cabinet who would have preferred to have seen the Government attempt more ambitious policies. The difficulty was that not all the members of the parliamentary Labour party were Socialists. If a few believed in Socialism, less were competent to work out the details of a Socialist, legislative programme. But in 1924, it was not Labour's political philosophy that was on trial, but the parliamentary party's capacity, for a strictly limited period, to form and maintain an administration. It was enough that a Labour Government should exist. One tentative step at a time towards the abyss of the unknown has always been the temper of British politics. Despite the rhetoric, the hopes, the impatient idealism, convention dictated that in office Labour was to play, not the bold swashbuckling pirate, but the timorous young bride. Trevelyan understood the hopes of back benchers who pressed for more aggressive and ambitious policies, but his days and thoughts were fully occupied with the problems and plans of his own department. Unlike MacDonald, however, he understood the reason for back bench frustration even if he did not altogether approve of the way that frustration sometimes showed itself. The satisfactions of office certainly induced patience.

Outside the Board of Education, Trevelyan concerned himself most with the Liberal party's future prospects as that might affect Labour's electoral fortunes. Labour remained in power, maintained for the most part* by Liberal votes in the House. Yet Labour never attempted to court Liberal favour. In the House, by a mixture of ill-mannered and incompetent behaviour, the Labour whips made life almost impossible for their Liberal counterparts. In by elections, even those Radical Liberals who were well disposed towards Labour were challenged. This effectively handed safe Liberal seats to the Tories. Intent upon forcing the Liberals as quickly as possible into the political wilderness, Labour discounted the immediate advantage this gave to the Conservatives. The enthusiasts were convinced that the Liberals were 'about to be snuffed out of existence'. Trevelyan doubted the immediacy of that prospect though he foresaw 'no *great* future for the Liberals'.[48] Even allowing for the Attorney General's political inexperience that first drew the hornets' nest of Campbell's case about the Government's ears, the handling of the subsequent parliamentary crisis suggests Labour's main motive was to create the maximum of embarrassment for the Liberals.

Just before Parliament had risen for the Summer recess, J.R. Campbell, editor of the Communist paper, *Worker's Weekly*, was arrested on a charge of incitement to mutiny by the publication of two articles. These had ended with the traditional revolutionary rhetorical appeal to the Army not to shoot down their fellow workers but to turn their weapons upon their common oppressors. Sir Patrick Hastings, having first indicated that the Government supported Campbell's arrest and prosecution, a few days later asked for his discharge. The Tories raised the cry of political interference with the course of justice, and when Parliament reassembled after the recess, they tabled a motion of censure. From the first, the Liberals had opposed Campbell's prosecution. Hoping to avoid defeat for the Government on the censure vote (Asquith could hardly support Labour, and yet for financial and political reasons he did not want an election), the Liberal leader moved for the appointment of a Select Committee to examine the whole issue. The ploy did not succeed. Labour, intent upon Liberal destruction, and not unaware of the advantage of being defeated on the Campbell issue rather than on its policy towards Soviet Russia which had run into serious difficulties, rushed lemming-like towards the precipice of dissolution. Trevelyan chronicled the race in his daily letters to Molly.

2 October:.... The party is full of beans and the Liberals very unbeany... The Liberals are riding for a fall and the only question is how soon we give it them. I think we may fairly expect to be in an election in a week or two.

*On 18 March 1924 it had been Tory votes that had saved the Labour Government when the Liberals divided the House against the proposal to speed up naval replacements.

But that no doubt will be decided within a few hours.

6 October: It looks to me mightily like an election. In any case I don't think we shall survive Wednesday [8 October]. But no one knows. We had a two hours Cabinet — rather excited — but very friendly with a very thorough discussion.

Ramsay will make a speech which will take things a stage further tomorrow. We have made up our minds to take both motions, Tory and Liberal, as they were meant, i.e. as Votes of Censure. If the Liberals acquiesce, it will be a very long climb down, too long for them to undertake I think...

7 October: Ramsay made a magnificent as well as skilful speech today. I think our defeat in some form or other is inevitable tomorrow. But who can tell? The Liberals are desperately anxious to get out of it.

8 October: So — we are beaten. Tomorrow Ramsay asks for a dissolution. Probably the King will give it, as probably no one else could form a Government to stay in. The Tories I think, all along must have intended to bring us down. They voted for the Liberal amendment to make sure. The Liberals looked liked whipped dogs. The Tories hardly cheered at all. Our people cheered vociferously. I never saw more hangdog victors.

There was a large crowd, mainly Labour men outside, cheering almost continuously. As I came out of the gate 'Good old Trevelyan' and a lot of cheering. There is no doubt..., that our people think no end of their chances. Money is the lack. I don't know how far it will injure us.[49]

Lack of finance was to be a concern of the Liberal party; but Labour in the 1924 election had to contend with a more unique problem.

In his own constituency, Trevelyan had no particular worries. The party workers were enthusiastic and the electoral machinery was well oiled by frequent use. Trevelyan's status had been enormously enhanced by his successes as President of the Board of Education. He did not lack for support in any quarter. One among many who wrote offering help was H.G. Wells.

With the accession of the Labour party to office, its possibilities in the propaganda of constructive ideas were necessarily subordinated to the give and take of administration and legislation, and its particular appeal to such supporters as myself disappeared. I had intended to take no part in the present very tiresome and unnecessary election. But I would like to make an exception, if I may, with regard to yourself. I think your work for education has been of outstanding value and that everyone who hopes for a happier, more civilized England should vote for you, irrespective of party associations. I have watched your proceedings with close interest and I am convinced that there has never been a better, more far sighted, harder working, and more unselfishly devoted Minister of Education than yourself.[50]

That was no bad testimonial for any man to receive.

As in the previous election, Trevelyan had a straight fight, and with the same Tory candidate, F.M.B. Fisher. The Central Newcastle division was not a solidly working class constituency and certain sections of the electorate, notably the ex-Liberal voters, might well have been persuaded to vote for Fisher. Trevelyan, while husbanding his Labour vote, wooed these Liberals. Indeed, there was little in Labour's governmental record to have caused concern to the traditional Liberal voter. Snowden's budget had been in the classic, Liberal, Free Trade mould. The single questionable area concerned Labour's policy towards Russia. Many wanted to believe that MacDonald and his colleagues were intent on handing over Britain and her empire to Lenin! The balance of electoral forces was fine, and in the heat of battle Trevelyan determined to discredit his opponent. He published information given him by New Zealand trade unionists that Fisher, when a Minister in that country before the war (despite his earlier pledges to the contrary), had enforced harsh Labour Laws. However, as the struggle for votes moved from issues to personalities, Fisher proved that he could give, if anything, better than he got.

> Mr. Trevelyan, who incidentally is under the Red Flag and is a great up-
> holder of the methods of the Soviet Government of Russia, in his extremity
> is compelled to resort to these methods... I am not the heir to a baronetcy,
> nor am I dependent upon means which I did not earn, but upon which
> my opponent is dependent for his existence. I am a self-made man, and I
> appeal to the electors..., to rely upon a worker rather than upon a drone.
> Even my opponents are not able to assert..., that I opposed my own
> country in the war, or that I ever flew the white feather or that I ever
> supported Bolshevism or German influence in the years 1914-18. [51]

But the noise of charge, counter-charge and insult between the rival candidates was as nothing compared with the furore stirred by the *Daily Mail* when four days before polling, in enormous and sensational headlines, it announced 'CIVIL WAR PLOT BY SOCIALISTS' MASTERS'. The so called Zinoviev Letter had been released by the Foreign Office.

The *Daily Mail's* violent political animus towards Labour was a matter of record, so the slanted and tendentious way in which it presented the news was to be expected. Of the two documents released by the Foreign Office, one purported to be a letter from Zinoviev, Secretary of the Communist International to the British Communist Party, urging them to undertake subversive activities in the Army and elsewhere. In a way, much more damaging was the second note from the Foreign Office to the Soviet *chargé-d'affaires* in London protesting at the Zinoviev letter but without expressing any reservations as to the authenticity of what was, in fact, a forgery. While MacDonald remained strangely silent on whether the letter was genuine (and by his evasiveness implied that it must be), Trevelyan, with a handful of other senior Labour colleagues, immediately attacked its authenticity. He declared it to be 'the usual white lie from Russia... I shall assume the letter is a fake until I know for certain.'[52] He had very good reason for taking this stand. Months earlier his friend George Young in an urgent letter had warned him 'that Crowe and Gregory had MacDonald mined'.* Even before Labour took office, Young had warned MacDonald repeatedly that 'he must have someone he could trust in charge of the private secretariat, of publicity, and of Russia'. MacDonald had ignored these warnings, in part undoubtedly because they were ascribed to Young's personal pique at his treatment by the diplomatic service. In the event, Young concluded, 'I let the vain man walk with wickedness to his own destruction... Cassandra was no doubt comforted for some inconvenience when the catastrophe came off according to prophesy.'[53]

Trevelyan was disliked by the permanent officials at the Foreign Office. They knew he suspected they exercised an undue influence upon MacDonald, who had taken on the almost impossible task of being both Prime Minister and Foreign Secretary. Also, Trevelyan's notorious opposition to the intelligence service, because its very *raison d'être* was an affront to his idealistic internationalism, made senior Foreign Office officials afraid that he would persuade MacDonald to dismantle the intelligence and foreign espionage services.

Within hours a myth grew about the Zinoviev letter. It was a stunt, engineered by the Foreign Office and the *Daily Mail* to trick Labour out of government. However, rather than the notorious Zinoviev letter, it was the Liberal decline and the unfair accidents of the British electoral system that determined Labour's fate in the 1924 election. Labour polled an extra million votes. In his constituency Trevelyan, like his opponent, increased his vote by a little more than two thousand, thus maintaining his majority at almost the same level as in December 1923.

C.P. Trevelyan 14,542
F.M.B. Fisher 13,646
Labour majority 896

Trevelyan wrote to his brother Robert: 'The Tories did their damndest in Newcastle and thought they had me out. But the poor never wavered. It is very hopeful for the future.'[54] Both Trevelyan's brothers, in the letters of congratulation they had sent him upon his re-election, recognised that the

---

*J.D. Gregory was Head of the Foreign Office, Northern Department. A fervent anti-Bolshevik he had been opposed to the Labour Government's policy of rapprochement with Russia. He was subsequently dismissed from the Foreign Office for currency speculation in 1928. Sir Eyre Crowe was Permanent Secretary at the Foreign Office. The ideal of the devoted British professional diplomat, though an anti-Bolshevik, he was better able to control his personal bias than Gregory.

crucial factor in his personal success had been his successful wooing of at least half the constituency's Liberal vote. In national terms, the demise of the Liberal party was, for George, a 'catastrophe... I have great distrust of both [Labour and Conservative parties] except when in leading strings to a middle party.'⁵⁵ Robert, on the other hand, thought it 'a great thing gained that the Liberals have been put out of the way. We shall have to now build up again with every hope of success.'⁵⁶ For the moment the Tories were triumphant. With less than fifty per cent of the total vote they had secured two thirds of the available seats with 419 members. Labour came next with 151, and the Liberals were left with a rump of forty, their leader, Asquith, banished to the Lords.

Trevelyan was pleased that the Liberals had done so badly, but he was convinced that the publication of the Zinoviev letter had seriously undermined Labour's fortunes. The whole incident had been handled as badly as possible, and a letter from Francis Hirst merely confirmed what already was Trevelyan's conviction. Hirst stated he would be 'utterly disgusted' if the Labour Cabinet 'timidly resign[ed] without probing the mystery and explaining it to Parliament'.

> I hope you will protest strongly against a hugger mugger. It's the biggest electoral swindle. I personally believe you were right in denouncing it boldly as a forgery. What has come over poor R. McD? The new Tory majority is I believe almost wholly due to the Bolshevik letter and it will be used against some good cause which you and I care for.⁵⁷

Labour did not resign straight away. At a stormy cabinet meeting, over which MacDonald soon lost control, Parmoor, enthusiastically backed by Trevelyan, Wedgwood and Thomson (all of them convinced there had been a plot) demanded an inquiry. Argument was heated; Haldane and Snowden in particular were concerned that if Parmoor and his supporters had their way, they would happily sacrifice the Foreign Office for an opportunity to cripple the hated secret service. They strove, therefore, to keep the inquiry secret. MacDonald supported the suggested secret inquiry by three Cabinet Ministers, but his choice of members — Thomas, Haldane and Henderson — did not please Trevelyan and Wedgwood who insisted on Thomas being replaced by Parmoor. This they achieved, but Parmoor and his associates were gagged effectively by MacDonald's instruction that the inquiry should concern itself with the authenticity of the Zinoviev letter only, and not question the role of the civil servants, the central issue if they wished to get at the truth. Trevelyan remained for ever convinced that MacDonald had handled the affair disastrously. He should immediately have sacked Gregory — Trevelyan had telegraphed this advice to MacDonald the day after the letter's publication. There would have been no scare at all had MacDonald known how to handle the permanent officials of the Foreign Office instead of being 'in awe of them'.[58]

MacDonald resigned on 4 November. The first Labour Government was ended. If there was cause for regret in the manner of its going, at the least the past months had been 'interesting and exciting', and not without reward. 'Hasn't it been enormously worth it?' Trevelyan asked Molly. 'Indeed, I don't so much care now how things move with me henceforward. I have done a good day's work.'[59]

DEFEAT:
1924-31

Baldwin's overwhelming electoral victory in October 1924 gave the Tories a handsome majority over the combined strength of the other parties, and a sound parliamentary base for five secure years of uninterrupted government. Molly Trevelyan was concerned how the prospect of the fruitless years in opposition, after so short and yet rewarding a period in office, might affect her restless, impatient husband. How would he support the tedium, the lack of any power to influence events, the inevitable inconveniences of London life, separated to such little apparent purpose from family, friends and the pleasures of rural life? In the event, Trevelyan bore the next four and a half years in opposition with resigned good humour. Molly was not alone in her surprise at this. Sidney Webb, who had told Hugh Dalton that Trevelyan had 'never really grown up', and that this accounted for his aggressiveness and impatience, nevertheless admitted Trevelyan 'had mellowed a bit with age'.[1] Trevelyan recognised and accepted this change, both in himself and the contribution that he could hope to bring to national politics. He told Molly:

> I have acquired a placid acceptance... which I hope will last my life amid all changes... For a little while, to be a Minister has added or will add pungency to our interests. To have a full life of things which you feel have got to be done, with the background of an important influence on a mass of friends, children and less fortunate folk than ourselves is quite as good a life as anyone could want.[2]

If Trevelyan appeared more 'mellow' increasing years was not the most important cause of the metamorphosis. Many factors, not all of his own making, promoted a greater sense of well-being both in private and public life than it had ever before been Trevelyan's fortune to experience. In his private thoughts he had been able finally to slough off the last persistent doubts, the nagging sense of guilt because he supposed it mattered that he should have disappointed a father's or a brother's expectations of him. Now he could freely admit to being the man he was, rather than the man others would have wished him to be. There were no regrets for the past, only a vision with new perspective of the future. His resolution had been sufficiently tempered by years of trial for him no longer to be wounded in spirit if his sworn fealty to the 'People' and the Labour party was mocked as romantic, misguided and sentimental.

Trevelyan could look back with considerable satisfaction to his Presidency of the Board of Education. His efforts for education and Wheatley's for housing had been the two domestic successes of the first Labour Administration. The feeling of well-being Trevelyan enjoyed because of his obvious popularity was enhanced by the difficulties experienced by his Tory successor. Lord Eustace Percy, twelfth of the Duke of Northumberland's thirteen children, had been born with — in his own words — 'the biggest of all possible silver spoons in [his] mouth'.[3] Sadly for Percy, the fortunate accident of birth into one of the richest and most noble families in the kingdom, which guaranteed unlimited largesse to cosset his private life, was reversed in his political life. The minor scion of another ducal family, Winston Churchill, as Chancellor of the Exchequer was to prove a very hard-hearted, parsimonious colleague. Snowden had curbed any costly exercise of enthusiasm that Trevelyan might have shown, but he had never been unsympathetic to the claims of secondary and elementary education upon the nation's budget. Churchill, however, was at the best impatient, and at the worst contemptuous of claims made for formal education. Therefore, it was not too difficult for Trevelyan to make capital — both personal and political — out of Percy's impossible position. That Minister was the victim not only of an unsympathetic Chancellor, but of a party hierarchy totally indifferent to, if not altogether unaware of, the disposition and expectations of the post-war electorate concerning education.

From the Opposition front bench Trevelyan had announced that for education, the entry of the Tories into Government meant it would never be 'glad confident morning again'. His gloomy forecast appeared confirmed when, at the insistence of a Cabinet committee on economy, Circular 1371 was issued by Percy's department proposing that local education authorities should make drastic checks upon any expansion. Trevelyan's image of generosity and his status with the teachers was enhanced by the penny-pinching image his Tory successor unwillingly earned at the behest of his political masters. 'Everywhere I go I get a great reception,' Trevelyan wrote to Molly after a bout of electioneering. 'I am a sort of myth. And I see today that my glorious successor has promulgated a fresh economic circular! As far as I can make out he is quite generally known as Lord Useless Percy.'[4]

With confidence born of acclaim came greater ease and relaxation in Trevelyan's parliamentary style. He found that he too could sometimes abandon earnestness and the heavy cannonade of serious debate for a sharp volley of humour. He discovered to his surprise that his new 'House-style' was rewarding; publicly it won him both more friends and arguments, and privately it gave him a great deal of personal satisfaction. It had always been his disposition to instruct. Now he could write that he had 'amused' the House. If he gave Percy a regular wigging, he also enjoyed scoring off Churchill, 'by pointing out that Winston would never have been able to win a free place [at a grammar school] as a working man's son before the age of 14'.[5] Speaking for the first time at a Labour Conference he was given 'a tremendous reception, quite the most marked after MacDonald's. It was some time before I could begin, and it appeared to be pretty general not only from the party delegates but from the Trade Unions.' At Warrington that same evening his speech was greeted with tumultuous applause. It was natural that Trevelyan should compare this reception with the one given him the last time he had been in the town during the war. Then he had been 'smuggled to a house in the outskirts of the town to meet twenty trembling pacifists while a mob howled around the advertized meeting place and broke its windows'.[6]

There was a lull in educational controversy during the first two years of Baldwin's Government. As much as anything this was because of the chronic economic and industrial troubles that culminated in the General Strike of 1926. Also, until the election brought an uneasy truce, there was a continuing debate within the Labour party about the ILP proposals contained in *Socialism in our time*. Controversy centred about the demand for a minimum living income for every citizen as the first charge upon the national product. This, the ILP argued, should be the mainspring of Labour's domestic policies. MacDonald contemptuously dismissed their demands as 'flashy futilities'. In his opinion they were a recipe for crushing electoral defeat. Trevelyan privately admitted his concern at MacDonald's timidity and he was far from happy about the general relationship between the leadership and the rank and file of the party. 'The leaders are dangerously near getting the Labour party quite out of touch with opinion.' If only MacDonald was 'less indecisive' on every issue. It was like 'perpetually having to pull a heavy load'. Nevertheless, Trevelyan had 'many good pals who want things done effectively', so when all was considered it remained 'quite good fun in some ways'.[7] MacDonald apart, what worried Trevelyan most in those years of opposition was the lack of new, young blood to invigorate the party. 'There are too many old men,' he told Molly. 'It is of enormous importance that the youth of the Socialist movement should feel that they are coming into their own. I have been irked at the slowness of youth coming to the front. I don't want a check now.' In this context, Jennie Lee's victory in a by election in the dying months of the Parliament afforded particular satisfaction, and he wrote at length of her 'great gifts of oratory, command over the House and sincerity'. 'Jennie's success comforts me for the subsequent want of grit in MacDonald. For it does mean, it really does, that the younger generation is coming to look after itself.'[8]

In December 1926, to the plaudits of the Association of Education Committees and the National Union of Teachers, the long awaited Hadow Report was published. In essence, the recommendations it made were no different from established Labour education policy. Nor was this altogether surprising, for the two most influential architects of the report were Percy Nunn and Tawney, both of whom were members of Labour's education advisory committee. In summary they recommended 'selection by differentiation' in place of 'selection by elimination'. Within six years, the leaving age should be raised from fourteen to fifteen, and every child should begin a distinct phase of its education at eleven, either in a grammar school, a central school (to become the secondary modern school under the 1944 Act) or a separate senior section in the old elementary schools. On behalf of the Government, Percy flatly rejected the Report's recommendations. Two educational philosophies were in direct opposition to one another: Labour's desire for a general all round improvement in a universal social service; the Tory emphasis on selective training for an able minority. Percy described the lacuna between the two party views as 'no more than a difference of taste'.[9] Trevelyan reaffirmed his party's commitment to raising the school leaving age, and in a letter to *The Times* added a new and important dimension to the debate. The expense of raising the school leaving age, he maintained, would be set off by 'the saving in unemployment benefit and poor relief for the fathers of families who are indirectly unemployed because 500,000 children are annually thrust into the labour market at 14'. To the party conference at Blackpool in 1927, he repeated his claim. If they supported the raising of the school leaving age to fifteen then 'they would have one of the biggest things on which they could go to the country. They had one of the biggest cries they could possibly have in deciding to pay for the efficient education of the children, the money which they now paid to keep their parents out of the workhouse.'[10] This appeared to be a neat solution, almost a case of something for nothing. When, as the responsible Minister, he had to grapple with the financial problem, Trevelyan was to find that the solution was not as easy as he had supposed. However, for the moment it served its purpose. Trevelyan was anxious that there should be general agreement in the Labour party to raise the school leaving age. There were those who wanted the limit set at sixteen rather than fifteen, but a not inconsiderable lobby of opinion in Yorkshire and Lancashire was against raising the school leaving age at all. Fifteen provided an obvious compromise, neither hopelessly reactionary nor merely 'a pious expression of opinion'. *Labour and the Nation*, the party's manifesto for the General Election, settled on fifteen as the leaving age, with a suitably vague expression of intention to 'raise to sixteen at a later date'. The significance of this resolution lay not in the arithmetic of compromise but in the fact that Trevelyan had inextricably bound Labour's promise on education to the unemployment issue. This last was to be the dominant domestic issue in the 1929 election campaign. It is an interesting commentary on the problems Labour was to face as the party of Government that when Baldwin chose to go to the country, Labour found the Liberals with their Yellow Book proposals for economic development had stolen the march on them. Only at the last moment did Labour produce a policy statement on the unemployment situation. The party seemed disposed to believe in verbal platitudes as solutions to problems, rather than work out in detail practical and more prosaic solutions. When, though they supposed the walls to be stout, the towers built in their imagination crumbled to dust, they sought explanations for the disaster which never encompassed the possibility that they were in any way to blame. Nor was Trevelyan as free of this sin as he supposed. This, in some part, accounts for his failures in his second period as Minister of Education. But, as yet, this lay in the future.

In January 1928, Trevelyan's mother died at Welcombe, the house she had inherited from her father, and where she and Sir George in their declining years chose to spend most of the year, visiting the Northumberland estate only for short periods in the summer. Sir George survived his wife by only seven months. So, at last, Sir Charles Trevelyan, as he now was styled, was master of Wallington. For more than a decade he and Molly with growing concern and impatience, had watched the estate slipping into a critical condition. The thirteen thousand acres had been too long neglected. Fences and gates were in ill repair, fields undrained, woods untended, necessary repairs to cottages had been left undone. The big house also was in urgent need of major repair. When architects were consulted, they confirmed the Trevelyans' worst fears: the roof over the main hall would have to be replaced entirely for there was imminent danger of its total collapse. All the lead flats on the rest of the roof needed replacing, and even some of the external walls were badly cracked because they had been built upon foundations inadequate to support their great weight. They had to be dismantled and rebuilt again. Inside, the alterations and decoration required could best be described as those needed to turn a dark, draughty mausoleum into a home for a lively family, and a genuine centre for an estate community. It was an inheritance that would have daunted many, or at the least have been accepted with reservation. Yet Trevelyan and his wife were only too eager to shoulder the burden. Undoubtedly there was something of both novelty and pride in their attitude, but their pleasure sprang much more from the vision they both shared of Wallington's future.

Since their marriage in 1904, the Trevelyans had spent as much time as parliamentary and public duties allowed living in their house in the tiny, model village of Cambo, part of the Wallington estate, a mile distant from the Hall. The four hundred or so people living on the estate were as well known to the new owners of the Hall and they in their turn knew the Trevelyans. In her memoirs, Molly was to recall of this period:

> We had walked and shot over most of the estate and made frequent visits to the farmers and cottagers. Several of our children had been to the village school... I had chatted with the village wives of our babies' ailments: we had both taken part in all the village activities and sat on the village committees — so that we felt ourselves part of the community.[11]

Now, even as their new status in the community was marked by the move from their comparatively humble house in Cambo to the dilapidated grandeur of the Hall, the Trevelyans determined there should be a new reforming spirit that would have nothing of past neglect. Being the couple they were, they personally wished to supervise and conduct the implementation of the reforms. To Molly fell the task of planning improvements for the houses of their estate workers. Trevelyan, dispensing with the services of his father's bailiff and farm manager, for the moment took over the whole management and responsibility for the estate. The fierce energy and determination with which the two halves of this formidable team tackled their tasks meant that in the first year at Wallington, including the major works on the Hall, no less than thirty one houses and cottages were repaired, and general improvements were made to the farms, out-buildings and lands. The scale and speed of these changes and the spirit that informed them, is best summed up in a speech Trevelyan made in April 1929 when, for the first time, they were able to invite all their tenants to a gathering at the Hall. The occasion was to celebrate the Trevelyans' silver wedding anniversary. The actual date should have been 6 January, but then the house had been in too great a state of disrepair. As it was, work on the great hall was still unfinished in April.

> We wish we could have given you a more worthy reception and a more beautiful banquet. It would have been fine if we could have sat down in the great hall to carve and eat a baron of beef and to drink to the memory of hard riding Fenwicks who feasted in the old castle in times past, and to dance till midnight under the portraits of the Blacketts who built and made beautiful this house. But builders, electricians, water engineers and plumbers possess our house. So we cannot do the honours of the old place thoroughly this time... However, we want this occasion at least to serve to

make you all feel that you are free of this house in a way that you have not been before.

You are all aware that I am no friend of the system which by pure chance makes me rich and a thousand others poor for life... I want you to know that I regard myself not as the owner of Wallington and the people of Wallington, but as a trustee of property which under wiser and humaner laws would belong to the community. It is for that reason that, while I put a new roof on Wallington for fear we should be crushed like Samson, Lady Trevelyan and I are busy making your houses more comfortable... I want you to feel that to come and see Wallington is on your part not an intrusion but a right... We would like to think that the pictures, the china, the books, the woods, the garden, are possessions for all the people around here to cherish or to use.

Lady Trevelyan and I have already told you that we intend that everyone employed on the estate shall have a week's holiday with pay every year arranged at a time to suit their wishes. We wish to make another announcement of a small advantage for some of our workmen. We have often expressed the opinion in public that it would be a fine thing if the Nation were to give family allowances where there are children in the family and that would be one of the best methods towards a wider and juster distribution of wealth. We intend to give an allowance to every family on the estate of 2/6 a week for every child from birth till such time as it leaves school or college. The allowance will be paid every month by Lady Trevelyan to the mother of the family. It will cease only when a boy or girl ceases to be educated or until such time as any future Government in this country shall provide maintenance allowances out of the public purse.[12]

The payment of allowances for children had been the subject of vexed debate within the Labour party. In 1926, an ILP resolution that Labour should commit itself to paying children's allowances had been defeated in Conference, mainly because of Trade Union opposition. They feared such allowances would be used to justify wage reductions. Other opponents favoured the development of social services in kind rather than the payment of cash allowances. Trevelyan's initiative caused a great deal of comment in the Commons. 'Most of our people are delighted,' Trevelyan wrote to Molly. 'A Tory Minister has already calculated that it is going to cost seventy millions to put into operation nationally.'[13] But Family Allowances as we now know them were not provided until after the Second World War, and then their provision was less generous than Trevelyan's private scheme.

The main structural alterations, repairs and redecoration of Wallington Hall took more than a year to complete. That first Summer, the Hall and gardens were opened to visitors free of charge every weekend and public holiday. Nothing gave Trevelyan and his wife more pleasure than to guide groups about the house and gardens, pointing out various treasures, sharing their delight and pride in the estate. For Trevelyan there was the satisfaction of

seeing the hopes he had so long cherished for Wallington at last beginning to
be realised. This work could not have been more congenial. He was hindered
by nothing save the length of his private purse (which was so long that on
occasion he would admit it embarrassed him) and the amount of activity that
could be crammed into each day. At Wallington there were no doubts and
hesitations, no placating the sensibilities of difficult colleagues, no interests to
cajole, no fools to suffer gladly or otherwise, no timorous leader to drag
reluctantly forward, only a personal vision and realisation of what was to be
achieved. The charms of Wallington made the prospect of a return to office
less and less attractive. Trevelyan confided in a letter to his daughter
Katherine:

> It is the devil, the prospect of a Labour Government. I gain whatever hap-
> pens. If we win enough then I become a Minister. If we don't win I have
> more than enough to do at Wallington. Which ought I to wish for? As a
> patriot I wish the first of course. When duty whispers low etc...![14]

Less than three months after writing this letter Baldwin had called an
election and for the first time Labour emerged as the majority party in the
Commons. Whether he would or not, for the moment Trevelyan's future
was decided for him.

The Franchise Act of 1928 had extended the vote to women on the same
terms as men. The 'flapper vote', together with a rise in population,
increased the total electorate by some seven million, and those who actually
voted increased from 1924's sixteen and a quarter million to twenty two and a
half million. However, this general increase in the numbers of voters was not
so marked in Central Newcastle. Nevertheless, fighting a somewhat low-key
campaign against a Tory opponent only — the Liberals having once for all
deserted the constituency — Trevelyan captured almost all the new votes,
while his opponent did marginally worse than had his predecessor in 1924.

> Rt. Hon Sir C Trevelyan (Labour).....17,580
> Viscount Adare (Conservative).......12,161
> Labour majority...................5,419

It came as no great surprise to Trevelyan that at a meeting with MacDonald
on 5 June he was offered, as in the previous Labour Administration, charge of
education. He had expected no more and no less. He accepted with alacrity.
It 'pleased [him] mightily', though he accepted less happily Morgan Jones as
his Under Secretary. Jones he considered 'quite useless' and would much
preferred to have had Arthur Shepherd, Phil Baker or Jennie Lee. 'I want a
young Under Secretary,' he told Molly, 'for youth is the great lack of our
party.' As to the composition of the new Cabinet, for the moment Trevelyan
seemed prepared to put aside his frequently expressed reservations about the

Labour leadership in general, and the inadequacies of MacDonald in particular. He would not deny there were 'fearful difficulties' facing MacDonald, 'but thought him seeming to thrive upon them'.[15] He very soon was to revert to his former poor opinion of Ramsay's qualities as a leader. Of his other Cabinet colleagues, Trevelyan expressed no reservation except if Jimmy Thomas was given the Foreign Office it would be 'a dreadful mistake', an opinion with which few, save Thomas, were likely to disagree.

Comparing Trevelyan's letters of this period to his wife, with those he wrote when first appointed a Minister in 1924, the confidence of the initial approach to the problems of Office had disappeared. This was to be no dawn in which it was bliss to be alive. The day after his appointment, he wrote, 'the two big jobs ahead are raising the school age and a denominational school settlement. The first will come off, *the second may not come off.*'[16] Even before the new parliament had assembled, Trevelyan had been defeated in Cabinet on the first of these issues. On a subject for which he had the support of the greater part of the Labour party, Trevelyan had been forced to concede defeat. He had told Molly beforehand that MacDonald would defeat him, not on political but personal grounds. 'See how I *know*,' Trevelyan stressed, 'the *real* factors in a *personal* situation.' In a second letter written later that same day, he told his wife not to worry over his defeat. The policy of raising the school leaving age to fifteen was 'the right one and will come again... my defeat is part of the situation. I cannot make JRM other than a "Safety First" man... George Lansbury says I fought as well as could be done. JRM must have the final say and I don't gird.'[17]

Before Parliament heard the King's speech, the character of the Labour Cabinet was established. 'This bloody Cabinet is far behind our Parliamentary Executive,' wrote Hugh Dalton in his diary. He had had a long *tête à tête* with Trevelyan. He admired Trevelyan's 'vigour and directness and the way he kept clear of personal quarrels within the party'. Dalton considered the Minister 'the best of political colleagues'.[18] In his turn, Trevelyan found Dalton 'a fine comrade', as he did Maxton, Jennie Lee, Ellen Wilkinson and Tom Johnston. They shared the same 'instinct for action', unlike 'our noble leaders who have to be shoved and pushed and pulled'.[19] None of this band would have denied that the second Labour Cabinet, lacking both Wheatley and Jowett, was, in its political sympathies, to the right of its predecessor. For the King's Speech it had produced a programme so moderate as scarce to whisper a hint of *Socialism in our Time*.

Given the hesitations and circumlocutions, the vanities and jealousies, the cautions and compromises of MacDonald, by comparison Trevelyan inevitably acquired the character and reputation of a militant leftist. Equally inevitable, there were some who wondered whether Trevelyan was playing a deep game for his own ends. Perhaps, reflected Sidney Webb — even more respectable now as Lord Passfield than as Beatrice's better half — Trevelyan calculated he might best capture the leadership of the party by cultivating a reputation as a leftist? The thought revealed nothing save Passfield's ignorance of Trevelyan's character. At no time did Trevelyan harbour any idea of usurping the Labour leadership. After a particularly difficult week in Parliament in November 1927, when the party had been caught in the toils of the Indian question, Trevelyan had written to Molly, 'I wouldn't be a leader for anything.' He did, however, add the *caveat* that the 'Leaders manufacture half their troubles.'[20] MacDonald's problem was that he 'lacked grit. Yet, God has given him to us. It might have been worse.' A little before the election in 1929, Trevelyan confided, 'I feel that if someone else [other than MacDonald] had been given such opportunities, the whole country would be on fire. Between you and me I *know* I could do it. But equally between you and me, I am profoundly thankful it never will fall to me to do it.'[21] Education was to prove quite hard enough a row to hoe without contemplating wresting the party leadership from MacDonald.

Raising the school leaving age, as far as the non-provided schools were concerned, made an acute problem impossible. New schools would have to be built, or at the least, more accommodation provided to house the extra pupils. The 1902 Act had made no financial provision for such expansion. The question of whether aid should be increased for the non provided schools had been an important side issue in the 1929 election. Trevelyan's attitude to the subject is made clear in letters he exchanged with Bertrand Russell in May of that year. Russell inquired:

> Is it likely that Labour..., will give more public money than hitherto to the non-provided schools, and in particular is it proposed to spend public money on the fabric of the schools? This, I know, is the policy of the Conservative party, but I shall be deeply disappointed if the Labour party also adopts a measure which as everybody knows is against educational efficiency and has no argument in its favour except the hope of getting the Catholic vote.[22]

Trevelyan's reply fell in two parts; the first a conventional response to Russell's inquiry. 'We have recommended the party to take [the] line..., that, while we sympathize with the difficulties of poor schools and shall treat *all* schools more liberally in the matter of maintenance, we will not scrap the 1902 compromise unless there is a settlement in sight.' Trevelyan continued in a more personal vein:

> I am absolutely determined that the Labour party shall not get into the hands of any religion, least of all the Catholic. I represent a constituency swarming with Irish Catholics. I would rather lose the seat than give the priesthood a bigger power in the schools. I have taken the above party line and I believe by indications that their laity are satisfied.

I want a better solution if I can get it. My anchor is the appointment of teachers. If I could get that into the hands of the public I would concede a great deal in other directions. Scotland has dealt with the question as well and tolerantly as it probably can be. The schools are wholly in the hands of the people and teachers are appointed by the local authority. But there is a denominational veto in the Catholic schools. This ensures a large proportion of Catholic teachers. Probably in this wicked world that is about as good a way out as is possible. The task is tougher in England with the old Church of England on our back and the 6000 single school areas.[23]

The task was to prove tougher than even Trevelyan supposed.

No one could pretend to be really satisfied with the existing Dual System that had emerged out of the heat of the educational debates at the beginning of the century. However, if there was no other apparent virtue, at least it seemed to have saved the country for almost thirty years from overt and bitter religious antagonism. Politically it would be most unwise to contemplate a breach of the existing system until a denominational settlement along new lines had been agreed freely by all parties. A realist would not have supposed this likely to be achieved easily. Yet some perceived, Trevelyan among them, certain signs that an agreed settlement no longer belonged entirely to the realm of pipe dreams. Like their hold upon the affections and loyalties of their disparate flocks, Anglican and Nonconformist leaders seemed prepared to give a little from the intransigent positions they had so long and so determinedly advocated. If there was less apparent weakening in the Catholic camp, the financial pains and penalties upon their community when they would be required to provide new schools meant that prudence suggested a new settlement of some sort, if only as a temporary measure.

After long and complicated discussions with the various interest groups, Trevelyan proposed that for a period of three years grants would be paid for alterations to schools that were needed to accommodate the raising of the school leaving age. In return for this generosity, the non provided school managers were to resign much of their control over their teachers to the local authorities. This last might have seemed like a concession won by Nonconformist pressure, but was no more nor less than Trevelyan had always wanted. Cardinal Bourne's response to the proposal indicated that the Catholic hierarchy would not readily accept. Nevertheless, Trevelyan went ahead and published his proposals, hoping the resultant publicity would force agreement. At the same time he recruited, among others, Fisher to smooth the path for an accommodation with the Liberals, and Tawney to explain the virtues of the proposal to the readers of the *Manchester Guardian*. These and other efforts to gain support were of no avail. The Catholics spurned the proposal, and even the Nonconformists declared that they were far from pleased.

Was Trevelyan anti-Catholic as some critics claimed? Religion, Trevelyan said, was 'really a thing for imaginative youngsters, a pretty fairy story which can do nothing but good, if only they were allowed to slough it off at the same time as Little Red Riding Hood and Rumple Stiltskin'.[24] In his private correspondence Trevelyan never showed any more *animus* towards one religious group than another. Today, the Archbishop of Canterbury was 'The Arch-bagger himself'; the next, 'a most gracious Cosmo'. He might be disposed to say, 'to Hell with intriguing Catholics'; but he said the same and as often of 'the Non-cons'. Perhaps Trevelyan's general disposition is best seen in the attitude he adopted in the great non debate over the reform of the Anglican Prayer Book in December 1927. At a meeting of the Parliamentary Committee (Labour's shadow Cabinet) chaired by Snowden, Trevelyan had been one of the three members who had indicated their intention was to abstain from voting. However, during the course of the debate he changed his mind. To Molly he wrote of how:

> Joynson Hicks spoke most excellently and roused all my Protestant blood. I hate chasubles and ritual. I began to feel the wrath of Cromwell rising in me against the Scarlet Woman... I deliberately prevented myself from deciding to vote until I heard (Lord Hugh) Cecil. He was very ineffective and disappointing. So now I have come down on the side of against. ...It has been great fun. I am such a long way off from all this farrago. But I am near Protestantism as the earth is near the sun from which came the original heat of life. Catholicism is some far off star, infinitely remote.[25]

By the Summer of 1930, though he had been in office for little more than a year, Trevelyan's position as Minister had become almost untenable. Twice, ostensibly because of time-tabling difficulties, he had been forced to withdraw an Education Bill. Should he be successful in a third attempt to introduce his proposed Bill, Trevelyan was not at all hopeful of its success. This was not because of the prejudices of religious bigots, or 'extreme advocates of the means test', but primarily because he feared 'hostile Premiers'. For Trevelyan, this last was 'the deciding factor'.[26] From the beginning of the Administration, Trevelyan had grown increasingly disenchanted with MacDonald's capacity as a leader. Nor was this simply because, on tactical grounds, MacDonald was against raising the school leaving age. In a nutshell, the man seemed to have set his face against anything that might be described as a Socialist measure. In February Trevelyan wrote to Molly, 'We are suffering severely from the defects in Ramsay's personality, his lack of push, decision and confidence... It is troublesome to see opportunities wasted with such a good party.'[27] In May 1930, in letters to his wife, Trevelyan's complaints against his leader reached a crescendo. 'The PM's up to his tricks again... You see if he doesn't do me in yet.' And the often repeated refrain was, 'The Prime Minister is outwitting me again.' In such circumstances it would have been impossible for Trevelyan to maintain a cheerful face but 'for the understanding and trust of the party'. With their support he would 'try to force the pace in the lobbies'.[28] However, in the Cabinet, Trevelyan was no more than a voice crying in the wilderness. Labour would achieve nothing while 'yoked to men without faith or daring in the key positions'. As to MacDonald, 'He detests me,' wrote Trevelyan, 'because I am always quite definite and won't shirk things in the approved style... He will let me down if he possibly can... the real wrecker is the PM with his timidity.' The only hope for the future was the rank and file of the party. 'Though I may blunder or am tripped the Labour party will see me through.'[29]

If June marked the high tide of Trevelyan's discontent in 1930, the following month his faith and hope were a little restored. In a Cabinet memorandum of late November 1929, Snowden had complained about the cost of raising the school leaving age because of the demand for maintenance allowances. To all the Tories and many of the Liberals, to pay maintenance grants as of right to the parents of children staying on the extra year at school was nothing less than a bribe. The only possible compromise would be to introduce a means test for the grants — a course favoured by the Local Education Authorities (LEA's) and that suited Snowden's disposition. The parliamentary Labour party, however, overwhelmingly rejected this idea. Trevelyan was not against the means test as such. He recognised that there was a need 'to be more moderate in our demands upon the Exchequer'. Surely the answer was 'to adopt a scale wide enough to eliminate the fear of inquisition and distribution among working class applicants'.   Snowden responded to Trevelyan's suggestion more favourably than he had hoped. 'It might have been worse,' Trevelyan wrote to Molly after an interview with the Chancellor. 'He is not impossible and I think something may be rastled out which the party will accept. At least it is not a *non possumus*. The Chancellor is direct, simple, intelligible. No jellyfish he!'[31]

The compliment to Snowden inferred criticism of MacDonald. Trevelyan's position was difficult enough without having to cope with a Prime Minister whose sole contribution seemed to be repeated warnings to 'take great care', to be 'very careful..., as we have been putting all sort of people's backs up recently in one way or another'. Even Morgan Jones, Trevelyan's Under Secretary, spoke of nothing save his fears that the opposition they could expect from the LEAs would wreck their Bill. A weak Prime Minister, Cabinet colleagues who seemed to have forgotten the primacy Labour traditionally gave to educational reform, hostile LEAs, extremists in all three parties determined that if they could not have their way no one else would either, and always in the background the very real threat of an outbreak of sectarian violence: the outlook for Trevelyan could not possibly have been bleaker. Yet, in September 1930, with the active support of Sankey, the Lord Chancellor, Trevelyan in the Cabinet won the assurance that his Bill would be given priority in the Government's timetable for the next parliamentary session. It was a measure of how low Trevelyan's hopes had sunk that this on occasion reckless optimist admitted it was difficult 'to get into a hopeful mood... Our Cabinets begin this morning. I hope all will go well. At any rate my own course is clear. I have got to have it.'[32] As he wrote the words Trevelyan must have known that if he was to hazard his future as a Minister upon the chance of guiding his Education Bill onto the statute book, the odds against a successful outcome were overwhelming.

The Education Bill introduced in the Commons in October 1930 made no provision for the church schools. The Tories were bound to fight upon this ground. However, much more real and dangerous was the possibility of revolt within Labour's ranks over the omission of aid for the non provided schools. The nub of the problem had been neatly expressed by Frank Betts in the *New Leader*. He had asked, 'What Labour candidate wants the Irish Catholics at his throat?' In many English cities the large Irish Catholic population traditionally voted Labour. The Catholic hierarchy, fully conscious of the power their flock provided, exerted the maximum pressure upon vulnerable Labour MPs to insure a settlement suitable to their interest. With John Scurr in the van, the Labour Catholic lobby warned Trevelyan and the Cabinet that if a suitable settlement was not forthcoming then they would move an amendment to postpone the Bill's operation. 'I am treating them with smiling courtesy,' Trevelyan wrote to Molly.[33] If only Trevelyan could have counted absolutely upon the Prime Minister's support. He knew that MacDonald had very little sympathy for the Catholic Labour group, but the wretched man refused to stand up and be counted on the issue. 'How I hate vain, timid people in great positions,' wrote Trevelyan. 'Just got a note from JRM. As hopelessly obstructive, hostile and unsympathetic as ever.'[34] However, with the approach of the Christmas recess and the season of goodwill, Trevelyan found that he was able to make at least some progress. He proposed a conference between all concerned parties that would meet before the Report stage of the Bill. Maybe the Catholics could be placated; at the least it meant the postponement of crisis until January. In private Trevelyan admitted that he took 'the blackest view of the prospects'.[35]

Not unexpectedly, when the conference met it proved a tense affair. Trevelyan, anxious to achieve a compromise, was prepared to go some little way towards placating the Catholics. The price paid for this initiative was the continued discontent of the Catholics and a violent reaction from the Free Churchmen who proved themselves as adept at moral and political blackmail as their opponents. Despite appeals by Lansbury and Greenwood, the Conference collapsed. Scurr gave notice that he would press his amendment;

MacDonald refused to intervene. In coalition with the Tories, the Catholic Labour MPs carried the Scurr amendment against the Government. The Education Bill having been mutilated by the Commons, what was left of it was rejected entirely by the Lords.

Why did the Education Bill fail? Was failure the inevitable result, or could Trevelyan, by more astute management, have avoided the wrecking of his Bill? Was the real problem the fact that Labour was a minority Government? Certainly, to get any measure through the House, the Government required support from at least part of the Opposition. The last thing Trevelyan was inclined to seek was an accommodation with the Liberals. He desired Labour, at whatever the cost, to stand upon its own feet. The distance between the two parties over education, however, was never so great that it could not be bridged. Trevelyan judged the relationship between the two progressive parties better than those who urged him to woo the Liberals. As the numerically weaker and the more uncertain members of the projected partnership, the Liberals were better fitted for the part of trimming principles and ignoring tender scruples. In any case, Trevelyan, who never recorded a favourable opinion of the Liberal party in Parliament if he could avoid it, in November 1930 noted that in the growing crisis, 'many of the Liberals are trying to be sensible'.[36] Trevelyan never counted possible Liberal opposition as a great obstacle to his Bill.

Was the sectarian problem the greatest obstacle to success? The Labour party had never really come to grips with the conundrum posed by their Catholic members. After Trevelyan had resigned, he received a letter from John Bromley, the Trade Union MP, stating the position in the baldest terms.

> Our Party..., has allowed itself to be made a nest for the Catholic party. It's an evil bird that fouls its own nest, which is what our Catholic section did when it defeated the Government... The Catholics will have to be fought by Socialists one day and it is as well that someone has made a start however ineffective it may appear at first. You can be sure that although many of our party may not tell you so, your action will gain much approbation... Unfortunately they will not all tell you so because they fear more for their seats than they do for the welfare of the Socialist cause.[37]

What is clear is that Trevelyan underestimated the intransigence of the majority of the Roman Catholic hierarchy. He listened more to the moderate, politic tones of the Bishop of Pella than the snarls of Cardinal Bourne. He also supposed that the majority of Catholic Labour MPs would put their Socialism before loyalty to their Church, or at the least, before selfish thoughts of maintaining their seats by wooing the Catholic vote. But bigotry and selfishness were never the prerogatives of the Catholics alone. The Free Church group within the party were just as quick to shout, pose, threaten when they supposed their own position to be undermined by the least concession to Catholic sensibilities.

To add to other possible causes of failure, the economic climate could not have been worse. However, in 1929 and again in 1930, Trevelyan considered that he had been fairly dealt with by Snowden. Only the last estimates Trevelyan submitted to the Chancellor before his resignation met with a very unsympathetic response. Trevelyan asked for more, and Snowden replied with a demand that he should 'make a substantial cut'. In reply Trevelyan declared that he felt he had already made enough sacrifices. He had reached the end of the road.

It would be a mistake to suppose the only reason Trevelyan decided to resign was because of the defeat of his Bill. That defeat was part only of a greater discontent and frustration. He had long contemplated the possibility of resignation. Six months earlier he had confided in Molly, 'I want very much to get out of it. But I should be a coward to do so till I know I can do no more.'[38] As the odds against him steadily and hopelessly mounted, the only factor that kept Trevelyan at his post was his sense of duty. 'What I should really like,' he wrote in November, 'is to be a private member and out of *this* Cabinet. Its incompetence haunts me.'[39] While the Lords were still debating the Education Bill, Trevelyan wrote to Molly;

> I am afraid I see no course for myself but resignation. It will lead to an outburst of ridicule led by our people. But I cannot see what other course is open to me, as I think the pusillanimity of the Government is the real reason for the Lords behaving as they do. But I am so placed that whatever I do is contemptible. I am not conscious of anything but being badly helped by our leaders. And of the various contempts I dread most the self-contempt of trying to go on in a hopeless position here and acquiescing in the ineffectiveness of the Government. I had better go ineffectively than stay ineffectively.[40]

The day after the Lords had rejected his Education Bill, Trevelyan wrote to MacDonald:

> I thought it right to remain in the Government as long as there was any chance of carrying the great reform which the Party wanted. But under the present circumstances I do not feel that I can usefully remain your Minister of Education.

So much was merely a preliminary to the main burden of his letter of resignation.

> For some time I have realised that I am very much out of sympathy with the general method of Government policy. In the present disastrous condition of trade it seems to me that the crisis requires big Socialist measures... We ought to be demonstrating to the country the alternatives to economy and

protection. Our value as a Government today should be to make people realise that Socialism is that alternative.[41]

MacDonald declared that Trevelyan's letter gave him 'some surprise. You have never indicated to me that you were contemplating such a step.'[42] The die was cast, and both men knew it. Because he was the man he was, MacDonald hesitated before accepting the inevitable. Because he was the man he was, Trevelyan did not retire quietly to the back benches. The impact of his resignation came not in his leaving the Cabinet but in his immediate actions thereafter.

Trevelyan was not disposed to free himself entirely of blame for the failure of his Bill. Nevertheless, he believed the major cause of that failure also explained why the Government had not succeeded in solving the problem of unemployment. Shortly after his resignation, Trevelyan at a meeting of the Parliamentary Labour Party spelled out in exact terms what he supposed was the real cause of Labour's failures in Government.

I should have been willing to go on administering a department where it had become impossible to make any Radical progress, *if I had been in entire sympathy with the general policy of the Government.* But I am not. I have for some time been painfully aware that I am utterly dissatisfied with the main strategy of the leaders of the party. But I thought it my duty to hold on *as long as I had a definite job in trying to pass the Education Bill.*

I never expected a complete breakthrough to Socialism in this Parliament. But I did expect it to prepare the way by a Government which in spirit and vigour made such a contrast with the Tories and Liberals that we should be sure of conclusive victory next time. But the first Session was a bitter disappointment...

And now we are plunged into an unexampled trade depression and suffering the appalling record of unemployment. It is a crisis almost as terrible as war... The people are in just the mood to accept a new and bold attempt to deal with radical evils. The Tories know it and are definite. They preach Protection louder and more confidently. If ever there was a chance of presenting the Socialist alternative it is today... But all we have got is a declaration of economy from the Chancellor of the Exchequer. We apparently have opted, almost without discussion, for a policy of economy... *It implies a faith, a faith that reduction of expenditure is the way to salvation...* You must bear all the implications of your new religion when you join a Church.

No Comrades. It is not good enough for a Socialist party to meet this crisis with economy. The very root of our faith is that prosperity comes from the high spending power of the people, and that public expenditure on the social services is always remunerative. I should have expected that in this crisis there would be a declaration, the reassuring announcement that no attempt at economy would be made in salaries, wages, benefits or social services — that they to us were sacrosanct. Then we could have begun to talk of patriotic sacrifice to those who can afford to pay even in bad times.

I owe a great deal to the Prime Minister — most of all that he helped me to enter the Labour party. Though I differ profoundly with the present leadership I have not the slightest sympathy with the action of men like Mosley. The Labour Party is going to be the power of the future however long it takes to evolve leaders who know how to act. But it is as in an army. The leaders for the time must settle the strategy. The officers who command the battalions can retire, but they must not rebel. I have taken the only step of protest open to me. I resign my position as an officer and become a private soldier. By that action I can speak. And once for all, my comrades, I will put into words what I think and I shall not say it again. I do not believe the Labour Party can succeed in breaking through to Socialism until the leadership is changed.[43]

This blunt attack, obviously primarily pointed towards MacDonald, was greeted with silence. In the political life murder by innuendo or the silent stab in the back are familiar tactics. But to rend the leadership publicly, not to hedge criticism about with polite ambiguities and equivocations, was a novel and highly uncomfortable experience. No one had ever doubted Trevelyan's moral courage, but tact had never been his strongest suit. 'You follow the light that is within you, and no one can ask more or less of you than that,' wrote Lansbury.[44] A few approved in private of what Trevelyan had been bold and resolute enough to say in public. But the majority of the party members resented his blunt attack upon MacDonald. There are none so blind as those who will not see. Phil Price, Trevelyan's young cousin and a recent recruit to Parliament, was deputed to sound reaction in the party to the speech. 'I must tell you frankly,' he wrote, 'their remarks are not favourable.'

They think you should have made a statement to the effect that you could do no more useful work in office, and left it at that. They think that you should have confined your remarks just to your resignation in so far as it was affected by the Cabinet's attitude on education and have left the general criticism of MacDonald's leadership and the progress towards Socialism till a later date.[45]

Many, as Agnes Hamilton was later to write, thought that Trevelyan was prepared to blame everyone and everything but himself for his failure. That explanation at least had the merit of being readily understood. Anticipation was sweeter for many Labour members than realisation. They would yet tarry on the road towards Socialism: it was not polite to show haste or anxiety to be at the end of a pilgrimage. As to their leader, their prophet and their guide, it was not yet time to admit that the only firm opinions he held were an enormous self regard and a determination to maintain himself in office whatever the cost. They watched their Government flounder deeper into disaster for want of applying a single, constructive, Socialist policy. They would not, however, countenance any man boldly pronouncing either on the nature of their ailment or its possible cure. Trevelyan, like the child in the fairy tale, had pointed out that the Emperor had no clothes. The party simply was not ready for such a heady exercise in honesty.

The coolly hostile reception given to his speech by most of his parliamentary Labour colleagues did not cause Trevelyan to stay away from the Commons and sulk. There was still work to do, work that could be done perhaps better from the third bench below the gangway than from the Government front bench. There was a comfortable familiarity at first in resuming the role of a rebel with a cause. More now would whisper in Trevelyan's ear, even if they still lacked the determination to pronounce it publicly, that he had been right in what he had said of MacDonald and the need for Socialist measures. Tom Johnston, the Lord Privy Seal, upbraided Trevelyan for resigning, 'as removing the most effective help he could have got for a forward Socialist policy in the Cabinet'. Outside Westminster, Trevelyan, in a long letter to his constituents, explained the reasons for his resignation from the Cabinet. He remained true to the promise he had given at the meeting of the Parliamentary Labour Party. There was no public word of criticism against the Labour leadership. There was, however, a clarion cry for constructive Socialist measures.

... The central need of the world is a better distribution of wealth. Our chief national disaster is poverty. As long as millions are impoverished, prosperity is impossible.

Was this simply a smug piece of vote-catching rhetoric by a man whose own financial circumstances were unlikely ever to be threatened? Many who did not know the man thought so, but they could not have been further from the truth. When Snowden, for instance, increased super tax in his 1930 budget, Trevelyan greeted the measure with undisguised joy. He wrote then to Molly of how the news had given pain to the Tories. 'On these sort of occasions I am aware of my real convictions. I feel a burst of satisfaction that more of the plunder is to be taken from me, and that as a consequence I might even be faced by inconvenience.'46 It might be easy to scoff at Trevelyan's attitude, but no one could impugn his sincerity. He concluded his letter to his constituents:

I represent in Parliament a constituency where poverty and economic insecurity are the normal condition of many thousands of families. The abounding wealth of the minority of the population is no advantage to them. There is not in a capitalist society more than a small gambling chance for any of them to secure comfort and security... A nation which continues to believe in capitalism cannot do battle against poverty with the conviction that it can be overcome. Socialism is the only policy which can bring up the depressed millions to a reasonable economic standard.

To make the changes necessary to reach for Socialism in time to help the lives of living electors in the Central Division of Newcastle, the Labour Party must devote itself to great measures at once... I joined the Labour Party because it holds out a vision of a new economic life based on co-operation and service. I only want to stay in politics to help to create a society reasonably free from destitution and freedom from the danger of war.[47]

Trevelyan called for Socialism. To that philosophy and those policies he had subcribed when he had solicited the votes of his constituents. But Labour's leader had no policy save faith in breaking faith. He toyed with each element of the programme upon which his party had been elected to power, and then rejected it. Having deserted his party's interest, he invented a national interest and the Government to serve it with himself, naturally, at its head. The National Government took office in August 1931 — a temporary coalition of all the 'talents' to solve Britain's immediate financial crisis. The Labour Party opposed this new Government's economy measures. In Government, Labour had been pusillanimous; in Opposition it proved equally faint-hearted. The Labour back benchers reserved their anger, not for their erstwhile leader MacDonald, but for the twisted, vengeful figure of Snowden who, in his turn, lashed them with a neurotic fury. Trevelyan judged Labour's new leader, a bewildered 'Uncle Arthur' Henderson, as 'good' in party meetings, and 'solid' on those few occasions that he was in the House. Most of Henderson's time was occupied with preparations for the election that everyone knew must come sooner rather than later. For his part, Trevelyan daily grew more disillusioned. It was not a happy lot to be a back bench member of an enfeebled, disorganised Opposition. The initial glamour of playing rebel had soon worn off. He was bored and impatient with Westminster antics when he knew his time could better and more constructively be spent on a proper task at Wallington.

In September, in a letter written to Molly, after another day in the Commons of party bickering, Trevelyan confided:

At home, I am happy and confident and have no thought but of pleasant love and active pursuits. I am no longer really happy here. I am beginning to see that I had better make a change before long. But you must not hurry me. I cannot desert the party that has meant so much to me or the people whom I am serving by no means so badly. I quite certainly intend to stand again and lead the party on the Tyne. I will settle later what I will do after that. But I am sure that I can do better with my main work at Wallington because I can be happy and confident there, and I am not happy here, and the value of my work has deteriorated. During the twenty years of vigorous life that may remain to me I had much better be flinging myself into a life where I have no distracting difficulties to sap my energy... In whatever I do, I do not want to have the sense that I am running away. Because that might be a permanent source of regret and disgrace when I had retired... I have got to be definitely sure that I am not wanted before I put it out of my power to help publicly in any great crisis.[48]

At the beginning of October, the timing of the General Election was finally decided. There was, however, to be one more illustration of how divided were Labour's ranks, even amongst those who had not crossed the floor to join MacDonald. For some time the ILP had been sparring with the National Executive. At the annual conference at Scarborough that year, but two days before Parliament was prorogued for the election, the ILP failed to have referred back a report by a joint committee on party discipline. Trevelyan, who never liked conferences at the best of times, reported to Molly that the defeat of the ILP would make things 'difficult for people like myself'. For his own part, however, 'I don't care how they voted. I am giving no pledge. It will not affect the election.' As to the spirit within the party generally, Trevelyan thought it to be 'very vigorous and hopeful', and everyone seemed pleased with their new leader, Henderson. 'Uncle Arthur received a great reception.'[49]

As a talisman for his party's success at the forthcoming election, Henderson could not have had a more miserable record. Almost invariably, no matter the constituency, Henderson lost his electoral contests. 1931 was to be no exception to that singular, sad record. The electorate of Burnley spurned Henderson but this time he was not to be alone in his misfortune. Of the Labour Cabinet Ministers, discounting Thomas and Snowden who had joined with MacDonald, only George Lansbury was returned to the Commons. Labour lost more than two million votes, and their representation in the Commons was reduced from their 289 of 1929, to fifty-one, or fifty-two if one added Jos Wedgwood, who had stood as an Independent. At Newcastle Central, Trevelyan was routed by the National Conservative candidate.

> Denville, A. (Nat. Con.)............20,309
> Trevelyan, Sir Charles (Socialist)......12,136
> National Conservative majority........8,173

'Sir Charles,' wrote a reporter for the *Journal & Northern Star,* without any exaggeration, 'was obviously a bitterly disappointed man.' Trevelyan had certainly not foreseen such a change of public opinion. 'I knew for the first time,' wrote Molly, 'what it meant to be "stunned by a blow".'[50] There was the usual flood of letters; from neighbours, friends, colleagues who had been defeated in the contest, and one from Jos Wedgwood.

Shall we never look upon your like again? These fools make me sick and I can imagine how they make you feel. If you were there with us, what fun it all would be; holding the bridge with Horatius, defying them 10 to 1. Without you there is no zest left.[51]

EPILOGUE:
'TYME TRYETH TROTH'

Though at the time his hands might well have seemed to have been more than full with the management and reconstruction of the Wallington estate together with his duties as a Minister, Trevelyan had, in 1930, accepted a further increment of public work when offered the Lord Lieutenancy of Northumberland. In some ways, his particular talents and sympathies better fitted him for a role in county rather than national affairs. The large private responsibilities of those whom it was once fashionable to recognise as the 'governing class', did provide a certain training for the world of affairs. Yet the talents exercised and the training tended to be restricted in their range to the management of men and the solution of problems that could be identified and measured personally. It was more the discharge of an intimate moral duty to a known neighbour of equal or dependent status. By tradition, the Dukes of Northumberland had acted as Lords Lieutenant for their county, and a Percy has described succinctly the limitations of the 'governing class'. It 'bred good regimental and ship's officers in the army and navy, but not so often good staff officers; good parish parsons, but not so often good bishops of a state church; good Indian civil servants who were more at home in their districts than at Simla; and for the same reasons, good local administrators who were more at home in County Councils than in Parliament'.[1]

When MacDonald proposed the Lord Lieutenancy, Trevelyan's immediate inclination was to refuse. However, he had to set against his total indifference to the dignity proferred, the strong feeling that the county needed to accustom itself to the Labour party holding positions in *every* part of the national life. Trevelyan warned MacDonald:

If you were to recommend me I think it is only right to say that, while I am reasonably popular with the commonalty of the county, the gentry might feel strong objection to the appointment. It would not in the least trouble me, and I think it would give them a useful lesson that they had got to make up their minds to a changed world. The Lord Lieutenants of the Counties ought to cease to be inevitably Tory peers. I am unable to see any obvious county magnate for you to appoint now that Grey has refused. I am, therefore, prepared to undertake the Lord Lieutenancy if you found the King had no objection to my taking the position.[2]

Sir Hugh Bell, Trevelyan's father-in-law, was Lord Lieutenant for the North Riding of Yorkshire, and he was consulted as to the duties and responsibilities of the office. On a serious level he was able to assure Trevelyan that he could interest himself in the business management of the Territorials without having to compromise his beliefs. On a less serious note, it was decided that Trevelyan need not purchase a Lord Lieutenant's uniform — a fine confection, rather like the dress uniform of an ambassador adorned with much gold — but share Sir Hugh's. In the unlikely event of the King visiting both counties on the same day, a fast car could ferry the uniform between one county potentate and the other so that both might preserve the sartorial dignity of their office. Fortunately, this arrangement never had to be tested.

Trevelyan was offered the Lord Lieutenancy of his county at the same time as Arthur Henderson had told him in confidence that his intention was to push Trevelyan 'for Viceroy of India for all he was worth'. This proposition horrified Trevelyan. He wrote to Molly, 'I said no at once. I don't know whether he will go on with the idea. I can't bear the notion.'[3] This in itself was enough to persuade Trevelyan to accept MacDonald's offer. There was too, one positive and attractive aspect; he would be able to strike a more favourable balance in magisterial appointments between Labour and Tory supporters.

The news of Trevelyan's appointment undoubtedly scandalised many Tory gentry in that still most feudal of English counties. What they considered tolerable behaviour for a Lord Lieutenant might conceivably have swallowed his eccentric attachment to left wing politics; but they couldn't be expected to understand a man who was so heedless of the necessary proprieties and dignity of his station in society as on one occasion to strip to the waist when out shooting rabbits on his estate on a warm day! Yet, if some were offended, more were pleased by Trevelyan's appointment. As one neighbour wrote:

> Please accept my warmest congratulations on the great honour that has been thrust upon you. It is a sign of the times that this high office, so jealously guarded as an appanage of the Peerage only since its inception in Northumberland in 1536, should for the first time pass to an avowed champion of the rights of democracy.[4]

Without doubt, the best comment on Trevelyan's assumption of his new dignity was made by his wife when writing her memoirs. 'His position as the foremost man in Northumberland made no difference in our way of life. We had always lived very simply and we saw no reason to alter our ways because of Charles' new status.'5 As Lord Lieutenant, Trevelyan was never required to do anything half so drastic as the first holder of his office who, after the Pilgrimage of Grace in 1536, hung the Prior of Hexham and his associates over the Abbey gates of the town. The Lord Lieutenant's flag fluttered as boldly over the estates of a Trevelyan as of a Percy, and despite rumours to the contrary, it remained a Union Jack and not the hammer and sickle. That things should remain more or less as they had always been was inevitable: that is the English disposition and the English way.

Late in 1932, reviewing the fate that had befallen the Labour party's leadership, Hugh Dalton wrote of Trevelyan that he seemed to have 'given up [politics] altogether, fascinated by the administration of his Northumberland estate'.6 The observation was not altogether true, but Trevelyan's defeat in the 1931 election did mark the beginning of a steady withdrawal from participation in national politics that within a few years was complete. The election disaster in 1931 had been an unexpected and hard blow, but Trevelyan very soon realised what he had experienced was not so much a catastrophe as a blessing. Now, with clear conscience he could concentrate most of his energies upon his work at Wallington. The compensations were considerable; regrets but a few. Molly, on a visit to the Commons had written of her sorrow that her husband was no longer a member of the House. 'I don't feel it,' replied Trevelyan. 'The earlier part of the time was only training when I was not worth much. Later, I have nothing to regret; though I wish the war had not been and that Labour had been better led. I am not in any way disappointed. I could go back there if I wanted, but I don't want.'7 Of course, there were the occasional moods of depression, but they were few and short lived, and when humour failed, a sense of the ridiculous gave ready relief.

> I never really repine over the failure of everything for me politically because I think it was as much outside circumstances and the hopelessly wrong men who were in chief places that made everything end in futility. And now these men hold what power there is and on all great questions can and will use it wrong. Only mass movements can do anything... But, if the Russian experiment is crushed, or more likely diverted into conquering militarism, there is an end to the best change that has ever come. It's the only thing I couldn't bear... The weather is damnable; the rivers are torrents, the trees drip, half the garden is undug. Damn God — I have half a mind to make Wallington over to the Coop and go and live in Russia where they don't believe in Him. At least the sun sometimes shines there and they have no unemployed.8

The tug of conscience, that would have dragged Trevelyan back into national

C.P. Trevelyan and Molly, Golden Wedding, 1954

politics, waned. 'I am not inclining towards Parliament any more than before. But, I think I ought to help to shove the Labour party into real Socialism; if the way occurs.'[9] He attended Labour Party Conferences and was a great deal cheered by the warmth of the reception he received. 'I have just had the biggest success of the Conference,' he wrote to Molly from Leicester in October 1932, after moving a resolution that the next Labour Government should immediately introduce Socialist measures. 'I swept the Assembly completely. Uncle Arthur simply wasn't listened to in asking for postponement. I got an unanimous vote, but what was more important, I moved them to their depths.'[10] But again came the affirmation, 'I don't feel the least inclination to give up my country life for politics again. I shall do my duty, and not too much more.'[11]

As a member of the Labour Party Executive, for the first years after leaving the Commons Trevelyan was obliged to attend party conferences. In the reaction against MacDonald and all that he was thought to stand for, it was natural that within the Labour party there was a period of left-wing revivalism. The politics of compromise for the moment were eschewed for the politics of absolutes. The grandest causes held sway, and even on education Trevelyan spoke with a greater violence than had ever before been known. For example, the new scale of fees for grammar school pupils introduced by the National Government in 1932 was not so much an economy measure but certain proof of their 'determination to prevent the class-system being undermined'.[12]

In 1933 Trevelyan enjoyed his greatest triumph at a Labour Conference. Despite every effort to stop him, he introduced a resolution committing the Labour Party to action in case of the threat of war by preparing for a General Strike. The resolution was passed by acclamation, accepted by the platform and formally blessed by Henderson.

> It is a quite immensely important decision. It puts the organic Labour movement against *all* war under any circumstances. And it is due to me alone that this feeling has been crystallised *now*. So I have been of some use... I now know the fine policy of a statesman is powerless. Mass passions and determinations, hatreds and new creeds of love sway the world... I don't make the Labour Party say it will have no part in war. If it does end by acting as it says, it will be because of the millions who see war is a fool's game and a horror not a pride.[13]

Trevelyan rejoiced in an atmosphere of international and political millenarianism; that is why he supported the Socialist League, and thought so highly of Cripps and Frank Wise. 'The party is determined to go really Socialist and timid leadership is at a discount,'[14] Trevelyan wrote in 1932. But within two years the atmosphere had changed; cautious counsels began to prevail, the 'revolutionaries' found themselves in a minority. Trevelyan welcomed his defeat when he failed to gain a place on the Executive in 1934. For him there would no longer be days 'beastly with violent personalities'. He had made his contribution. It was for youth to take the banner forward. The miners of Morpeth pressed him to become their candidate. It would be the safest of safe Labour seats. He refused. 'I won't go into politics again unless there are signs of a Rooseveltian energy in leadership and a Socialist policy in practice,' he told Molly. 'No, I pine for home, not politics.'[15] Many wrote to try and persuade Trevelyan to change his resolve never to stand for the Commons again. 'Your decision is absolutely wrong,' wrote MacNeill Weir. 'You were the only [Labour Cabinet Minister] who had any idea what Socialism meant.'

> How many of your colleagues have learned the lesson of 1931? Not a single one except yourself, and then you left. If ever duty was plain and clear it is in your case. With every temptation to go towards the Right you have stood firm. I wish I could induce Achilles to leave his tent... Alan Breck was not a bonnier fechter than you. Come on! Take up your sword![16]

Trevelyan was tempted; Morpeth after all was the perfect constituency. He was still very fit despite his sixty-four years. 'Am I lazy? Am I a coward? Or, am I wise and falling back into the niche which is really made for me in the world?'[17]

About the time when he was most undecided whether he should accept the miners' invitation and stand for Morpeth as a Labour candidate, Trevelyan had occasion to pass through his first constituency, Brighouse and Elland. 'It was exceedingly unchanged and familiar,' he told Molly, 'but it seems rather a long way off doesn't it? I feel that what we are doing now is much more worthwhile than those day of easy politics. Yet, I don't regret anything. It would have been better if we had been given a job like Wallington earlier to get our teeth into it. But we are learning. And now — well I hope that we are entering upon a new period.' The time that was yet left would better be spent on work at Wallington than Westminster. 'I still am not nearly content with the use we make of Wallington. I want to try more definitely to make it a resort for socialist and international minded people.'[18]

The years were kind to Trevelyan. They did not diminish his physical or intellectual vigour. Most important, they did not quench his optimism. His vision was always of the future. When he thought of the past it was without rancour. All his plans for Wallington were realised. It became a focal point in the North as a meeting place for young people who were interested in politics, and the rebels who dared to dream dreams and found, often to their surprise, their youthful hopes shared by their elderly host. Trevelyan's home was a cultural centre where adult education courses flourished, where the People's Theatre of Newcastle had a second home, where the Youth Hostel

Movement was given its greatest encouragement. Wallington, the house, its treasures, the gardens, enjoyed by so many visitors as by friends, was given by Trevelyan to the National Trust in 1941, subject only to a life interest. He gave too the large estate to insure that future generations might enjoy (and share) the splendours that he had been privileged to know. The spirit of Wallington was the spirit of youth. Visitors would not find an old, disappointed politician pining for days gone by, of things that might have been, with talk of men and measures long gone. Surrounded by a host of children and grandchildren, Trevelyan remained young at heart. He was a countryman, proud to show anyone his estates; to exult in the beauties of his proud border country, to talk of Swinburne and Otterburn. A visitor might be shown in the library the soap splashed pages of *Thucydides* that Macaulay had read while shaving, or as likely be cross-examined with an engaging concern on a current interest. There was, too, talk of politics, of the pleasure in hopes realised in the great Labour Ministry after the Second World War, and of plans for the future. And in the evening, by the fireside in the Library while Molly stitched at her embroidery, there was yet time to read aloud in that firm voice and with undiminshed vigour, the *Border Ballads* he loved so well.

At Wallington on Thursday, 24th January 1958, in his eighty-eighth year, Charles Trevelyan died.

> *Ergo vivida vis animi pervicit et extra*
> *Processit longe flammantia moenia mundi*
> *Atque omne immensum peragravit mente animoque.*[19]

SOURCES AND
REFERENCES

The following abbreviations are used for the various members of the Trevelyan family, and to identify the various Trevelyan papers which are held at Newcastle University Library.

CPT. = Charles Philips Trevelyan, and the C.P. Trevelyan Mss.
GOT. = George Otto Trevelyan, and the G.O. Trevelyan Mss.
CT.   = Caroline Trevelyan.
RCT. = Robert Trevelyan.
GMT. = George Macaulay Trevelyan.
MKT. = Molly Trevelyan.

Other persons are identified in full, and references to other manuscript sources when first cited include the location of the manuscript.

CHAPTER 1: HERITAGE AND EDUCATION OF A RADICAL

1. G.M. Trevelyan, *An Autobiography and other essays*. (London, 1949), pp. 3-4.
2. Rev. C.G. Chittenden to CT., 31 August 1880. GOT. 133.
3. CPT. to CT., 23 September 1880. GOT. 34.
4. CPT. to RCT., 19 September 1880. GOT. 34.
5. Chittenden to GOT., 20 April 1881. GOT. 133.
6. CPT. to GOT., (n.d.). GOT. 34.
7. Chittenden to GOT., 27 December 1880 and 3 January 1881. GOT. 133.
8. CPT. to Robert Philips, 18 June 1883. GOT. 135.
9. CPT. to GOT., (n.d.). GOT. 35.
10. CPT. to CT., (n.d.). GOT. 35.
11. Chittenden to CT., 7 August 1883. GOT. 133.
12. Chittenden to CT., 26 December 1883. GOT. 133.
13. Chittenden to CT., 31 January 1884. GOT. 133.
14. Chittenden to GOT., 2 and 14 August 1884. GOT. 133.
15. G.M. Trevelyan, *Sir G.O. Trevelyan: A Memoir*. (London, 1932), pp. 20-21.
16. CPT.'s *Diary*, 26 December 1887. CPT. Ex. 96.
17. CPT. to GOT., (n.d.). GOT. 36, and GOT. 39.
18. CPT.'s *Diary*, 15 November 1887. CPT. Ex. 96.
19. CPT. to GOT., 8 November 1885. GOT. 37.
20. CPT. to GOT., 29 November 1885. GOT. 37.
21. G.M. Trevelyan, *Sir G.O. Trevelyan*, p. 31.
22. G.M. Trevelyan, *Autobiography*, p. 19.
23. Bertrand Russell, *Autobiography*. (London, 1967), Vol. 1, p. 66.
24. CPT. to CT., 15 June 1892. GOT 45.
25. H.G. Wells, *The New Machiavelli* (Penguin Edn., 1946), p. 214.
26. CPT. to CT., 27 March 1892. GOT. 45.
27. CPT. to GOT., 30 October 1889. GOT. 42.
28. CPT. to GOT., 24 November 1889. GOT. 42.
29. CPT. to GOT., 26 February 1890. GOT. 43.
30. CPT. to GOT., 9 June 1890. GOT. 43.
31. CPT. to GOT., 18 January 1891. GOT. 44.
32. CPT. to GOT., 4 February 1891. GOT. 44.
33. CPT. to GOT., (n.d.), February (?) 1892. GOT. 45.
34. CPT. to GOT., 22 May 1892. GOT. 45.
35. CPT. to CT., 10 May 1892. GOT. 45.
36. CPT. to CT., 15 June 1892. GOT. 45.
37. CPT. to CT., 2 October 1892. CPT. Ex. 42.

38. CPT. to CT., 6 February 1893. GOT. 46.
39. CPT. to CT., 9 February 1893. GOT. 46.
40. CPT. to CT., 11 February 1893. GOT. 46, and CPT. to Mary Bell, 3 October 1903. CPT. Ex. 18.
41. CPT. to MKT., 3 October 1903. CPT. Ex. 18.

42. CPT. to CT., 16 November 1892. CPT. Ex. 42.
43. CPT. to CT., 22 February 1893. GOT. 46.
44. CPT. to GOT., 17 January 1893. GOT. 46.
45. CPT. to CT., 3 March 1893. GOT. 46.
46. CPT. to CT., 17 August 1893. GOT. 46.

CHAPTER 2: MAKING A BEGINNING IN POLITICS

1. CPT. to GOT., 28 July 1893. CPT. Ex. 42.
2. CPT. to CT., 13 October 1893. CPT. Ex. 42.
3. CPT. to GOT., 30 November 1893. GOT. 46.
4. CPT. to CT., 30 November 1893. GOT. 46.
5. CPT. to GOT., 29 November 1893. GOT. 46.
6. See, G.M. Trevelyan, Autobiography, pp. 7-8.
7. Quoted, Byron Farwell, The Man Who Presumed (London, 1958), p. 307.
8. CPT. to CT., 18 May 1890. GOT. 43.
9. Farwell, op. cit., pp. 309-10.
10. CPT. to North London Radical Association, April 1894, CPT. 50.
11. CPT. to GOT., 12 December 1894. CPT. Ex. 43.
12. Farwell, op. cit., p. 310.
13. The Standard, 16 July 1895. Cutting in GOT. 169.
14. South London Press, July 1895. Cutting in CPT. 50.
15. Ibid.
16. CPT. to CT., 26 January 1896. GOT. 49.
17. CPT.'s Journal, December 1896. CPT. Ex. 2.
18. H.G. Wells, op. cit., p. 150.
19. Ibid, p. 188.
20. CPT. to CT., 12 April 1895. CPT. Ex. 1.
21. CPT. to GOT., 15 April 1895. CPT. Ex. 1.
22. CPT. to CT., 12 April 1895. CPT. Ex. 1.
23. CPT. to CT., 5 October 1895. CPT Ex. 43.
24. CPT. to GOT., 15 November 1889. GOT. 42.
25. C.P. Trevelyan, From Liberalism to Labour (London, 1921), pp. 19-21.
26. Speech to Sheffield Liberal Association, January 1896. CPT. 52.
27. Manchester Guardian, January 1896. Cutting in CPT. 52.
28. Speech at Boston, February 1896. CPT. 52
29. CPT.'s Notebook, 'Suggestions', 27 May and 14 October 1896. CPT. Ex. 2.
30. CPT. to CT., 5 December 1895. GOT. 48.
31. Herbert Samuel to CPT., 24 October 1901. Herbert Samuel Mss., A/14, Library of the House of Lords.
32. CPT. to Samuel, 12 and 18 May, and 11 November 1895. CPT. 2.

33. CPT. to GOT., 9 December 1895, and to CT., 17 and 24 December 1895. GOT. 48.
34. C.P. Trevelyan, The Cause of the Children (London, 1897), pp. 35-40.
35. CPT. to Samuel, 13 September 1896. CPT. 2.
36. CPT. to CT., 24 November 1897. GOT. 50.
37. CPT. to GOT., 27 November 1897. GOT. 50.
38. Ibid.
39. CPT. to Samuel, 25 September 1897. CPT. 2.
40. CPT. to Samuel, 2 February 1897. CPT. 2.
41. CPT. to CT., 2 December 1897. GOT. 50.
42. CPT. to CT., 20 February 1898. GOT. 51.
43. Bradford Observer, 8 March 1899. Cutting in CPT. 50.
44. Brighouse Echo, (n.d.). Cutting in CPT. 50.
45. CPT. to CT., 2 December 1897. GOT. 50.
46. CPT. to GOT., 23 February 1898. GOT. 51.
47. CPT. to CT., 25 February 1898. GOT. 51.
48. CPT. to CT., 11 March 1898. GOT. 51.
49. CPT. to CT., (n.d.), 24 (?) March 1898. CPT. 3.
50. CPT. to Trevelyan family, 8 May 1898. CPT. 3.
51. See, published Diary, pp. 137-41.
52. CPT. to Trevelyan family, 15 August 1898. CPT. 1, (2nd. pkt.).
53. Diary, p. 167.
54. CPT. to Samuel, 2 October 1898. CPT. 2.
55. CPT. to Samuel, 19 December 1898. CPT. 2.
56. Manchester Examiner, (n.d.), February 1899. Cutting in CPT. 51.
57. CPT. to CT., 21 January 1899. GOT. 52.
58. CPT. to Samuel, 5 February 1899. CPT. 2.
59. CPT. to Samuel, 5 and 7 February 1899. CPT. 2.
60. Brighouse Echo, 17 February 1899. Cutting in CPT. 51.
61. Ibid, 11 March 1899. Cutting in CPT. 51.
62. GOT. and CT. to CPT., 9 March 1899. GOT. 139.
63. Mrs. Prestwich to CPT., 9 March 1899. CPT. 6.

CHAPTER 3: OF LIBERALISM, LEADERS AND WAR

1. CPT.'s 'Weekly Parliamentary Letter', 21 March 1899. Cutting in CPT. 51.
2. The Times, 23 March 1899.
3. CPT. to CT., 20 July 1900. CPT. Ex. Misc. Letters, 1890-1902.
4. 'Silhouettes of Celebrities', (n.d.), 1899. Cutting in CPT. 51.

5. CPT. to Samuel, 19 December 1898. CPT. 2.
6. CPT. to CT., 2 December 1899, CPT. Ex. Misc. Letters, 1890-1902.
7. 7 February 1900. Cutting in CPT. 52.
8. 14 March 1900. Cutting in CPT. 52.
9. Walter Runciman to CPT., 27 July 1900. CPT. 3.
10. CPT. to Runciman, 1 August 1900. CPT. 3.

11. *Brighouse Echo*, (n.d.). Cutting in CPT. 50.
12. CPT. to GOT., 25 September 1900. CPT. Ex. Misc. Letters, 1890-1902.
13. GMT. to GOT., (n.d.), CPT. Ex. Misc. Letters, 1890-1902.
14. Trevelyan's Election Address, 1900. CPT. 50.
15. CPT. to GOT., 10 October 1900. CPT. Ex. Misc. Letters, 1890-1902.
16. Runciman to CPT., 10 October 1900. CPT. 83.
17. Fred Maddison to CPT., 11 October 1900. CPT. 83.
18. CPT. to Lord Crewe, 22 November 1900. Crewe Mss.c/50/1900, Cambridge University Library.
19. *Ibid.*
20. CPT. to Rosebery, 20 November 1900. CPT. 3.
21. CPT. to Crewe, 22 November 1900. Crewe Mss.c/ 50/1900.
22. CPT. to Samuel, 29 June 1901. CPT. 2.
23. CPT. to Editor, *Westminster Gazette*. 30 June 1901.
24. CPT.'s 'Weekly Parliamentary Letter', 4 July 1901. Cutting in CPT. 51.
25. Sir Henry Campbell-Bannerman to Henry Asquith, 10 July 1901. Asquith Mss. Vol. X, Bodleian Library, Oxford.

26. Asquith to Campbell-Bannerman, 11 July 1901. Campbell-Bannerman Mss. B.Mus.Add.Mss.41210, British Museum Library.
27. Asquith to CPT., 27 August 1901. CPT. 3.
28. Newspaper report of speech, unidentified, (n.d.). Cutting in CPT. 52.
29. *Ibid.*
30. CPT. to Runciman, 21 November 1901. Runciman Mss. R5/2, University Library, Newcastle.
31. A.J. Lawrie to CPT., 8 November 1901. CPT. 3.
32. Asquith to CPT., 17 November 1901. CPT. 3.
33. A.J. Lawrie to CPT., 9 December 1901. CPT. 3.
34. CPT. to Nomination Ctte. Eighty Club, (Draft), (n.d.). CPT. 3.
35. R.B. Haldane to CPT., 19 December 1901. CPT. 3.
36. Quoted, J.A. Spender, *Life of Sir Henry Campbell-Bannerman* (London, 1933), Vol. 2, p. 17.
37. Rosebery to CPT., 25 December 1901. CPT. 3.
38. Rosebery to CPT., 28 December 1901. CPT. 3.
39. Unidentified newspaper report, (n.d.), 25 February 1902. Cutting in CPT. 51.
40. See, CPT. to Samuel, 31 January 1905. CPT. 2.

CHAPTER 4: CONFUSION, RESURGENCE, VICTORY

1. *The Catholic Times*, 28 September 1900.
2. Quoted, W.W. Davies, *Lloyd George: 1863-1914* (London, 1939), p. 111.
3. Speech at Elland, 27 September 1902. Cutting in CPT. 52.
4. Speech at Halifax, (n.d.), December 1902. Cutting in CPT. 52.
5. CPT.'s 'Weekly Parliamentary Letter', 5 August 1902. CPT. 51.
6. CPT. to CT., 9 July 1902. CPT. Ex. 47.
7. Speech at Selby, 23 May 1903. Cutting in CPT. 52.
8. Quoted, W.S. Adams, *Edwardian Heritage* (London, 1949), p. 187.
9. Margot Asquith, *Autobiography* (Penguin Edn., 1936), Vol. 2, p. 46.
10. Speech at Northowram, 3 October 1903. Cutting in CPT. 54.
11. Speech to 99 Club, 15 October 1903. Cutting in CPT. 54.
12. Campbell-Bannerman to CPT., 6 October 1903. CPT. 5.
13. See, John Brown, 'Ideas concerning Social Policy and their influence on legislation in Britain, 1902-11', Ph.D. thesis, London, 1964.
14. CPT to CT., 2 February 1904. GOT. 57.
15. Speech at Glasgow, 16 November 1903. Cutting in CPT. 54.
16. Report of *Fifteenth Annual Meeting of Land Law Reform Association*, 24 April 1902. CPT. 52.
17. *Daily News*, 19 December 1904.
18. Speech, (n.d.), May 1905. Cutting in CPT. 52.

19. C.P. Trevelyan, 'Wanted — Talent', in, *British Empire Review*, May 1901.
20. *Daily News*, 6 August 1903.
21. Speech at Saltaire, March 1901. Cutting in CPT. 52.
22. P. Mackenzie to CPT., 11 August 1903. CPT. 5.
23. Philip Poirier, *The Advent of the Labour Party* (London, 1958), p. 166.
24. Hubert Beaumont to CPT., 3 July 1903. CPT. 5.
25. T. Catterall to Chairman, Beaumont's election committee, 2 July 1903, (copy). CPT. 5.
26. CPT. to CT., 17 March 1901. GOT. 54.
27. CPT.'s 'Weekly Parliamentary Letter', 26 July 1905. CPT. 53.
28. R.C.K. Ensor, *England: 1870-1914* (Oxford, 1936), p. 377.
29. CPT.'s 'Weekly Parliamentary Letter', 17 February 1904. CPT. 53.
30. Speech at Brighouse, February 1904. CPT. 54.
31. Speech at Brighouse, June 1904. CPT. 54.
32. Viscount Samuel, *Memoirs* (London, 1945), p. 45.
33. Samuel to CPT., 3 February 1905. CPT. 6.
34. J.E.B. Seely to CPT., 14 September 1905. CPT. 6.
35. Samuel to CPT., 18 September 1905. CPT. 6.
36. Seely, Trevelyan, Wells, et. al. to A.J. Balfour, November 1905, Mottistone Mss., Vol. viii, f. 248, Nuffield College.
37. H.G. Wells, *op. cit.*, pp. 204-05.
38. CPT. to CT., 17 July 1901. CPT. Ex. Misc. Letters, 1890-1902.
39. Mary, Lady Trevelyan, *The Number of My Days* (Privately printed, 1963), p. 23.

40. *Ibid*, p. 40.
41. *Ibid*, pp. 41-42.
42. *Ibid*, p. 43.
43. CPT. to MKT., 3 September 1903. CPT. Ex. 8.
44. CPT. to MKT., 27 December 1903. CPT. Ex. 8.
45. CPT. to MKT., 20 December 1903. CPT. Ex. 8.
46. CPT. to MKT., 12 July 1905. CPT. Ex. 20.

47. Mary, Lady Trevelyan, *op. cit.*, p. 57.
48. CPT. to Samuel, 31 January 1905. CPT. 2.
49. Report of Adoption Meeting, 3 January 1906. Cutting in CPT. 50.
50. CPT. to GOT., 18 January 1906. GOT. 59.
51. CPT. to CT., 14 January 1906. GOT. 59.

CHAPTER 5: OF LAND, LORDS, LABOUR AND IRELAND

1. CT. to GMT., 7 December 1905. CPT. Ex. 52.
2. J.C. Wedgwood to Ralph Wedgwood, 1 November 1905. Josh. Wedgwood Mss., courtesy of Mrs. Helen Bowen Pease.
3. Runciman to CPT., 9 December 1905. CPT. Ex. 51.
4. CPT. to GOT., 11 December 1905. GOT. 58.
5. CPT. to MKT., 13 and 14 December 1905. CPT. Ex. 20.
6. CT. to CPT., 18 December 1905. CPT. Ex. 52.
7. Runciman to CPT., 19 December 1905. CPT. Ex. 51.
8. CPT. to GOT., 21 December 1905. GOT. 58.
9. CPT. to GOT., 8 February 1906. GOT. 59.
10. CPT. to MKT., 14 December 1906. CPT. Ex. 21.
11. J.C. Wedgwood to CPT., 8 February 1907. CPT. 7.
12. Janet Trevelyan to MKT., 17 April 1908. CPT. 274.
13. Wedgwood to CPT., 13 April 1908. CPT. 9.
14. GOT. to H.H. Asquith, 15 April 1908. Asquith Mss., Vol. XI, f. 100.
15. Asquith to CPT., 13 April 1908. CPT. 9.
16. Runciman to CPT., 13 April 1908. CPT. 9.
17. GMT. to MKT., 16 December 1907. CPT. 274.
18. CPT. to MKT., 10, 14 and 17 December 1907. CPT. Ex. 23.
19. Unidentified newspaper report, (n.d.). Cutting in CPT. 50.
20. CPT. to GOT., 19 October 1908. GOT. 61.
21. CPT. to CT., 7 July 1909. GOT. 62.
22. See, CPT. to GOT., 21 and 25 October 1911. GOT. 64.
23. CPT. to MKT., 20 July 1908. CPT. Ex. 25.
24. Loreburn to CPT., 21 September 1906. CPT. 6.
25. CPT. to CT., 18 December 1911. GOT. 64.
26. CPT. to MKT., 26 July 1906. CPT. Ex. 21.
27. CPT. to MKT., 18 December 1906. CPT. Ex. 21.
28. CPT. to CT., (n.d.), June 1907. GOT. 60.
29. CPT. to GOT., 12 December 1908. GOT. 61.
30. GOT. to CPT., 12 December 1908. CPT. Ex. 58.
31. See, Spender & Asquith, *Life of Lord Oxford and Asquith* (London, 1932) Vol. 1, p. 241.
32. See, CPT. to MKT., 16 and 17 February 1909. CPT. Ex. 27.
33. CPT. to MKT., 29 April 1909. CPT. Ex. 27.
34. CPT. to MKT., 30 April and 1 May 1909. CPT. Ex. 28.
35. CPT. to CT., 21 July 1909. GOT. 62.
36. CPT. to CT., 29 July 1909. GOT. 62.
37. CPT. to MKT., 20 September 1909. CPT. Ex. 30.

38. CPT. to MKT., 22 September 1909. CPT. Ex. 30.
39. CPT. to MKT., 23 September 1909. CPT. Ex. 30.
40. CPT. to MKT., 4 October 1909. CPT. Ex. 31.
41. CPT. to CT., 20 October 1909. GOT. 62.
42. CPT. to Runciman, 20 November 1909. Runciman Mss. R1/12.
43. CPT. to MKT., 18 July 1907. CPT. Ex. 22.
44. Wedgwood to CPT., 31 August 1907. CPT. Ex. 56.
45. CPT. to MKT., 4 September 1908. CPT. Ex. 26.
46. CPT. to MKT., 15 September 1909. CPT. Ex. 30.
47. GOT. to CPT., 7 November 1909, CPT. Ex. 62.
48. CPT.'s 'Manifesto to Constituents', 10 December 1909. CPT. 25.
49. GOT. to CPT., 20 January 1910. CPT. Ex. 32.
50. CPT. to MKT., 23 January 1910. CPT. Ex. 32.
51. R.L Outhwaite to CPT., 1 February 1910. CPT. 14.
52. Sir Edward Grey to CPT., 10 February 1910. CPT. 14.
53. CPT. to Runciman, 2 February 1910. Runciman Mss. R1/12.
54. CPT. to MKT., 15 February 1910. CPT. Ex. 68.
55. CPT. to CT., 24 February 1910. GOT. 63.
56. CPT. to CT., 9 June 1910. GOT. 63.
57. CPT. to CT., 11 July 1910. GOT. 63.
58. CPT. to CT., 13 November 1910. GOT. 63.
59. CT. to CPT., 15 November 1910. CPT. Ex. 64.
60. CPT. to CT., 28 November 1910. GOT. 63.
61. CPT. to GOT., 17 November 1910. GOT. 63.
62. CPT. to CT., 30 November 1910. GOT. 63.
63. Speech at Brighouse, 7 December 1910. Cutting in CPT. 25.
64. Speech at Adoption Meeting, 20 November 1910. Cutting in CPT. 25.
65. *Brighouse Echo*, 9 December 1910.
66. CPT. to MKT., 16 December 1910. CPT. Ex. 15.
67. CPT. to CT., 11 April 1911. GOT. 64.
68. CPT. to MKT., 23 July 1911. CPT. Ex. 16.
69. CPT. to CT., 25 July 1911. GOT. 64.
70. CPT. to MKT., 9 August 1911. CPT. Ex. 16.
71. CPT. to MKT., 15 August 1911. CPT. Ex. 16.
72. CPT. to MKT., 20 April 1909. CPT. Ex. 28.
73. CPT. to MKT., 16 August 1911. CPT. Ex. 16.
74. Wedgwood to CPT., 3 October 1911. CPT. Ex. 65.
75. Note by CPT. to Runciman added to Memorandum, 25 March 1912. Runciman Mss. R2/5/1.
76. CPT. Memorandum to Morley, Runciman et. al., 25 March 1912 (copy). CPT. 16.
77. John Morley to CPT., 25 March 1912. CPT. 16.

78. CPT. to Bishop of Oxford, 2 April 1912. CPT. 16.
79. CPT. to MKT., 10 June 1913. CPT. Ex. 105.
80. A.C. Murray's Diary, 19 July 1912. Elibank Mss.
    Add. Mss. 8814, National Library of Scotland.
81. CPT. to MKT., 6 January 1913. CPT. Ex. 100.
82. E.T. John to C.E. Breese, 7 September 1913.
    E.T. John Mss., National Library of Wales, Aberystwyth.
83. A.C. Murray, *supra*, 25 July 1912.
84. CPT. to MKT., 30 September 1913. CPT. Ex. 105.
85. CPT. to D.Ll. George, 2 November 1913.
    Ll. George Mss. c/4/12/4, Beaverbrook Library.
86. CPT. to Wilson Raffan, 8 November 1913. CPT. 26.
87. Raffan to CPT., 17 November 1913. CPT. 26.
88. CPT. to MKT., 26 November 1913. CPT. Ex. 99.
89. CPT. to Runciman, 3 November 1913. Runciman Mss. R1/17/1.

90. *Ibid.*
91. George Dangerfield, *The Strange Death of Liberal England*. (Paladin Paperback Edn., 1970), p. 76.
92. CPT. to MKT., 2 July 1912. CPT. Ex. 68.
93. CPT. to CT., 16 February 1911. GOT. 64.
94. CPT. to MKT., 17 January 1913. CPT. Ex. 100.
95. CPT. to CT., 10 January 1913. GOT. 66.
96. CPT. to GOT., 12 February 1914. GOT. 67.
97. CPT. to CT., 3 March 1914. GOT. 67.
98. CPT. to GOT., 19 March 1914. GOT. 67.
99. CPT. to CT., 4 April 1914. GOT. 67.
100. CPT. to MKT., 22 July 1914. CPT. Ex. 106.
101. CPT. to MKT., 24 July 1914. CPT. Ex. 106.
102. CPT. to MKT., 27 July 1914. CPT. Ex. 106.
103. CPT. to MKT., 28 July 1914. CPT. Ex. 106.
104. CPT. to MKT., 30 July 1914. CPT. Ex. 106.

CHAPTER 6: RESIGNATION

1. CPT. to H.H. Asquith, 3 August 1914 (Draft). CPT. Ex. 106.
2. Runciman to CPT., 4 August 1914. CPT. 17.
3. Typescript of Trevelyan's *Memorandum on Beginning of War*, p. 6.
4. *Ibid.*
5. See, Trevelyan's 'Election Address', 1906. CPT. 50.
6. Draft of article, 'England and Peace'. CPT. 42.
7. CPT. to MKT., 29 November 1913. CPT. Ex. 105.
8. Trevelyan's 'Parliamentary Diary', (n.d.), 1907. CPT. Ex. 71.
9. CPT. to CT., 18 December 1907. GOT. 60.
10. Speech at Elland, 24 March 1909. Cutting in CPT. 54.
11. CPT. to GOT., 19 October 1908. GOT. 61.
12. A.D. Sanger to CPT., 2 June 1907. CPT. 7.
13. George Young to CPT., 25 June 1906. CPT. 6.
14. Grey to CPT., 22 June 1906. CPT. 6.
15. CPT. to Grey, (n.d.), 23 (?) June 1906. CPT. 6.
16. CPT. to MKT., 23 July 1906. CPT. Ex. 21.
17. Draft in CPT. 6.
18. See, CPT. to E.D. Morel, 19 and 31 March 1908. Morel Mss., F. 8, British Library of Economic & Political Science, London.
19. E.D. Morel to CPT., 24 October 1908. CPT. 10.
20. CPT. to MKT., 17 June 1913. CPT. Ex. 100.
21. See, GOT. to CPT., 21 December 1909. CPT. Ex. 52.
22. CPT. to CT., 28 July 1911. CPT. Ex. 66.
23. CPT. to MKT., 31 August 1911. CPT. Ex. 16.
24. Runciman to CPT., 18 September 1911. CPT. Ex. 65.
25. CPT. to Runciman, 17 September 1911. Runciman Mss. R18/11.
26. Morel to CPT., 8 September 1913. CPT. Ex. 35.
27. CPT. to MKT., 28 November 1911. CPT. Ex. 16.
28. CPT. to MKT., 16 July 1912. CPT. Ex. 68.

29. CPT. to MKT., 22 October 1912. CPT. 'Ex. 99.
30. GOT. & CT. to CPT., 27 October 1912. CPT. Ex. 67.
31. CPT. to MKT., 26 October 1912. CPT. Ex. 99.
32. CPT. to MKT., 22 July 1912. CPT. Ex. 68.
33. CPT. to MKT., 14 July 1912. CPT. Ex. 68.
34. Dudley Ward to CPT., 16 March 1913. CPT. 26.
35. Morel to CPT., 21 February 1913. CPT. 26.
36. See, N. Angell to CPT., 18 April and 1 August 1913. CPT. 26, and, CPT. Ex. 35.
37. CPT. to Morel, 20 February 1913. Morel Mss. F. 8.
38. CPT. to Runciman, 10 September 1913. Runciman Mss. R/1/17/1-22.
39. Runciman to CPT., 4 January 1914. CPT. 17.
40. Richard Holt to CPT., 16 November 1913. CPT. 26.
41. *The Nation*, 29 November 1913.
42. CPT. to D.Ll. George, 6 January 1914. Ll. George Mss. c/4/12/4.
43. Runciman to CPT., 4 January 1914. CPT. 17.
44. Quoted, Roy Jenkins, *Asquith* (London, 1964), p. 299.
45. CPT. to Runciman, 5 January 1914. Runciman Mss. R1/17/1-22.
46. CPT. to MKT., 24 July 1914. CPT. Ex. 106.
47. CPT. to MKT., 27 July 1914. CPT. Ex. 106.
48. CPT. to MKT., 28 July 1914. CPT. Ex. 106.
49. CPT. to CT., 2 August 1914. CPT. Ex. 69.
50. Typescript of Trevelyan's *Memorandum on Beginning of War*, p. 1.
51. CPT. to MKT., 29 July and 1 August 1914. CPT. Ex. 106.
52. *Ibid.*
53. CPT. to MKT., 2 August 1914 (1st letter). CPT. Ex. 106.
54. CPT. to MKT., (n.d.), 31 (?) July 1914. CPT. Ex. 106.
55. CPT. to MKT., 1 August 1914. CPT. Ex. 106.

56. CPT. to MKT., 2 August 1914 (1st letter). CPT. Ex. 106.
57. CPT. to MKT., 2 August 1914 (2nd letter). CPT. Ex. 106.
58. Richard Holt's *Diary*, 9 August 1914. Holt Mss., Liverpool Public Library.
59. CPT. to MKT., 3 August 1914. CPT. Ex. 106.
60. *Hansard*, v:65:1809.
61. CPT. to MKT., 4 August 1914 (1st letter). CPT. Ex. 106.

CHAPTER 7: *WARRIOR FOR PEACE*

1. CPT. to CT., 4 August 1914. GOT. 67.
2. C.P. Trevelyan, 'Letter to Constituents', 5 August 1914. Cutting in CPT. 42.
3. Kate Courtney, *Diary*, 9 August 1914. Courtney Papers, British Library of Economic & Political Science, London.
4. CPT. to MKT., 5 and 11 August 1914. CPT. Ex. 106.
5. John Gulland to MKT., 5 August 1914. CPT. Ex. 70.
6. CPT. to MKT., 5 August 1914. CPT. Ex. 106.
7. Bertrand Russell, 'Some Psychological Difficulties etc.', in Julian Bell (Ed.), *We Did Not Fight* (London, 1935), p. 329.
8. Kate Courtney, *Diary*, 9 August 1914. Courtney Papers.
9. *Labour Leader*, 6 August 1914.
10. *The Nation*, 8 August 1914.
11. *New Age,* 13 August 1914.
12. CPT. to George Lansbury, 7 August 1914. Lansbury Collection, Vol. 17, f. 170, British Library of Economic & Political Science.
13. Lansbury to CPT., 2 October 1914. CPT. 73.
14. CPT. to Morel, 5 August 1914. Morel Mss. F. 6, file 1.
15. CPT. to MKT., 7 August 1914. CPT. Ex. 106.
16. *Ibid.*
17. Bertrand Russel, *Autobiography*, (London, 1968), Vol. 2, p. 17.
18. Arnold Rowntree to CPT., 15 August 1914. CPT. 73.
19. Lord Bryce to CPT., 4 September 1914. CPT. 73.
20. CPT. to MKT., 31 August 1914. CPT. Ex. 106.
21. C.P. Scott's *Diary*, 3/4 August 1914, in T. Wilson (Ed.), *Scott's Diary* (London, 1971), p. 103.
22. C.P. Scott to CPT., 5 September 1914. CPT. 73.
23. Arthur Ponsonby to CPT., 11 September 1914. CPT. 73.
24. CPT. to MKT., 7 September 1914. CPT. Ex. 107.
25. CPT. to MKT., 10 September 1914. CPT. Ex. 107.
26. The letter had been published already in the *Investor's Review*, 22 August 1914.
27. T.E. Harvey to CPT., 14 August 1914. CPT. 73.
28. CPT. to Scott, 13 September 1914. Copy from C.P. Scott Papers, courtesy of Prof. Howard Weinroth.
29. Ramsay MacDonald to CPT., 10 September 1914. CPT. 73.
30. Quoted, Frank Owen, *Tempestuous Journey* (London, 1954), p. 276.
31. Ponsonby to CPT., 11 September 1914. CPT. 73.
32. C.P. Scott to E.D. Morel, 24 September 1914. Morel Mss.
33. L. Upcott Gill to CPT., 11 September 1914. CPT. 73.
34. CPT. to MKT., 14 September 1914. CPT. Ex. 107.
35. CPT. to Ponsonby, 14 September 1914. Ponsonby Papers, Shulbrede Priory, courtesy the late Baron Ponsonby.
36. See, A.J. P. Taylor, *The Trouble Makers* (Panther Edn., 1969), p. 123.
37. *Manchester Guardian*, 18 September 1914.
38. Holford Knight to Graham Wallas, 7 August 1914. Wallas Collection, British Library of Economic & Political Science, London.
39. *New Witness*, 17 September 1914.
40. *John Bull*, 14 November 1914.
41. CPT. to MKT., 29 September and 6 October 1914. CPT. Ex. 107.
42. Gerald France to CPT., 27 September 1914. CPT. 73.
43. Claude Bichnell (?) to CPT., 27 October 1950. CPT. Misc. Letters 1950.
44. Draft in Trevelyan's hand of reply to Bichnell (?), (n.d.), October 1950. CPT. Misc. Letters, 1950.
45. GMT. to CPT., (n.d.), August 1914. CPT. 60.
46. CPT. to RCT., 22 September 1914. CPT. 230.
47. See, G.M. Trevelyan, *Sir G.O. Trevelyan: A Memoir* (London, 1932), p. 145.
48. CPT. to MKT., 14 September 1914. CPT. Ex. 107.
49. CPT. to MKT., 26 December 1914. CPT. Ex. 107.
50. *Brighouse Echo*, 8 October 1915. Cutting in CPT. 42.
51. CPT. to CT., 29 August 1914. CPT. 220.
52. CPT. to Ponsonby, 22 October 1914. Ponsonby Papers.
53. CPT. to CT., 22 November 1914. GOT. 67.
54. *Brighouse Echo*, 27 November 1914. Cutting in CPT. 42.
55. CPT. to M. Philips Price, 4 March 1915. CPT. 76.
56. *Daily Sketch* (n.d.). Cutting in CPT. 42.
57. The Times (n.d.). Cutting in CPT. 42.
58. *Herald* (n.d.). Cutting in CPT. 42.
59. C.P. Trevelyan's reply to Elland Constituency Association Resolution, 7 May 1915. CPT. 42.

60. *Brighouse Echo*, 17 December 1915. Cutting in CPT. 42.
61. Harold Stead to CPT., 15 May 1916. CPT. 67.
62. CPT. to MKT., 26 December 1914. CPT. Ex. 107.
63. CPT. to MKT., 14 September 1914. CPT. Ex. 107.
64. J.C. Wedgwood to E.D. Morel, 18 September 1915. CPT. 76.
65. Note enclosed in Morel to CPT., 17 April 1916. CPT. 77.
66. CPT. to RCT., 11 August 1915. CPT. 230.
67. CPT. to Sydney Knutsford, 5 October 1914. CPT. 73.
68. Robin Price to CPT., 11 May 1915. CPT. Ex. 73.
69. Robin Price to CPT., 1 November 1917. CPT. Ex. 77.
70. CPT. to Ponsonby, 24 July 1915. Ponsonby Papers.
71. CPT. to MKT., 4 November 1914. CPT. Ex. 107.
72. CPT. to MKT., 9 September 1914. CPT. Ex. 107.
73. CPT. to MKT., 5 November 1914. CPT. Ex. 107.
74. CPT. to MKT., 6 November 1914. CPT. Ex. 107.
75. Notes for Letchworth speech, (n.d.), October 1915. CPT. 44.
76. Unidentified newspaper cutting, (n.d.), October (?) 1915. CPT. 42.
77. Leonard Courtney to CPT., 15 October 1915. CPT. 76.
78. Ponsonby to CPT., 24 July 1915. CPT. 74.
79. CPT. to John Simon, 25 November 1915, (copy). CPT. 76.
80. See, J.B.W. Chapman to CPT., 30 November 1915. CPT. 76.
81. CPT. to RCT., 19 June 1918. CPT. 230.
82. CPT. to CT., 28 May 1915. GOT. 68.
83. CPT. to GOT., 29 May 1915. GOT. 68.
84. CPT. to Ponsonby, 27 May 1915. Ponsonby Papers.
85. Ponsonby to CPT., 22 May 1915. CPT. 74.
86. Ponsonby to CPT., 16 June 1915. CPT. 74.
87. Morel to CPT., 2 November 1915. CPT. Ex. 73.
88. P. Snowden, *Autobiography* (London, 1934), Vol. 1, p. 430.
89. Ponsonby to MKT., 16 November 1915. CPT. 76.
90. J. Hoggan to CPT., 7 December 1915. CPT. 76.
91. CPT. to C.P. Scott, 14 October 1916. Scott Papers, copy courtesy of Professor Howard Weinroth.
92. CPT. to Ponsonby, 12 August 1918. Ponsonby Papers.
93. G.B. Shaw to CPT., 16 November 1917. CPT. 78.
94. Shaw to CPT., 28 February 1918. CPT. 83.
95. CPT. to Shaw, 7 March 1918, (copy). CPT. 83.
96. Shaw to CPT., 14 March 1918. CPT. 83.
97. CPT. to Ponsonby, 12 August 1917. Ponsonby Papers.
98. CPT. to RCT., 15 November 1917. CPT. 230.
99. CPT. to H.W. Massingham, 23 January 1918, (copy). CPT. 83.
100. *The Nation*, 2 February 1918, pp. 566-67.
101. J.B. Pollok McCale to CPT., 3 February 1918. CPT. 83.
102. CPT. to Col. Harold Greenfell, 8 February 1918. CPT. 83.
103. C.H. Wilson to CPT., 25 March 1918. CPT. 83.
104. Ponsonby to CPT., 3 February 1918. CPT. 79.
105. Notes by Trevelyan for Speech, 'Reasons for leaving Liber', (n.d.). CPT. 79.
106. CT. to CPT., 28 November 1918. CPT. 223
107. CPT. to CT., 30 November 1918. GOT. 71.
108. MKT. to CT., 6 December 1918. GOT. 71.
109. CPT. to CT., (n.d.), December 1918. GOT. 71.
110. CPT. to CT., 30 December 1918. GOT. 71.
111. CPT. to RCT., 11 January 1919. CPT. 230.
112. Morel to MKT., (n.d.), December (?) 1918. CPT. Ex. 70.

CHAPTER 8: FROM LIBERALISM TO LABOUR

1. K. Trevelyan, *Fool in Love* (London, 1962), p. 48.
2. CPT. to GOT., 12 January 1919. GOT. 141.
3. GMT. to CPT., 29 January 1919. GOT. 141.
4. CPT. to GOT., 27 January 1919. GOT. 141.
5. Ponsonby to CPT., 30 December 1918. CPT. Ex. 79.
6. E. Laprik to CPT., 30 December 1918. CPT. Ex. 79.
7. CPT. to J.A. Taylor, 31 May 1919. CPT. 70.
8. CPT. to Eleanor Acland, 24 May 1919. Richard Acland Mss., copy courtesy of Dr. Roy Douglas.
9. W.E. Moll to CPT., 2 June 1919. CPT. 70.
10. CPT. to Eleanor Acland, 24 May 1919. Richard Acland Mss.
11. Unless otherwise ascribed, quotations in this section are from C.P. Trevelyan, *From Liberalism to Labour* (London, 1921).
12. Loreburn to CPT., 26 March 1921. CPT. 103.
13. Sir John Fry to CPT., 16 January 1922. CPT. 104.
14. CPT. to Fry, 16 January 1922. CPT. 104.
15. CPT. to Eleanor Acland, 5 June 1919. Richard Acland Mss.
16. C.P. Trevelyan, 'Preface' to H. Langshaw, *Socialism and the historic function of Liberalism* (London, 1925), pp. vi-vii.
17. *Ibid*. pp. vii-ix.
18. CPT. to Prince Max of Baden, (n.d.), March (?), 1922, (copy). CPT. 104.
19. CPT. to MKT., 27 March 1921. CPT. Ex. 115.
20. CPT. to MKT., 29 March 1921. CPT. Ex. 115.
21. CPT. to RCT., 29 October 1922. CPT. 231.
22. CPT. to RCT., 20 November 1922. CPT. 231.
23. CPT. to CT., 1 March 1923. GOT. 76.
24. CPT. to GOT., 10 November 1923. GOT. 76.
25. Mary, Lady Trevelyan. *op. cit.*, p. 92.
26. Ramsay MacDonald to CPT., 13 December 1923. CPT. 94.

27. Quoted, H. Nicolson, *King George V: his life and reign* (London, 1952), pp. 384-85.
28. Mary, Lady Trevelyan, *op. cit.*, p. 93.
29. CPT. to MKT., 29 July 1923. CPT. Ex. 117.
30. Based upon quotations from Professor Richard Lyman's *Notes*, copy to the author by courtesy of Prof. Lyman.
31. CPT. to C.A. Cline, 4 September 1956, by courtesy of Professor Cline.
32. GOT. to CPT., 23 January 1924. CPT. 108.
33. CPT. to MKT., 30 July 1924. CPT. Ex. 118.
34. R.B. Haldane, 'Education & Democracy', in, H.B. Lees-Smith (Ed.), *The Encyclopaedia of the Labour Movement* (London, 1926), Vol. i. p. 228.
35. See, *Hansard*, v:16:2239-30.
36 C.P. Trevelyan, 'Labour's Record at the Board of Education', in, H.B. Lees-Smith (Ed.), *op. cit.*, Vol. i, p. 231.
37. See, M. Cole (Ed.), *B. Webb's Diaries: 1924-32* (London, 1956), p. 2. Cf. Rodney Barker, *Education & Politics: 1900-51* (Oxford, 1972), p. 50, n. 6.
38. *Secondary Education for All: A Policy for Labour* (London, 1922), p. 30.
39. R. Lyman's, *Notes*, 9 June 1952.

40. CPT. to MKT., 4 March 1924. CPT. Ex. 118.
41. CPT. to MKT., 19 July 1927. CPT. Ex. 121.
42. CPT. to GOT., 12 April 1927. GOT. 80.
43. GOT. to CPT., 25 July 1924. CPT. 118.
44. CPT. to MKT., 22 April 1924. CPT. Ex. 118.
45. CPT. to MKT., 24 April 1924. CPT. Ex. 118.
46. CPT. to MKT., 22 July 1923. CPT. Ex. 117.
47. See, Fenner Brockway, *Inside the Left* (London, 1942), p. 202.
48. CPT. to MKT., 20 June 1924. CPT. Ex. 118.
49. CPT. to MKT., 2, 6, 7, and 8 October 1924. CPT. Ex. 118.
50. H.G. Wells to CPT., 21 October 1924. CPT. 108.
51. Report of Fisher's speech, (n.d.). Unidentified newspaper cutting in CPT. 224.
52. Quoted, Chester, Fay and Young, *The Zinoviev Letter: a political intrigue* (London, 1967), p. 131.
53. George Young to CPT., 31 October 1924. CPT. 96.
54. CPT. to RCT., 4 November 1924. CPT. 231.
55. GMT. to CPT., 30 October 1924. CPT. 96.
56. RCT. to CPT., 1 November 1924. CPT. 96.
57. F. Hirst to CPT., 3 November 1924. CPT. 96.
58. R. Lyman's, *Notes*.
59. CPT. to MKT., 6 October 1924. CPT. Ex. 118.

CHAPTER 9: DEFEAT

1. See, Hugh Dalton, *Memoirs* (London, 1953), Vol. 1, p. 180.
2. CPT. to MKT., 27 November 1926. CPT. Ex. 120.
3. Eustace Percy, *Some Memories* (London, 1958), p. 9.
4. CPT. to MKT., 14 February 1927. CPT. Ex. 121.
5. CPT. to MKT., 9 April 1925. CPT. Ex. 119.
6. CPT. to MKT., 30 September 1925. CPT. Ex. 119.
7. CPT. to MKT., 22 and 23 November 1927. CPT. Ex. 121.
8. CPT. to MKT., 21 March, 26 and 28 April 1929. CPT. Ex. 123.
9. Eustace Percy, *op. cit.*, p. 102.
10. Quoted, R. Barker, *op. cit.*, p. 59, n.3.
11. Mary, Lady Trevelyan, *op. cit.*, p. 102.
12. Copy of Speech, (n.d.), April 1929, CPT. 275.
13. CPT. to MKT., 26 April 1929, CPT. Ex. 123.
14. CPT. to K. Trevelyan, 20 March 1929. CPT. Ex. 123.
15. CPT. to MKT., 5 and 6 June 1929. CPT. Ex. 123.
16. CPT. to MKT., 6 June 1929, (my italics). CPT. Ex. 123.
17. CPT. to MKT., 27 June 1929. CPT. Ex. 123.
18. Hugh Dalton, *op. cit.*, Vol. 1, pp. 170, 180 and 223.
19. CPT. to MKT., 23 November 1927. CPT. Ex. 121.
20. CPT. to MKT., 24 November 1927. CPT. Ex. 121.
21. CPT. to MKT., 28 April 1929. CPT. Ex. 123.
22. Bertrand Russell to CPT., 14 May 1929. CPT. 138.
23. CPT. to Russell, (n.d.), May 1929. CPT. 138.

24. CPT. to MKT., 17 March 1937. CPT. Ex. 131.
25. CPT. to MKT., 15 December 1927. CPT. Ex. 121.
26. CPT. to MKT., 19 June 1930. CPT. Ex. 124.
27. CPT. to MKT., 24 February 1930, CPT. Ex. 124.
28. See, for example, CPT. to MKT., 2, 6 and 19 June (2nd letter) 1930. CPT. Ex. 124.
29. CPT. to MKT., 16 November 1930. CPT. Ex. 124.
30. CPT. to P. Snowden, Ed. 24/1140.
31. CPT. to MKT., 21 July 1930. CPT. Ex. 124.
32. CPT. to MKT., 17 September 1930. CPT. Ex. 124.
33. CPT. to MKT., 28 November 1930. CPT. Ex. 124.
34. CPT. to MKT., 15 December 1930. CPT. Ex. 124.
35. CPT. to MKT., 17 December 1930 (1st. letter). CPT. Ex. 124.
36. CPT. to MKT., 18 December 1930 (2nd. letter). CPT. Ex. 124.
37. John Bromley to CPT., 3 March 1931. CPT. 142.
38. CPT. to MKT., 18 September 1930. CPT. Ex. 124.
39. CPT. to MKT., 15 November 1930. CPT. Ex. 124.
40. CPT. to MKT., 16 February 1931. CPT. Ex. 125.
41. CPT. to MacDonald, 19 February 1931, (Draft, copy). CPT. Ex. 125.
42. MacDonald to CPT., 20 February 1931. CPT. 142.
43. Draft notes for speech to parliamentary Labour party (n.d.). CPT. 142.
44. George Lansbury to CPT., 17 March 1931. CPT. 142.
45. Phil Price to CPT., 4 March 1931. CPT. 142.
46. CPT. to MKT., 15 April 1930. CPT. Ex. 124.
47. Draft of letter to constituents, (n.d.), April 1931.

CPT. 142.

48. CPT. to MKT., 14 September 1931. CPT. Ex. 125.
49. CPT. to MKT., 5 October 1931. CPT. Ex. 125.

50. Mary, Lady Trevelyan, *op. cit.*, p. 130.
51. J.C. Wedgwood to CPT., 29 October 1931. CPT. 98.

EPILOGUE: 'TYME TRYETH TROTH'

1. Eustace Percy, *op. cit.*, p. 16
2. CPT. to MacDonald, 20 October 1930, (copy). CPT. 276.
3. CPT. to MKT., 15 October 1930. CPT. Ex. 124.
4. E.R. Keith to CPT., 2 November 1930, (copy). CPT. 276.
5. Mary, Lady Trevelyan, *op. cit.*, p. 125.
6. Hugh Dalton, *op. cit.*, Vol. 2. p. 25.
7. CPT. to MKT., 31 May 1932. CPT. Ex. 126.
8. CPT. to MKT., 29 May 1932. CPT. Ex. 126.
9. CPT. to MKT., 30 July 1932. CPT. Ex. 126.
10. CPT. to MKT., 5 October 1932. CPT. Ex. 126.
11. CPT. to MKT., 3 October 1932. CPT. Ex. 126.
12. See, R. Barker, *op. cit.*, pp. 66ff.
13. CPT. to MKT., 4 October 1933. CPT. Ex. 127.
14. CPT. to MKT., 3 October 1932. CPT. Ex. 126.
15. CPT. to MKT., 30 September 1934. CPT. Ex. 128.
16. L. MacNeill Weir to CPT., (n.d.). CPT. 146.
17. CPT. to MKT., 30 September 1934. CPT. Ex. 128.
18. CPT. to MKT., 28 September 1934. CPT. Ex. 128.
19. Lucretius, *De Rerum Natura*, i. 72.

And thus, his mind's lively force won its victory,
And he passed on far beyond this world's fiery walls,
And in his mind and spirit he encompassed everything.

INDEX